For my wife, April, and our three awesome dudes,

>   You inspire me every day to be
>   a better husband and father.

FOREWORD

Daily Mormon is meant to be read for daily study or inspiration. Each chapter is short, one or two pages, and takes just a few minutes to read. However, with questions to ponder and daily challenges, the effect is that you start your day off in an uplifting way, and the feeling lasts as you ponder the scripture.

It can be used as a stepping stone to establishing a daily scripture study habit for those who have struggled to do so in the past, or as a companion to your current study. Many readers read the daily messages first thing in the morning, others late at night, and others once they get to work or after they start their day. It can fit into your daily routine however you choose, and will help guarantee that you get a dose of The Book of Mormon every day in a simple, accessible way.

Daily Mormon started out as a daily email that was written while I was in the research phase on another project. I had highlighted more than 300 verses in The Book of Mormon and felt like while the book would take over a year to write, I wanted to share what I had found right away.

The email took off and soon hundreds of people were getting daily messages sent to their inbox. (You can sign up for free at http://dailymormon.email)

Realizing there was only around 300 or so emails, I knew the series would ultimately come to an end. Many of the readers had asked me to put the emails into book form so that they could study at their own pace and in their own order. I then compiled all 300+ emails into a physical book so that readers could continue their daily practice of studying, pondering, and working to become better at understanding and living the gospel.

TABLE OF CONTENTS

1 NEPHI 1
1 Nephi 1:20. 1
1 Nephi 2:20 3
1 Nephi 3:7 5
1 Nephi 10:18 6
1 Nephi 10:19 7
1 Nephi 13:37 8
1 Nephi 14:1-2 9
1 Nephi 15:11 10
1 Nephi 15:24 11
1 Nephi 16:2-3 12
1 Nephi 17:3 14
1 Nephi 17:13-14 15
1 Nephi 17:36-40 16
1 Nephi 17:46 17
1 Nephi 19:14-15 18
1 Nephi 20:18 19
1 Nephi 22:1-2 20
1 Nephi 22:17 21
1 Nephi 22:19-20 22
1 Nephi 22:22, 27, 31. 23

2 NEPHI.................... 24
2 Nephi 1:9 24
2 Nephi 1:19 25
2 Nephi 1:20 26
2 Nephi 2:1-2. 27
2 Nephi 2:6-9. 29
2 Nephi 2:11 31
2 Nephi 2:13 32
2 Nephi 2:16 33
2 Nephi 2:21-27 35
2 Nephi 3:12 37
2 Nephi 3:19 38
2 Nephi 4:4 39
2 Nephi 6:12-13 40
2 Nephi 6:17-18 42
2 Nephi 8:3 43
2 Nephi 8:7-8. 44
2 Nephi 8:11 45
2 Nephi 9:7 46
2 Nephi 9:17-39 47
2 Nephi 9:41-42 50
2 Nephi 10:14 52
2 Nephi 13:10-11 53
2 Nephi 15:20 54
2 Nephi 25:23 55
2 Nephi 25:28-29 56
2 Nephi 26:11 58
2 Nephi 26:23-24 59
2 Nephi 27:23 60
2 Nephi 28:15-17 61
2 Nephi 28:30 63
2 Nephi 28:32 65
2 Nephi 29:9 66
2 Nephi 29:11 67
2 Nephi 30:1-2 68
2 Nephi 31:3 69
2 Nephi 31:12-17 70
2 Nephi 31:20 72
2 Nephi 32:3 73
2 Nephi 32:5 74
2 Nephi 32:8-9 75
2 Nephi 33:1 77

JACOB..................... 78
Jacob 2:18-19 78
Jacob 2:29 79
Jacob 3:1 80
Jacob 4:6-7 81
Jacob 4:10-11 83
Jacob 4:13 85

Jacob 6:4 86	Mosiah 23:7-8 127
Jacob 6:6 87	Mosiah 23:21-22 129
Jacob 6:11-12 88	Mosiah 26:3 130
Jacob 7:9-11 89	Mosiah 26:29-31. 131
	Mosiah 27:25-26 133
ENOS **90**	Mosiah 29:27. 135
Enos 1:15 90	
	ALMA. **137**
JAROM **91**	Alma 1:12 137
Jarom 1:4 91	Alma 3:19 139
	Alma 5:21 140
OMNI. **92**	Alma 5:33-36 141
Omni 1:25-26 92	Alma 5:38 143
	Alma 5:40-41 144
MOSIAH **93**	Alma 5:51 145
Mosiah 1:3 94	Alma 7:9 146
Mosiah 1:7 95	Alma 7:14-16 147
Mosiah 1:13 96	Alma 7:20-21 149
Mosiah 2:17 97	Alma 7:23-24. 150
Mosiah 2:20-21. 98	Alma 9:12-13. 153
Mosiah 2:22 99	Alma 9:15 155
Mosiah 2:32-33 100	Alma 9:25 156
Mosiah 2:36-39 101	Alma 9:27-28 157
Mosiah 2:41 102	Alma 10:19. 158
Mosiah 3:12 103	Alma 11:37. 159
Mosiah 3:17 104	Alma 11:40-41. 160
Mosiah 3:24-27 106	Alma 12:9-11 161
Mosiah 4:8-10 108	Alma 12:16-18 164
Mosiah 4:11-12 109	Alma 12:24-25. 165
Mosiah 4:26 110	Alma 12:33-36. 167
Mosiah 4:30 111	Alma 13:27-29. 169
Mosiah 7:33 112	Alma 14:11. 170
Mosiah 8:16-18 114	Alma 19:36. 171
Mosiah 8:20-21 116	Alma 22:6. 172
Mosiah 11:20-21 117	Alma 22:16. 173
Mosiah 11:25 118	Alma 24:27 - 25 174
Mosiah 13:28 119	Alma 24:30. 175
Mosiah 15:11-12 120	Alma 26:21-22 176
Mosiah 16:8-12 122	Alma 26:35. 177
Mosiah 18:21 124	Alma 26:37... 178

Alma 29:4-5	179
Alma 29:7	180
Alma 30:47	182
Alma 30:60	183
Alma 32:15-16	184
Alma 32:21	185
Alma 32:22	187
Alma 32:27	188
Alma 32:41-43	189
Alma 34:16-28	190
Alma 34:36	192
Alma 36:6-7	193
Alma 37:12	195
Alma 37:13	197
Alma 37:15-17	198
Alma 37:28	199
Alma 37:33-37	200
Alma 37:46	202
Alma 38:1	203
Alma 38:5	204
Alma 38:9	205
Alma 39:6	206
Alma 39:8	207
Alma 39:14	208
Alma 40:26	209
Alma 41:3-6	210
Alma 41:8	211
Alma 41:10	212
Alma 41:14-15	214
Alma 42:15-16	215
Alma 42:20	216
Alma 42:22-24	217
Alma 43:46	219
Alma 44:4	220
Alma 48:17	221
Alma 50:19-20:	222
Alma 57:26	223
Alma 61:14	224

HELAMAN ... 225

Helaman 3:27-30	225
Helaman 3:34-36	227
Helaman 4:11-13	229
Helaman 4:15	231
Helaman 5:9	232
Helaman 5:12	233
Helaman 5:29	235
Helaman 6:23-31	236
Helaman 6:35-36	238
Helaman 7:17-28	239
Helaman 8:15	241
Helaman 12:1	242
Helaman 12:2	243
Helaman 12:3	244
Helaman 12:4-6	245
Helaman 12:7-21	247
Helaman 12:22	249
Helaman 12:23-24	250
Helaman 12:25-26	252
Helaman 13:6	253
Helaman 13:11	254
Helaman 13:13	255
Helaman 13:18-20	256
Helaman 14:8	258
Helaman 14:13	259
Helaman 14:17	260
Helaman 14:19	261
Helaman 14:30	262

3 NEPHI ... 264

3 Nephi 5:22	264
3 Nephi 9:2	265
3 Nephi 9:12	266
3 Nephi 9:14-15	267
3 Nephi 9:17	268
3 Nephi 9:20-22	269
3 Nephi 10:6-7	271
3 Nephi 10:14	272
3 Nephi 11:11	273

3 Nephi 11:14 274	3 Nephi 20:8 340
3 Nephi 11:23-28 276	3 Nephi 23:1 341
3 Nephi 11:29-30 278	3 Nephi 27:6 342
3 Nephi 11:31-41 279	3 Nephi 27:16-17 343
3 Nephi 12:1 282	3 Nephi 27:19-20 344
3 Nephi 12:2 284	3 Nephi 27:27 346
3 Nephi 12:3-12 286	3 Nephi 27:28-29 347
3 Nephi 12:14-16 288	3 Nephi 27:33 348
3 Nephi 12:17-20 289	3 Nephi 28:34 349
3 Nephi 12:21-26 290	3 Nephi 29:9-7 351
3 Nephi 12:27-30 292	3 Nephi 29:9 353
3 Nephi 12:31-48 293	3 Nephi 30:2 355
3 Nephi 13:1-8 295	
3 Nephi 13:14-15 297	**MORMON** **356**
3 Nephi 13:16-18 299	Mormon 3:20-22 356
3 Nephi 13:19-21 300	Mormon 4:5 358
3 Nephi 13:22-24 302	Mormon 5:24 360
3 Nephi 13:25-34 303	Mormon 6:17-21 361
3 Nephi 14:1-5 305	Mormon 7:1-2 362
3 Nephi 14:6 307	Mormon 7:3 363
3 Nephi 14:7-12 308	Mormon 7:4 364
3 Nephi 14:13-14 310	Mormon 7:5-8 365
3 Nephi 14:15-20 312	Mormon 7:9-10 367
3 Nephi 14:21-27 314	Mormon 8:12 369
3 Nephi 15:1 316	Mormon 8:17 370
3 Nephi 15:3 9 317	Mormon 8:20 371
3 Nephi 15:10 15 319	Mormon 9:1 373
3 Nephi 15:16-17 321	Mormon 9:6 374
3 Nephi 15:18 322	Mormon 9:8 375
3 Nephi 16:6-8 323	Mormon 9:10 377
3 Nephi 16:10 324	Mormon 9:20-21 378
3 Nephi 16:12 326	Mormon 9:23-25 380
3 Nephi 16:13-14 327	Mormon 9:27-29 381
3 Nephi 16:15 328	
3 Nephi 17:3 329	**ETHER** **382**
3 Nephi 17:4 330	Ether 2:9-12 382
3 Nephi 18:10-16 331	Ether 2:15 384
3 Nephi 18:18-23 333	Ether 2:24 385
3 Nephi 18:24-25 335	Ether 3:2 387
3 Nephi 18:28-34 337	Ether 3:14 388

Ether 3:15-16 389	Ether 12:26-29 419
Ether 3:19-20 390	Ether 12:30-31 421
Ether 3:26. 391	Ether 12:32-35 422
Ether 4:7. 392	Ether 12:41 424
Ether 4:9-12. 393	
Ether 4:13-16 395	**MORONI** **425**
Ether 4:18-19 397	Moroni 6:8 425
Ether 6:22-23 399	Moroni 7:5-19 426
Ether 7:26... 401	Moroni 7:22-24. 429
Ether 8:19. 402	Moroni 7:25 431
Ether 8:22-26 403	Moroni 7:26. 432
Ether 11:8. 405	Moroni 7:33-34. 433
Ether 12:6-22 406	Moroni 7:37-38. 434
Ether 12:6 408	Moroni 7:41-44. 436
Ether 12:7. 409	Moroni 7:44-48. 438
Ether 12:8. 410	Moroni 8:8-17 440
Ether 12:9. 411	Moroni 8:25-27 442
Ether 12: 10-11. 412	Moroni 10:3-8 443
Ether 12:12-18 414	Moroni 10:18-19. 445
Ether 12:19-21 416	Moroni 10:20-23 446
Ether 12:22 418	Moroni 10:32-33 447

1 NEPHI

Make Them Mighty

> *1 Nephi 1:20 - But behold, I, Nephi, will show unto you that the tender mercies of the Lord are over all those whom he hath chosen, because of their faith, to make them mighty even unto the power of deliverance.*

After Lehi's vision earlier in chapter 1 of the first book of Nephi, he "went forth among the people, and began to prophesy".

"...and the Jews did mock him."(v. 18-19). These are the same people that had cast out, and stoned, and slain the prophets of old (v. 20).

Now, many of us have been persecuted in our lifetimes, some more than others.

The worst I've experienced was on my mission in Washington D.C., where as a 19-year-old serving in southern Maryland I had to deal with a number of "less-than-Christlike" human beings who decided that it was a good idea to drive through large puddles and drench us head to toe with icy water in the middle of winter, throw half empty beer bottles at my face while riding my bike up a steep hill, spit in my face, call me the devil, etc.

Now, one could argue I was asking for it, as I was dressed the part of a missionary hell-bent on serving my fellow man and bringing the light of Christ into their lives.

You don't have to look far outside of my own experience to see that persecution, discrimination, bigotry, and hatred are experiencing a hay-day as I type this at the end of 2016. We have just come through one of the worst elections of my lifetime, not because of the outcome, but because of the actions of people on both sides. We've seen an escalation in hate crimes since election day, and there are countless numbers of individuals who have expressed their fear of what has become more common and, in some instances, accepted: bigotry, hatred, sexism, racism, and verbal and physical abuse to others deemed deserving of such treatment.

I'm aware of the privilege I experience sitting here as a middle-aged white male in the United States. I haven't had to fear about much in my life. I'm sure many of you reading this are in the same situation. But, unless you're living in a bubble - virtual or otherwise - you've seen the evidence of this all around us.

What to do if you're afraid?

According to this promise of the Book of Mormon, have faith, and make sure that faith is centered on the Lord Jesus Christ. Does that mean we won't take a beer bottle to the head? No, the Lord's promises typically have a wider or longer perspective than a specific incident. The promise, however, is that we will be made mighty even unto the power of deliverance.

While we cannot control the actions of others, we can control the actions we take, and that they are coming from our desire to act in faith and hope, not fear or hatred. This doesn't answer the obvious questions like "why does God let bad things happen to good people?", but it does give me faith that in the long run things will work out and we will be blessed for our faithfulness.

Question to Ponder: How would you act differently if tough situations if you had a strong knowledge of this promise?

Keep My Commandments And Ye Shall Prosper

> *1 Nephi 2:20 - And inasmuch as ye shall keep my commandments, ye shall prosper.*

Here in the first chapters of the book of Nephi in The Book Of Mormon, the Lord is speaking directly to Nephi. He's praising him for his righteous choices: *Blessed art thou, Nephi, because of thy faith, for thou hast sought me diligently, with lowliness of heart.*(v. 19). Ultimately Nephi is chosen to rule over his (older) brothers, Laman and Lemuel.

This statement occurs a number of times throughout The Book of Mormon. It felt like every other week in Gospel Doctrine class I'd stand in front of the class saying, "Remember a few weeks ago when the lesson was also about the blessings that come from keeping the commandments?"

It often occurs in a similar manner as well: IF you keep the commandments, THEN [insert incredible blessing here].

Sometimes it's hard, in the moment, to choose between righteousness and sin or transgression. We're briefly putting something of worldly value over things that have a more eternal and significant - but possibly far removed - value, and it's easy to understand why. That's part of why we're here on earth, to be presented with temptations and trials where our faith is able to be tested and tried; only by going through these experiences will we ever grow and become better.

I think this is, in part, why we're often encouraged to follow the basics of the gospel. What is the gospel? Christ himself outlined it when he spoke to the people in Bountiful after his resurrection:

> *3 Nephi 27:*
> *13 Behold I have given unto you my gospel, and this is the gospel which I have given unto you—that I came into the world to do the will of my Father, because my Father sent me.*

> *14 And my Father sent me that I might be lifted up upon the cross; and after that I had been lifted up upon the cross, that I might draw all men unto me, that as I have been lifted up by men even so should men be lifted up by the Father, to stand before me, to be judged of their works, whether they be good or whether they be evil—*

> *15 And for this cause have I been lifted up; therefore, according to the power of the Father I will draw all men unto me, that they may be judged according to their works.*

> *16 And it shall come to pass, that whoso repenteth and is baptized in my name shall be filled; and if he endureth to the end, behold, him will I hold guiltless before my Father at that day when I shall stand to judge the world.*

The atonement. Faith, repentance, baptism, enduring to the end. We are reminded every week as we partake of the sacrament of Christ's sacrifice for us. We are taught the gospel weekly, but it is not enough to prevent us from sinning throughout the week. The only way to improve in that regard is to spend more time thinking about the gospel and how to better live it, and we do that through daily scripture study and striving to have the Holy Ghost as our constant companion.

"Keep the commandments" seems like a simple, binary commandment. It's kind of pass/fail. But any amount of improvement on our part will result in blessings from God; we don't need to be perfect today to qualify.

It's a reminder to find ways to better live the gospel on a daily basis. As we keep the commandments, we will prosper.

Questions to Ponder: What does faith in this promise look like in your life? How would you change your actions to better align with the belief that if we are obedient, we will be blessed?

He Shall Prepare A Way

> *1 Nephi 3:7 ...the Lord giveth no commandments unto the children of men, save he shall prepare a way for them that they may accomplish the thing which he commandeth them.*

At times, as a member of The Church of Jesus Christ of Latter-day Saints, it may seem impossible to do everything that has been asked of us. Twice a year we sit and listen to our leaders who teach us to repent, to do our home teaching, to serve others, pay tithing, keep the commandments, and on and on. (I don't want to sound glib, I'm just trying to be brief).

This verse in 1 Nephi chapter 3 has always brought me comfort in times that I have felt overwhelmed. I was called to be an elder's quorum president when I was 18 in my student ward, and I felt utterly inadequate to lead a ward of elders who were mostly older than I was. About a month later in the October 2002 conference, Elder Eyring gave a memorable talk titled Rise To Your Call, which echoed the same sentiments as this statement from Nephi.

One quote among many favorites from that talk:

> *"the Lord will guide you by revelation just as He called you. You must ask in faith for revelation to know what you are to do. With your call comes the promise that answers will come. But that guidance will come only when the Lord is sure you will obey. To know His will you must be committed to do it. The words "Thy will be done", written in the heart, are the window to revelation."*

The Lord knows each of us, personally and intimately, and we can take comfort from that fact in those times that we need it. We are not alone in this world, though it may feel that way at times if we are not living righteously, or we are going through a trial that we need to get through to strengthen our faith. But we can be confident that the Lord is there watching over us, always.

Question to ponder: How would your life be different with the understanding that the Lord has prepared a way for us to accomplish everything he's asked us? What would be the most significant change in your day to day life?

For He Is The Same

> 1 Nephi 10:18 - *For he is the same yesterday, today, and forever; and the way is prepared for all men from the foundation of the world, if it so be that they repent and come unto him.*

There is something incredibly comforting about this attribute of our Savior, that he is unchanging and eternal, that he is the same, forever. If you're going to place your faith in a Savior, if you're going to believe in an atonement and the power of resurrection, you'd want that to be unchanging. When times get tough, we can always turn to our Savior and the fact that he gave his life for us, and know that the reality of that statement will never change.

Our lives, however, change on a daily basis. How many of us have had a bad day because of a negative comment on social media that we just couldn't let go? Every day brings new challenges and new temptations, and Satan is actively fighting to mislead us and make us doubt our testimonies and our faith. Don't let him. Spend time each day remembering our Savior, his Gospel, and his Atonement for us.

Question to Ponder: What blessings have come into your life because of the Atonement? How has your faith helped you in the past?

The Mysteries Of God

> *1 Nephi 10:19 - For he that diligently seeketh shall find; and the mysteries of God shall be unfolded unto them, by the power of the Holy Ghost, as well in these times as in times of old, and as well in times of old as in times to come; wherefore, the course of the Lord is one eternal round.*

This has been a favorite verse of mine since my teenage years when a youth leader used it in a lesson during a stake youth conference. It was a principle with a promise - diligently seek...and the mysteries of God shall be unfolded.

What does that even mean? The possibilities lie beyond what I think we can even comprehend. If the Holy Ghost can unfold the mysteries of God, what else can he teach us?

Do you think Noah knew how to build an ark, or Nephi a boat before they were commanded to do so? NO! They had no idea!

So today's Questions to Ponder are: what do you need help with, where in life are you stuck? How would you feel if the Holy Ghost could guide you through it? Do you believe that it's possible? And how can you make some extra time to diligently seek the answers that you're looking for?

For Whoso Shall Publish Peace

> 1 Nephi 13:37 - "And blessed are they who shall seek to bring forth my Zion at that day, for they shall have the gift and the power of the Holy Ghost; and if they endure unto the end they shall be lifted up at the last day, and shall be saved in the everlasting kingdom of the Lamb; and whoso shall publish peace, yea, tidings of great joy, how beautiful upon the mountains shall they be."

I wonder if the prophets in the Book of Mormon - when speaking about seeing us and our day - if they saw things like Facebook and Twitter, blogs and YouTube. (Were they able to figure out how to use SnapChat??)

If they did see the ubiquity of social media in our time, and how much of our lives it has become, how would they feel about it? Would they see it as good or evil?

I've noticed in my own life the hesitancy to post about gospel-related topics. I catch myself wondering what my "followers" and friends will think if I post a picture of a verse from the scriptures. But you know what happens nearly every time? The highest amount of engagement of any other posts. (And I have some CUTE kids...)

A recent post had 4-5x as many people engaged with that photo, and it had more comments than any other post this year. It's a somewhat silly, yet still incredibly convincing, faith-confirming way to realize the truth of the promises that come to those who seek to bring forth [his] Zion and publish peace.

Question to Ponder: How are you using social media? Is it positive or negative? Building or tearing down? In what ways can you make changes to improve and to "publish peace"?

BONUS CHALLENGE: What's your favorite verse of scripture? I challenge you to post it online today with the story of why it is so meaningful to you. Let me know how it goes! (And if you're really savvy you can even use the hashtag #dailymormon to find others that are posting as well.

The Taking Away Of Their Stumbling Blocks

> 1 Nephi 14:1-2 - 1 And it shall come to pass, that if the Gentiles shall hearken unto the Lamb of God in that day that he shall manifest himself unto them in word, and also in power, in very deed, unto the taking away of their stumbling blocks

> 2 And harden not their hearts against the Lamb of God, they shall be numbered among the seed of thy father; yea, they shall be numbered among the house of Israel; and they shall be a blessed people upon the promised land forever; they shall be no more brought down into captivity; and the house of Israel shall no more be confounded.

It always seems so simple when I read scriptures like this. "If they hearken unto the Lord", or "harden not their hearts". Seems pretty simple, right? Yet when I've actually sat and pondered, I get that feeling in my gut that I could do better, that I haven't been as diligent or as humble as I could be, and that I haven't been paying enough attention to the promptings of the spirit, or giving enough time to pondering and meditation to allow the Spirit the opportunity to speak and be heard in the first place.

As simple as it may seem in the scriptures, it can be hard in practice. It is possible to start feeling the weight of all of these things that we "should" be doing on a daily basis and feel that we're not as good as we "should" be. As a mentor once told me, "stop should-ing all over yourself and do what you can. That's the only way to progress."

Questions to Ponder: What can you do today to be just 1% better than yesterday? What distractions can you remove from your life so that you have more room for pondering and for the Spirit to teach, guide, and comfort you?

Quote: From Elder Scott's conference talk in 2013:

"We need not worry if we can't simultaneously do all of the things that the Lord has counseled us to do. He has spoken of a time and a season for all things. In response to our sincere prayers for guidance, He will direct us in what should be emphasized at each phase of our life. We can learn, grow, and become like Him one consistent step at a time."

(Thanks to Nate for sharing the quote :)

These Things Shall Be Made Known Unto You

> *1 Nephi 15:11 - Do ye not remember the things which the Lord hath said? If ye will not harden your hearts, and ask me in faith, believing that ye shall receive, with diligence in keeping my commandments, surely these things shall be made known unto you.*

What could you use help with in your life right now? Finances? Your career? Your calling? Your relationship? What if there was a process by which you could have all these things made known unto you?

There is, and it appears numerous times throughout the scriptures. It requires humility and faith, and that you're actively and diligently keeping the commandments. The promise is clear, that these things will be made known unto you.

Just recently, while preparing this email newsletter, I read through The Book of Mormon again and rediscovered how often this divine book of scripture mentions the need to keep the commandments, repent, have faith and be humble, and I realized I had a long way to go in every single one of those areas.

I made a decision to get back into the habit of repenting every day, praying daily, and keeping the commandments as well as I could, and it was incredible how quickly the Spirit came back into my life in such an increased measure. It was dramatic - you should see my morning journal where I track all of my ideas and what I'm working on. I was receiving such specific inspiration as to how to be a better father, a better husband, a better disciple, and even a better business owner. What could happen for you?

Questions to Ponder: Each of us can improve, no matter how great we are and how diligent we are. This is not to make you feel bad, but to inspire you to try and do more. How can you be more diligent in keeping the commandments? How can you remove pride from your life so that you become more humble? How can you act in faith so that the Lord sees that faith and can reward you for it?

Whoso Would Hearken Unto The Word Of God

> 1 Nephi 15:24 - ...and whoso would hearken unto the word of God, and would hold fast unto it, they would never perish; neither could the temptations and the fiery darts of the adversary overpower them unto blindness, to lead them away to destruction.

How many of us have friends or family members that have left the church? I'd venture a guess that all of us have someone close to us in that situation. How did that happen? And are we immune?

According to the scriptures, we're all targets of Satan when it comes to being led astray. In the Doctrine and Covenants section 50 verses 2-3, we're taught that "there are many spirits which are false spirits, which have gone forth in the earth, deceiving the world. And also Satan hath sought to deceive you, that he might overthrow you." Most instances (possibly all..) of people leaving the church can be traced back to an issue with pride seeping into their lives. Whether it's rationalizing disobedience and sin, ignoring the words of the prophets, being critical of the imperfections of our leaders, or being offended, they all stem from pride.

The antidote, the protectant from all of these deceptions is reading the scriptures and hearkening to the word of God and holding fast to it. This promise from Nephi to his brothers is applicable today as it was then, if not more so.

Questions to Ponder: Where in our lives are we being lax, or letting pride into our lives? How can we find more time each day (even if it's just five minutes to read a short email from a friend ;)) to read and ponder the scriptures, and humble ourselves to where we live its teachings?

The Guilty Taketh The Truth To Be Hard

> 1 Nephi 16:2-3 - 2 And it came to pass that I said unto them that I knew that I had spoken hard things against the wicked, according to the truth; and the righteous have I justified, and testified that they should be lifted up at the last day; wherefore, the guilty taketh the truth to be hard, for it cutteth them to the very center.

> 3 And now my brethren, if ye were righteous and were willing to hearken to the truth, and give heed unto it, that ye might walk uprightly before God, then ye would not murmur because of the truth, and say: Thou speakest hard things against us.

Some tough love from Nephi, but a statement of truth nonetheless. I've come to learn that, like fear, we can use this feeling of "that's hard" to gauge where we're at on that spectrum of righteous to unrighteous...The truth is the truth. In D&C 93:24 we read that "...truth is knowledge of things as they are, and as they were, and as they are to come;" ... there's no bias when it comes to the truth. If we feel that it's hard to take, or that it isn't lining up with our personal beliefs, that is saying more about us than the truth that has been revealed, and we need to prayerfully and humbly make some adjustments.

Questions to Ponder: Given this dichotomy, would you rather be like Nephi or his brethren? What gospel truths do you find hard at the moment? How can you find opportunities to humble yourself and gain a testimony of those truths so that we are following our Heavenly Father, Christ, and the gospel to the fullest extent possible?

By Small Means

> *1 Nephi 16:28-29 - 28 And it came to pass that I, Nephi, beheld the pointers which were in the ball, that they did work according to the faith and diligence and heed which we did give unto them.*

> *29 And there was also written upon them a new writing, which was plain to be read, which did give us understanding concerning the ways of the Lord; and it was written and changed from time to time, according to the faith and diligence which we gave unto it. And thus we see that by small means the Lord can bring about great things.*

This section of the history of Nephi and his family is one of my favorite in The Book Of Mormon. Imagine the stress that they were under, out in the wilderness, no food, broken bow. Yet Nephi is as stoic as ever -- before stoicism had even been created...

Nephi's words here are powerful. He was the opposite of his doubting brothers: full of faith, ready at every moment to heed the Lord's commands. He realized that sometimes answers to prayers come in small and simple ways, but that great things can still come from those seemingly insignificant beginnings.

Questions to Ponder: Do we expect too much from the Lord when looking for answers to our prayers? Are we seeking "great signs and wonders"? How can we become more sensitive to the promptings of the Spirit? And how can we increase our faith in the Lord when it comes to his ability to answer our prayers?

If It So Be...

> 1 Nephi 17:3 - And thus we see that the commandments of God must be fulfilled. And if it so be that the children of men keep the commandments of God he doth nourish them, and strengthen them, and provide means whereby they can accomplish the thing which he has commanded them;

This was one of the first scriptures that sparked this idea of "statement" verses in The Book Of Mormon. It all hinges on the "if" in the second sentence. IF it so be that we keep the commandments, [THEN] he doth nourish and strengthen us, and provide means to accomplish anything.

I've asked before, but we're going to start seeing recurring themes and statements in this email series, which is why we're starting from the beginning and going forward through the book as if we were reading it straight through. It's interesting to see which prophets focus on what topics and to what extent. Nephi spoke often on the importance of keeping the commandments because for him that's where a lot of his spiritual strength came from.

Questions to Ponder: Do we care about/value the blessings promised in this verse? If so, what are we doing about it? Our actions reveal our values, so how can we better keep the commandments to show our Heavenly Father that we value nourishment, strength, and accomplishing the things which he has commanded us?

**Bonus / Daily Challenge: A few readers have asked for something along the lines of a daily action item, or what I'll call a daily challenge (it's the type-A personality in me...) These are optional, but hopefully, they will help as we all try and be better at living the gospel.

Today's challenge is to ask a friend or loved one: "what is one way you think I could be better at living the gospel?"

Be ready for some brutal honesty, a gut check on your humility, and a great opportunity to grow and become more diligent in keeping the commandments.

Thank you for reading! I'd love any feedback you may have on whether or not you're finding value in these emails and how they could be better. Just respond to this email, I read every single one.

Inasmuch As Ye Shall Keep My Commandments...

> 1 Nephi 17:13-14 - 13 And I will also be your light in the wilderness; and I will prepare the way before you, if it so be that ye shall keep my commandments; wherefore, inasmuch as ye shall keep my commandments ye shall be led towards the promised land; and ye shall know that it is by me that ye are led.

> 14 ... After ye have arrived in the promised land, ye shall know that I, the Lord, am God; and that I, the Lord, did deliver you from destruction; yea, that I did bring you out of the land of Jerusalem.

I "warned" you yesterday that the book of 1st Nephi mentions the commandments a lot. This time, it's the Lord speaking directly to Nephi. He's commanded him to build a boat, a task that Nephi is completely unfamiliar with. Yet, in true Nephi fashion, his faith trumps his fear, and he famously asks "whither shall I go that I may find ore to molten, that I may make tools to construct the ship after the manner which thou hast shown unto me?" (v. 9).

Questions to Ponder: What is the parallel in our own life for how Nephi responded to this situation? How can we do the same? The Lord mentioned as one of the blessings of keeping the commandments that "ye shall know that I, the Lord, am God;" - wouldn't Nephi have already known that, given everything he has seen up to this point? Why would the Lord promise that?

Daily Challenge: Read through 1 Nephi 16-18 and focus on Nephi's actions and reactions to the situation they're in. What does it mean for you? What should you do about it?

And He Loveth Those...

> *1 Nephi 17:36-40 - 36 Behold, the Lord hath created the earth that it should be inhabited; and he hath created his children that they should possess it.*

> *37 And he raiseth up a righteous nation, and destroyeth the nations of the wicked.*

> *38 And he leadeth away the righteous into precious lands, and the wicked he destroyeth, and curseth the land unto them for their sakes.*

> *39 He ruleth high in the heavens, for it is his throne, and this earth is his footstool.*

> *40 And he loveth those who will have him to be their God. Behold, he loved our fathers, and he covenanted with them, yea, even Abraham, Isaac, and Jacob; and he remembered the covenants which he had made; wherefore, he did bring them out of the land of Egypt.*

Nephi is still prophesying to his brothers at this point, and we get this great section of Scripture that teaches us about some of the attributes of God. How comforting is it to know that we have a Father in Heaven and a Savior in Jesus Christ who love us, and who keep covenants with us as long as we remain worthy.

One of my favorite times reading through The Book of Mormon was when I highlighted every verse that described the attributes of our Heavenly Father and/or Jesus Christ, our Savior. The book truly is another testament of Jesus Christ.

Questions to Ponder: How well do you know your Heavenly Father? What can we do to strengthen our relationship with him?

Daily Challenge: If you haven't read through The Book of Mormon in a while, start today. Find a few minutes, and start simple. Make a pact with yourself to read just one chapter a day.

Why Is It That Ye Can Be So Hard In Your Hearts?

> *1 Nephi 17:46 - ...by the power of his almighty word he can cause the earth that it shall pass away; yea, and ye know that by his word he can cause the rough places to be made smooth, and smooth places shall be broken up. O, then, why is it that ye can be so hard in your hearts?*

Can you imagine how it must have felt to be rebuked by Nephi? I think it would be a pretty humbling experience. Even here, the words "why is it that ye can be so hard in your hearts" stings a bit, doesn't it? Or it that just me?

This verse is a great way to measure where we are in our faith. If the Lord can do all of these things, then why are we not asking for his help with the little things? Being a better parent, or serving more, or avoiding temptation. Sometimes it's easier to have faith in the big things because they're so far removed from our daily reality. But the true test of our faith is to do the daily, simple things, that show our Heavenly Father that we truly value the many blessings he's given us, the greatest of which is the Atonement of Christ.

Questions to Ponder: How did it feel when you read that verse? Read it again as if Nephi was talking directly to you. What areas in our lives can we soften our hearts, be more humble, and more diligent?

Daily Challenge: Act in faith. Find something small that you can do today that is an action that shows your faith in our Heavenly Father. Say a prayer. Schedule a visiting teaching visit. Fast for something you need help with. Take ten minutes to meditate and listen for inspiration from the Holy Ghost.

Because They Turn Their Hearts Aside

> *1 Nephi 19:14-15 - 14 And because they turn their hearts aside, saith the prophet, and have despised the Holy One of Israel, they shall wander in the flesh, and perish, and become a hiss and a byword, and be hated among all nations.*

> *15 Nevertheless, when that day cometh, saith the prophet, that they no more turn aside their hearts against the Holy One of Israel, then will he remember the covenants which he made to their fathers.*

Up to today we've focused on mainly positive principles and promises from The Book of Mormon. Yet, as I was studying over the last six months, I realized that there are just as many warnings for those that are prideful, or disobedient, or who fail to hearken to the word of the Lord.

The word "perish" was one I never paid much attention to. However, the concept came up over and over again, and I'm excited to dive into what the book teaches as a whole on this subject. The warning here is a very serious one, which you can tell even by the tone. There's a noticeable difference from the other verses that are filled with hope and positive vibes.

There's a clear line drawn here between those that turn their hearts aside, and those that repent or have repented. The latter group qualifies for the blessings that have been promised under the Abrahamic covenant, which are many.

Questions to Ponder: What does it mean to "turn your hearts aside"? How have we been guilty of doing so? What can we do to repent, to change, and to humble ourselves enough to turn our hearts to the Lord?

Daily Challenge: Spend a few minutes today just pondering, thinking about these verses, thinking about the magnitude of the Book of Mormon coming forth, in our time, for us. To guide us and help us and comfort us, to give us more knowledge and understanding and hope.

Then Had Thy Peace Been As A River

> *1 Nephi 20:18 - O that thou hadst hearkened to my commandments— then had thy peace been as a river, and thy righteousness as the waves of the sea.*

Can you feel the tinge of sorrow in this verse? I read it and I immediately feel empathy for the Lord and Isaiah as these words were spoken and written down. Then, there's the reinforcement of the principle of receiving blessings when we keep the commandments. Anyone else here feel like they'd benefit from peace like a river? How much of our lives are filled with stress, with too many decisions, or a constant, low-level hum from all of the inputs on the internet and our phones?

"Keep the commandments" is what we're told. But that's such a simple statement that sometimes I think we take it for granted - ok, I KNOW that *I* take it for granted.

Questions to Ponder: Are there things we can do to be better at keeping the commandments? When was the last time we studied the many commandments that the Lord has given us? Are we doing everything we can?

Daily Challenge: Go on a mini scripture hunt. Turn to the Topical Guide under Commandments of God, find the first verse that stands out to you, and go from there. Follow the footnotes, or go to the next verse. What did you learn? What inspiration came from it? I'd love to know - just reply to this email and let me know!

By The Spirit Are All Things Made Known

> *1 Nephi 22:1-2 - 1 And now it came to pass that after I, Nephi, had read these things which were engraven upon the plates of brass, my brethren came unto me and said unto me: What meaneth these things which ye have read? Behold, are they to be understood according to things which are spiritual, which shall come to pass according to the spirit and not the flesh?*

> *2 And I, Nephi, said unto them: Behold they were manifest unto the prophet by the voice of the Spirit; for by the Spirit are all things made known unto the prophets, which shall come upon the children of men according to the flesh.*

Nephi is speaking to his brothers after reciting some chapters from the book of Isaiah. They were rightly confused (I mean, who isn't confused by the Isaiah chapters the first time they come in contact with them...?) and ask "how are we supposed to understand this stuff"?

Nephi answers with this great principle, that by the Spirit are all things made known unto the prophets. The important place to focus is not on the prophets, but what comes before that. Rather, that by the spirit are things made known. Nephi is teaching us about the attributes of the Holy Ghost, that he's a revelator, yes, but also that he can make ALL things known unto us.

Again: all things.

Questions to Ponder: If we truly believe that our Heavenly Father is all-knowing and that he can communicate with us through the Holy Ghost, then what is possible at that point? Are there any contingencies there that we are placing on that belief? Such as: well, God wouldn't want to help me with this addiction I'm struggling with, or this frustration I have with my job, or how to break this next chapter of my novel... If there's nothing that He can't know, nothing he can't reveal to us, how does that change how we use prayer and fasting, our relationship with the Spirit, and things like pondering and meditation?

Daily Challenge: Put this to the test. Think of something, big or small, that you're struggling with and ask the Lord for help.

The Righteous Need Not Fear

> *1 Nephi 22:17 - Wherefore, he will preserve the righteous by his power, even if it so be that the fulness of his wrath must come, and the righteous be preserved, even unto the destruction of their enemies by fire. Wherefore, the righteous need not fear; for thus saith the prophet, they shall be saved, even if it so be as by fire.*

We've been told that fear is the opposite of faith, both in the scriptures and in general conference, and it makes sense, right? If we're consumed with fear, whether it be of the second coming, or the destruction of our country by elements we have no control over, or any other of a number of things we could be afraid of, it prevents us from taking certain actions. Why would you ever go out on the road in your car if you didn't have faith in the other drivers of the road not crossing the line into your lane of traffic? It would absolutely prevent you from ever driving another inch if you had that fear.

It is our faith in God and the gospel that allows us to progress because with faith comes action. Beyond that, however, and in the bigger picture, we're told in this scripture that we need not fear if we are righteous because the righteous shall be saved. For me, at least, that's an incredibly comforting thought.

Questions to Ponder: Where in our lives are we letting fear prevent and paralyze us from taking action? It could be anything from tithing (I'm afraid I won't have enough to pay my bills...) to marriage (too many of my friends' marriages have ended in divorce and I don't want that to happen to me...) to anything in between. How would life be different if our choices were made out of faith rather than fear?

Daily Challenge: Post something online today about how your faith allows you to act, and a blessing that has come from being faithful in the past. If you're having trouble thinking of something, you can use this link to share Daily Mormon with your friends. It's scary sometimes to post about our faith online, but it's my belief that the world will be better off for it. And you'll never know if you don't try...

The Righteous Shall Not Perish

> *1 Nephi 22:19-20 - 19 For behold, the righteous shall not perish; for the time surely must come that all they who fight against Zion shall be cut off.*

> *20 And the Lord will surely prepare a way for his people, unto the fulfilling of the words of Moses.*

There is so much comfort that comes from promises like this from the Lord and His prophets. Sometimes our focus is so narrow on how hard things are, or we may feel that there's no way out of whatever trial we're going through. Yet, we know that the Lord will never abandon us.

It's important to remember in these times the truth taught in verses like these. That broader perspective has been extremely helpful in my life as I've gone through tough times like a divorce and my mother passing away from cancer. It would have been easy to think that the Lord had abandoned me and that these experiences were proof of that, but the truth was that I was the one distancing myself from him in those situations. As soon as I remembered the promises I'd made to live the gospel fully, to repent, to turn to the scriptures and invite the spirit into my life, it wasn't long till those truths were revealed.

If we're righteous, the Lord will be with us. He will preserve us, he will prepare a way for us.

Questions to Ponder: Do you believe these scriptures to their fullest extent? Do you believe they apply to you individually, and not just as one member of the church as a whole? How has this perspective helped you in the past?

Daily Challenge: Find a friend or family member that's struggling, and see if you can add some perspective to their situation. It will certainly be scary, but if they're willing to listen, the added testimony from you will undoubtedly help them get through it with the added comfort from the spirit.

The Righteous Need Not Fear...

> *1 Nephi 22:22, 27, 31 - 22 And the righteous need not fear, for they are those who shall not be confounded...*

> *27 But, behold, all nations, kindreds, tongues, and people shall dwell safely in the Holy One of Israel if it so be that they will repent.*

> *31 ...if ye shall be obedient to the commandments, and endure to the end, ye shall be saved at the last day.*

In this chapter, Nephi has been answering the question posed by his brothers: What meaneth these things which thou has read? (V.1) Nephi then spends the rest of this chapter expounding truth to them and ends with these emphatic promises for those that are righteous, who repent, and who keep the commandments.

It helps, at times, to imagine that Nephi or other prophets are speaking directly to us. Not through the scriptures, but literally imagining standing in front of them and being told these words straight to our faces.

Questions to Ponder: Can you imagine Nephi saying these words directly to you? How does it feel? Where does your mind go to? Where do we need to be more obedient, or more repentant?

Daily Challenge: Sit for 5-10 minutes today thinking of everything you've seen so far from the scriptures through this daily email. Nephi has spoken at length about obedience, righteousness, and repentance. How can you be better at any one of those things from now on?

2 NEPHI

They Shall Dwell Safely Forever

> 2 Nephi 1:9 - ...And if it so be that they shall keep his commandments they shall be blessed upon the face of this land, and there shall be none to molest them, nor to take away the land of their inheritance, and they shall dwell safely forever.

The chapter heading for 2 Nephi 1 states that Lehi was prophesying of a land of liberty, what we know now is the United States, or at very least the American continent. It's always been a question of mine when a prophet is speaking about a group of people as a whole, such as "they shall keep his commandments...their inheritance", where the cutoff is. What I mean is, does the Lord expect 100% compliance? (Obviously not). If not, then is there a cutoff point where the people as a whole are considered "righteous" or "wicked"? But, and more importantly, what does that mean for us individually? What is our responsibility as part of the group, part of the blessed, part of the chosen, etc. It adds some extra perspective to our roles and our covenants as members of the church.

Questions to Ponder: How can we be more faithful in keeping the commandments? How can we influence others to do the same, through our actions and our example?

Daily Challenge: Some of us struggle with home and visiting teaching, and this one's for you/us. Reach out to one of your families today, ask how they are, and set up a time to connect with them, to talk about the gospel, their lives, your lives, and the blessings that have come into your life because of the scriptures.

His Will Be Done

> *2 Nephi 1:19 - ...But behold, his will be done; for his ways are righteousness forever.*

The subtitle of The Book of Mormon is Another Testament of Jesus Christ, yet we haven't spent much time talking about our Savior in this email series. The truth of the matter is that after reading the entire book, highlighting each and every statement I could find, and then categorizing them, I found over 125 verses that had some mention of the attributes of Christ - nearly half of the verses I highlighted.

The book is truly another testament.

Sometimes, however, we gloss over verses like this that have a short, simple attribute like this one. We're taught "his ways are righteous forever". Numerous conference talks have expounded on this concept, and I'm sure many articles and other writings have covered it as well. It's a concept so deep that it can't be properly handled in a short daily email such as this one. Yet, that doesn't diminish its importance.

Questions to Ponder: What are the implications of that truth - that the Lord's ways are righteousness forever? What does it mean? How does that effect your life?

Daily Challenge: Spend some time pondering/meditating on that principle, that attribute of the Lord.

Inasmuch As Ye Shall Keep My Commandments...

> 2 Nephi 1:20 - ...Inasmuch as ye shall keep my commandments ye shall prosper in the land; but inasmuch as ye will not keep my commandments ye shall be cut off from my presence.

When you look at what is going on in the world today, with our nation so divided and so much chaos, so much hatred all so pervasive, I often wonder how much longer it will last. Are we primed for a big event where a group of people grows so wicked that they get wiped out? I don't think we're there yet, but yeah, that's where my mind goes sometimes.

What is comforting in times like these is verses like this one, where we are given a promise that if we will keep the commandments we shall prosper. I think that can apply not only to us as a nation, but to us as communities, as families, and as individuals. If we remain faithful in keeping the commandments we will prosper. It helps us focus on obedience and faith rather than fear, which also makes these tough times easier to get through.

Questions to Ponder: What does prosperity look like? Is it worth working for by keeping the commandments?

Daily Challenge: Look for someone, online or in person, who is currently focusing on fear with the things they are sharing with others. Offer a different perspective: one of faith.

He Shall Consecrate Thine Afflictions For Thy Gain

> *2 Nephi 2:1-2 - 1 And now, Jacob, I speak unto you: Thou art my firstborn in the days of my tribulation in the wilderness. And behold, in thy childhood thou hast suffered afflictions and much sorrow, because of the rudeness of thy brethren.*

> *2 Nevertheless, Jacob, my firstborn in the wilderness, thou knowest the greatness of God; and he shall consecrate thine afflictions for thy gain.*

It felt like too short of a verse to just quote that last bit, so here it is in context. It's important, at times, to substitute our own names in the place of the person being spoken to - in this case Jacob. Lehi is sort of going around giving his last bit of advice to each of his children, and we get this great truth as he's speaking to Jacob.

How many of us have suffered "afflictions and much sorrow"? I lost my mother back in 2011 to cancer - it's probably my greatest "sorrow" in my life. Yet I can look back now and see how if we remain focused on the gospel and the things we know to be true, we can find that those moments of sorrow and affliction can teach us, and sometimes even motivate us. Personally, the knowledge of the plan of salvation and eternal families motivates me to live the gospel as fully as possible so that one day I can be reunited with my incredible mother.

Similarly, the Lord spoke to Joseph Smith when he was in the pit of despair in Liberty Jail. In Doctrine & Covenants section 121 we read the prophet's pleading with the Lord: "where art thou? ... how long shall thy hand be stayed?" to which the Lord replies:

> *7 My son, peace be unto thy soul; thine adversity and thine afflictions shall be but a small moment;*

> *8 And then, if thou endure it well, God shall exalt thee on high;*

This promise is real. Times get tough, but if we endure it well and with the proper perspective, we are promised greater blessings on the other side of these sorrows and afflictions.

Questions to Ponder: What is a trial or affliction you're going through right now? Is there another way to look at the situation? One that focuses on faith rather than sorrow?

Daily Challenge: In your prayers today ask the Lord for help putting this principle into practice. Ask for help to "endure it well", and see how much comfort comes from asking for that help.

The Importance to Make These Things Known

> 2 Nephi 2:6-9 - 6 Wherefore, redemption cometh in and through the Holy Messiah; for he is full of grace and truth.

> 7 Behold, he offered himself a sacrifice for sin, to answer the ends of the law, unto all those who have a broken heart and a contrite spirit; and unto none else can the ends of the law be answered.

> 8 Wherefore, how great the importance to make these things known unto the inhabitants of the earth, that they may know that there is no flesh that can dwell in the presence of God, save it be through the merits, and mercy, and grace of the Holy Messiah, who layeth down his life according to the flesh, and taketh it again by the power of the Spirit, that he may bring to pass the resurrection of the dead, being the first that should rise.

> 9 Wherefore he is the first fruits unto God, inasmuch as he shall make intercession for all the children of men; and they that believe in him shall be saved.

Given the context from yesterday's email, Lehi is still speaking to his son Jacob, potentially some of the last words he will speak to him this directly. One of the first things he does is to testify of the Savior and his atonement.

Think of all the things Lehi and Nephi saw in their dreams and their visions. There likely aren't many others that have lived on this earth that have seen the things they saw. And the faith that was required of them - this was all to happen in the future! Whereas for us, this is something that happened 2000 years ago. I'm not sure which situation is easier when it comes to faith, but to hear Lehi testify of our Savior always helps reinforce my testimony.

Honestly it's one of the reasons I felt it important to write these emails every day - "how great the importance to make these things known unto the inhabitants of the earth".

Questions to Ponder: Given your testimony, how can you help others learn about the truths that you know about from the scriptures? Who can you tell about The Book of Mormon, of Joseph Smith, and the restoration of the gospel, the priesthood, and the Lord's true church on the earth today?

Daily Challenge: You guessed it - go and tell that person you just thought of. Tell them something. Offer your testimony of a gospel truth that you think can help their lives. Send them a copy of The Book of Mormon with some of your favorite verses highlighted. Send them a video produced by the church with an inspirational message. Then let me know how it goes! I'm excited to see how it works out for you and your friend.

Opposition in All Things

> *2 Nephi 2:11 - For it must needs be, that there is an opposition in all things. If not so, my firstborn in the wilderness, righteousness could not be brought to pass, neither wickedness, neither holiness nor misery, neither good or bad.*

There's so much to unpack in this section of Lehi's words to his son Jacob. First of all, the context. Lehi is speaking of the plan of salvation, about the creation, the fall, and the Atonement, and how all of these things were worked out long before they occurred. We know from the book of Abraham that the Lord was chosen to come down before the earth was even created. That knowledge is expanded upon in the temple.

The big takeaway for me is how much hinges on this idea of opposition. Without it we don't have agency, which means we don't have a fall, we don't have (or need) an atonement, which leaves us without a way to return to live with our Heavenly Father again. So much of the plan of salvation doesn't work if there's no opposition - which is why the Savior's plan was chosen over Lucifer/Satan's.

Even he is an integral part of the plan, as he's the source of much of the opposition we face in this life. In Doctrine & Covenants 29:39 it says, "and it must needs be that the devil should tempt the children of men, or they could not be agents unto themselves; for if they never should have bitter they could not know the sweet--"

Questions to Ponder: With this perspective in mind, how does that change how we deal with opposition, with trials and afflictions, with hardship, and when things don't go the way we planned. Could there be a bigger reason that these things are happening? There's no progress without opposition, so what is the Lord trying to help you get to?

Daily Challenge: Dig a little deeper on this one. Go into the scriptures, look at the footnotes, the topical guide, and wherever else you can find more discussion on this topic of opposition. A great place to start is this conference talk from April 2016 by Elder Oaks.

If Ye Shall Say There Is No Law...

> 2 Nephi 2:13 - "And if ye shall say there is no law, ye shall also say there is no sin. If ye say there is no sin, ye shall also say there is no righteousness. And if there be no righteousness there can be no happiness. And if there be no righteousness nor happiness there be no punishment nor misery. And if these things are not there is no God. And if there is no God we are not, neither the earth; for there could have been no creation of things, neither to act nor to be acted upon; wherefore, all things must have vanished away."

I think we learn a lot about Satan and his motivations here. If he can effectively get us to believe that the gospel isn't true - that there is no law, no sin, no happiness, no God - then he wins. It's the epitome of pride to work this hard to get us to fail, just because his plan wasn't chosen in the pre-mortal existence. But think about how effective he's already been. I would bet that every single one of us has a friend or family member who has fallen for one or more of these deceptions. "Ah, it's just coffee." "There is no God". What's the point right? If you believe any of these things, then there's no meaning to any of it and why even try?

Later in the chapter we learn that his goal is to make us miserable. This is a super effective method that the adversary uses to lead strong members away from the gospel and to forfeit their salvation. How pathetic do you have to believe that YOU win if you can make it so that OTHERS lose? That's what we're dealing with here, a petulant little child who's still mad that he didn't win.

Don't. Let. Him. Win.

Questions to Ponder: What gospel truths and principles have you questioned or struggled with? How can we "doubt our doubts" and work to strengthen our testimonies on those topics?

Daily Challenge: Pick one doubt, one thing you struggle with, and do something today to study, expand your perspective, put it into action, and try your faith on it. We have to be active in maintaining and growing our testimonies or we are headed toward the other end of the spectrum outlined in today's verse.

Act For Himself

> *2 Nephi 2:16 - Wherefore, the Lord God gave unto man that he should act for himself. Wherefore, man could not act for himself save it should be that he was enticed by the one or the other.*

Yes, we're continuing our deep dive on 2 Nephi 2 this week. There are just so many great verses that teach us incredible truths that I can't leave them out.

This verse is a call back to the email from two or three days ago about the need for opposition in all things. We are taught about agency, and that agency is contingent upon there being choices, and to have different choices you have to have opposition. We're also taught that this gift of agency came from God, that he gave us this ability as part of the plan of salvation. It's not happenstance or coincidence, it is an integral part of how the plan works.

Knowing that this was all thought out before we came here can be an incredibly strengthening principle of the gospel. It's easy at times to feel alone, or even abandoned. The truth is that we've likely just made choices that have altered our relationship with God, from OUR end, not His. Choices have consequences, but the right choices also have blessings that follow. It's up to us to use our agency in the right way to get the desired result.

Questions to Ponder: How does this perspective change the choices you make on a daily basis? Are there simple things that can be changed that would bring us closer to God?

I love this story from President Hinckley that he's shared a few times in General Conference:

> *I recall a bishop telling me of a woman who came to get a recommend. When asked if she observed the Word of Wisdom, she said that she occasionally drank a cup of coffee. She said, "Now, bishop, you're not going to let that keep me from going to the temple, are you?" To which he replied, "Sister, surely you will not let a cup of coffee stand between you and the House of the Lord." (emphasis added).*

Daily Challenge: Drop something that's holding you back. Ask the Lord for help in prayer if you can't think of something. None of us are perfect and we can all do better. Find somethings simple you can choose to change, today.

That They Might Have Joy

2 Nephi 2:21-27 - 21...wherefore, their state became a state of probation, and their time was lengthened, according to the commandments which the Lord God gave unto the children of men. For he gave commandment that all men must repent; for he showed unto all men that they were lost, because of the transgression of their parents.

22 And now, behold, if Adam had not transgressed he would not have fallen, but he would have remained in the garden of Eden. And all things which were created must have remained in the same state in which they were after they were created; and they must have remained forever, and had no end.

23 And they would have had no children; wherefore they would have remained in a state of innocence, having no joy, for they knew no misery; doing no good, for they knew no sin.

24 But behold, all things have been done in the wisdom of him who knoweth all things.

25 Adam fell that men might be, and men are, that they might have joy.

26 And the Messiah cometh in the fulness of time, that he may redeem the children of men from the fall. And because that they are redeemed from the fall they have become free forever, knowing good from evil; to act for themselves and not be acted upon, save it be by the punishment of the law at the great and last day, according to the commandments which God hath given.

27 Wherefore, men are free according to the flesh; and all things are given them which are expedient unto man. And they are free to choose liberty and eternal life, through the great Mediator of all men, or to choose captivity and death, according to the captivity and power of the devil; for he seeketh that all men might be miserable like unto himself.

I know, it's a lot today. Sorry? Not sorry? I'm undecided on that one.

I guess I could have broken this section up into seven different emails, but I thought it nice to put them together to give some extra perspective to the plan our Heavenly Father has for us, specifically how all of these things are perfectly connected and interdependent. In these handful of verses we learn about repentance, the fallen state of man, the plan of salvation, the atonement, redemption from the fall, agency, laws and obedience, and Satan's motivation. Whew!

It's almost like this was all thought through ahead of time, rather than life being a strange confluence of unrelated events which ends when we die... hmm...

The bird's-eye-view takeaway for me from these verses is that our Heavenly Father truly does have a plan for us. That he has infinite wisdom, and that we are in good hands. Yes, sometimes bad things happen. Sometimes we falter as we journey along through our lives. But literally everything has been thought of, stress tested, and proven. There is a plan that works, and it works for US. How incredible is that?

Questions to Ponder: How do you feel after reading these verses? Where does your mind go? What is the Spirit helping reveal and testify?

Daily Challenge: Reread the 2nd chapter of Nephi that we've been pulling verses from over the last few days. Get the full context, then ask the same ponder questions from today. How do you feel? What verses stand out to you? Why do you think that is? Let me know how it goes, I love talking to others about this chapter, because there's so much in there to talk about!

The Knowledge Of My Covenants

> *2 Nephi 3:12 - Wherefore, the fruit of thy loins shall write; and the fruit of the loins of Judah shall write; and that which shall be written by the fruit of thy loins, and also that which shall be written by the fruit of the loins of Judah, shall grow together, unto the confounding of false doctrines and laying down of contentions, and establishing peace among the fruit of thy loins, and bringing them to the knowledge of their fathers in the latter days, and also the the knowledge of my covenants, saith the Lord.*

Here's a verse that has brought me so much comfort over the last few years, specifically as I've gotten more into politics. Think about that - you can basically describe politics as "false doctrines, contentions, and lack of knowledge". How often do we hear about things like fake news and propaganda, living in a "post-truth" society, and being lied to on a consistent basis.

It's almost like the prophets in The Book of Mormon saw our day and included words specifically for our time...

ANY time that I find myself drowning in a sea of confusion and doubt, fear and contention, I am so grateful that I can turn to the scriptures. The Bible and The Book of Mormon together exist to help us find peace and knowledge. And isn't it interesting that the solution to so many of these problems we're facing in the world is just that: knowledge.

Questions to Ponder: Where in your life are you confused, or experiencing contention with others? What scriptures can help you overcome those feelings?

Daily Challenge: Do something today to strengthen your testimony of the scriptures as the word of God. You can pray, read, ponder, study - for any amount of time - but with the goal of deepening your testimony in these sacred texts.

The Words Which He Shall Write

> 2 Nephi 3:19 - And the words which he shall write shall be the words which are expedient in my wisdom should go forth unto the fruit of thy loins. And it shall be as if the fruit of they loins had cried unto them from the dust; for I know their faith.

Here, a simple promise: The Book of Mormon was written for our day. Specifically compiled by Mormon from the writings of numerous prophets, hidden up for hundreds of years, translated by the prophet Joseph Smith, and now sitting before us, available anywhere, for free. That's not even the coolest part: the principles and promises contained in this book were chosen specifically for our time... but how does that work?

Our time is certainly different than the time of Joseph Smith. Or the early 1900s. Or even just a few decades ago. So how is it that it was written for our time?

Because the principles and promises contained in the Book of Mormon are true principles, and true principles don't change. They can be applied to anyone, at any time, in any situation. That's the "expedient in my wisdom" part - at least that's how I read it. At times it's helpful to picture Kind Benjamin, or Moroni, or Alma speaking directly to us as we read their words - because that's how it's intended.

Questions to Ponder: What are your favorite verses in the scriptures? Why? Was there a scripture that was particularly helpful during a stressful or arduous time in your life? What is the principle in that verse that helped you?

Daily Challenge: Re-read a few of your favorite scriptures throughout the day. Remember where you were when they became important to you. See how the Lord was helping you through the scriptures, and tease out the principles in those verses.

Ye Shall Prosper In The Land

> *2 Nephi 4:4 - For the Lord God hath said that: Inasmuch as ye shall keep my commandments ye shall prosper in the land; and inasmuch as ye will not keep my commandments ye shall be cut off from my presence.*

This was one of the first verses that stood out to me as I was reading through The Book Of Mormon this year that lead me down the path that has brought me to here, writing this email. Such a straightforward statement. Keep the commandments, and you'll be good.

It's SO simple, right? Now, simple doesn't always mean easy... I've learned that too many times, and I bet we all have. None of us are perfect, and our Heavenly Father knows that. He's also told us that it's about doing everything we can do, not about being perfect. It's nice to know that this isn't binary. Yes, keeping A commandment is pretty binary - either you kept the word of wisdom or you didn't; either you stole or you didn't... But knowing that none of us will have a perfect score at the end of our life, it's more about doing what we can.

Then there's that second part: prosper in the land. At the time, I imagine that was one of the most important things the Lord could tell someone; an incredible blessing as a reward for keeping the commandments. I often think about what that means in our day, for me in my life, for my family, for my business. Seems like a pretty good bet, right? Keep the commandments and I'll bless your life.

I'm in!

Questions to Ponder: What's a commandment or gospel principle you're struggling with? Can the added perspective of promised blessings - "prospering in the land" - help you overcome that temptation? What does prosper in the land mean for you, for your family, for your life?

Daily Challenge: Give up a temptation, cold turkey, for the next week. That's it. 7 days. If at the end of those 7 days you still feel the need to go back to that thing - then sure, go ahead. (I'm not condoning sin here, just saying...sometimes things are hard.) My guess is that, rather, after a week of giving it up, you'll barely miss it, and wonder why you hadn't done it sooner.

Fight Not Against Zion

> 2 Nephi 6:12-13 - 12 And blessed are the Gentiles, they of whom the prophet has written; for behold, if it so be that they shall repent and fight not against Zion, and do not unite themselves to that great and abominable church, they shall be saved; for the Lord God will fulfill his covenants which he has made unto his children; and for this cause the prophet has written these things.

> 13 Wherefore, they that fight against Zion and the covenant people of the Lord shall lick up the dust of their feet; and the people of the Lord shall not be ashamed. For the people of the Lord are they who wait for him; for they shall wait for the coming of the Messiah.

In this section, Jacob is teaching us using the words of Isaiah. In chapter 6 verse 4-5 he gives us some introductory context:

> 4 And now, behold, I would speak unto you concerning things which are, and which are to come; wherefore, I will read you the words of Isaiah... And I speak unto you for your sakes, that ye may learn and glorify the name of your God.

> 5 And now, the words which I shall read are they which Isaiah spake concerning all the house of Israel; wherefore, they may be likened unto you, for ye are of the house of Israel...

The words of Isaiah are important because we are of the house of Israel. The words directly apply to us in our day. So let's break it down.

Gentiles: us.

Great and abominable church: check out 1 Nephi 13

Lick up the dust of their feet: sounds about as gross now as it would be back then

Wait: From the church's Book of Mormon Study Guide:

The word wait, as used by Isaiah, means to remain strongly attached while staying put, or still, until something expected occurs. To "wait upon the Lord" is to remain true to Him until the time when He sees fit to pour out the full measure of His blessings.

It's often difficult to parse out the teachings from the Isaiah sections quoted in The Book of Mormon, but I've found that if we can modernize it, then figure out the imagery that doesn't directly translate because we live in such a different time, that it makes it possible.

These verses stuck out to me because of everything that's going on in our world right now, especially within the church. We have this extremely direct warning for those who would choose to fight against Zion. What happens to them is not pretty, yet people still choose that path.

It's important for us to remember to wait when things happen. To remain strongly attached while staying put. To remain true until the time that the blessings come.

Questions to Ponder: Who is Isaiah speaking to now? Why is Jacob quoting these sections? Why would Mormon choose to include these verses?

The Mighty One of Jacob

> *2 Nephi 6:17-18 - 17...for the Mighty God shall deliver his covenant people. For thus saith the Lord: I will contend with them that contendeth with thee—*

> *18 And I will feed them that press thee, with their own flesh; and they shall be drunken with their own blood as with sweet wine; and all flesh shall know that I the Lord am thy Savior and thy Redeemer, the Mighty One of Jacob.*

Continuing on yesterday's thread, this is more Isaiah. (Guy sure knew how to paint a picture, am I right?)

And again, we get this promise that God shall deliver his covenant people. Not only that, he says, but the Lord will contend with them that contendeth with thee. In other words, those that "fight against" you.

Over the last few days I've received a bunch of emails from readers of this daily "newsletter", and a common thread of why people had signed up was that they were struggling - either with life, or their faith, or a number of other things. It's verses like this that I hope will help those that are struggling. It's part of the scriptures, I think, because these prophets knew what we would deal with in our lives, and wanted to have these "records" help us through them. God will deliver his covenant people, those that are keeping their covenants and striving to live the gospel. Whatever we're going through in our lives, we can take comfort in the power and strength of our Mighty Savior and Redeemer.

Questions to Ponder: What else can we do to more strongly be defined as the Lord's "covenant people"? What other words are used to describe our Savior, Jesus Christ? Which one's stand out to you, and why do you think that is?

Daily Challenge: Read through the whole chapter, 2 Nephi 6. For further reference you can check out the church's Book of Mormon Study Guide.

The Lord Shall Comfort Zion

> *2 Nephi 8:3 - For the Lord shall comfort Zion, he will comfort all her waste places; and he will make her wilderness like Eden, and her desert like the garden of the Lord. Joy and gladness shall be found therein, thanksgiving and the voice of melody.*

Jacob is still quoting Isaiah here, and he's specifically talking about he last days. For me, this is another comforting scripture - the Lord shall comfort Zion. Look at the promises in this verse - sure, the world is a scary place right now, so much uncertainty, so much pride, so much unrighteousness. But we can choose to focus on those things, or we can choose to focus on our own lives, the choices we make, and the blessings that come to those who choose to keep the commandments and follow the Lord.

Zion sounds like a much better option.

Questions to Ponder: Why is it so effective for Satan to get us faithful saints to focus on all of the negative aspects of the world? What happens when we forget all of these promised blessings for Zion? How do we spend more time thinking about the latter?

Daily Challenge: Go a day without social media. Without news. Without tweets. Without the negativity that shows up in our news feeds. See how you feel at the end of the day :)

Ye That Know Righteousness

> *2 Nephi 8:7-8 - 7 Hearken unto me, ye that know righteousness, the people in whose heart I have written my law, fear ye not the reproach of men, neither be ye afraid of their reviling.*

> *8 For the moth shall eat them up like a garment, and the worm shall eat them like wool. But my righteousness shall be forever, and my salvation from generation to generation.*

The big takeaway for me from these verses is that we get some more detail about our Savior and his attributes. His righteousness shall be forever.

Isaiah is still talking about the last days in this chapter, and specifically about the gathering of Israel. He's speaking about the time, but also about the people that will be redeemed. So he uses phrases like "ye that know righteousness, the people in whose heart I have written my law". And what does he say to them (us)? Fear not.

Then teaches us a principle, that his righteousness is forever. Doesn't it help to know that the things we believe in, the things we are told to have faith in are not fleeting dogmas, not fads, not trends - but real, true principles? It does for me.

Questions to Ponder: Why did Isaiah include these words in his writings? Why did Jacob quote them, and Mormon select them to be a part of the record? Why do those who are righteous need not fear the "reproach of men...or their reviling"?

Daily Challenge: Dig a little deeper into these chapters. A good place to start is in the Book of Mormon Student Manual.

Sorrow and Mourning Shall Flee Away

> *2 Nephi 8:11 - Therefore, the redeemed of the Lord shall return, and come with singing unto Zion; and everlasting joy and holiness shall be upon their heads; and they shall obtain gladness and joy; sorrow and mourning shall flee away.*

Another promise verse from Isaiah and Jacob (and Mormon, since he included it in the record... :)

Even if you don't translate the verse into modern language, it still sounds incredible. Everlasting joy and holiness. Gladness and joy. No more sorrow and morning. It sounds exactly what we are all looking for in our own lives RIGHT NOW doesn't it?

Like I mentioned before, nearly half of the responses I get from people as to why they signed up was because they were struggling, and needed something. (I respond with "dive into the scriptures", but hopefully these daily emails help as a stepping stone...)

The answers are right here though. If we're struggling, if our life could be described as the opposite of this verse, then this chapter, this book is for us. Righteousness. Obedience to the commandments. Humility, faith, repentance, diligence...all of these things lead to joy and gladness and the removal of sorrow and mourning. And, from my experience, we start seeing those blessings come into our lives the moment we begin to try. There's no threshold for righteousness that qualifies us for blessings. We don't have to be 83% righteous in order to qualify for blessings. We have to try. It's binary - either we are or we aren't trying to better live the gospel. Let's all do better, try a little harder, help each other out and make our lives more joyful and holy in the process.

Questions to Ponder: Reading over that verse, how does it sound to you? How great would it be to receive those blessings? What can we do to put things into the proper perspective, so that the blessings outweigh the hard stuff we're going to have to go through to get them?

Daily Challenge: Spend some time today meditating - sitting quietly, phone off, not in front of any computer or tv or devices, just quiet and alone. Think about the weight of it all - that we have a Savior. That it's part of an incredible plan, one that was agreed upon before we came to this earth. Try and put it all into perspective.

An Infinite Atonement

> 2 Nephi 9:7 - *Wherefore, it must needs be an infinite atonement—save it should be an infinite atonement this corruption could not put on incorruption. Wherefore, the first judgment which came upon man must needs have remained to an endless duration. And if so, this flesh must have laid down to rot and crumble to its mother earth, to rise no more.*

Here Jacob continues speaking to his brothers about our Heavenly Father's plan, and honestly, going through the scriptures this way has given me a ton of new perspective about Jacob. I love the way he teaches, I love how blunt and straightforward he is, and especially how logical he is in the way he understands and teaches these doctrines.

He's talking about how if there were no atonement, we wouldn't even be here. The first judgment, or physical death, would be permanent without the atonement. So many things hang on this atonement that our Savior provided, and we learn even more, that it had to be an infinite atonement - not merely a sacrifice of a man or an animal, but of our Savior. He was the only one that could have provided such an atonement, and he chose to do so, in part because of you and I.

Think about how personal that is. It's truly incredible.

Questions to Ponder: Why did the plan require an infinite atonement? What does this say about our Savior? About our Heavenly Father? About the plan of salvation?

Daily Challenge: Take a moment today, whether in your thoughts or on your knees, to offer a prayer of gratitude. Strictly gratitude, no requests, just gratitude for our Savior, for his sacrifice, and for the plan of salvation. Give yourself time after your prayer to listen for the Spirit and his testimony of these truths.

An Experiment

2 Nephi 9:17-39 - 17 O the greatness and the justice of our God! For he executeth all his words, and they have gone forth out of his mouth, and his law must be fulfilled.

18 But, behold, the righteous, the saints of the Holy One of Israel, they who have believed in the Holy One of Israel, they who have endured the crosses of the world, and despised the shame of it, they shall inherit the kingdom of God, which was prepared for them from the foundation of the world, and their joy shall be full forever.

19 O the greatness of the mercy of our God, the Holy One of Israel! For he delivereth his saints from that awful monster the devil, and death, and hell, and that lake of fire and brimstone, which is endless torment.

20 O how great the holiness of our God! For he knoweth all things, and there is not anything save he knows it.

21 And he cometh into the world that he may save all men if they will hearken unto his voice; for behold, he suffereth the pains of all men, yea, the pains of every living creature, both men, women, and children, who belong to the family of Adam.

22 And he suffereth this that the resurrection might pass upon all men, that all might stand before him at the great and judgment day.

23 And he commandeth all men that they must repent, and be baptized in his name, having perfect faith in the Holy One of Israel, or they cannot be saved in the kingdom of God.

24 And if they will not repent and believe in his name, and be baptized in his name, and endure to the end, they must be damned; for the Lord God, the Holy One of Israel, has spoken it.

25 Wherefore, he has given a law; and where there is no law given there is no punishment; and where there is no punishment there is no condemnation; and where there is no condemnation the mercies of the Holy One of Israel have claim upon them, because of the atonement; for they are delivered by the power of him.

26 For the atonement satisfieth the demands of his justice upon all those who have not the law given to them, that they are delivered from that awful monster, death and hell, and the devil, and the lake of fire and brimstone, which is endless torment; and they are restored to that God who gave them breath, which is the Holy One of Israel.

27 But wo unto him that has the law given, yea, that has all the commandments of God, like unto us, and that transgresseth them, and that wasteth the days of his probation, for awful is his state!

28 O that cunning plan of the evil one! O the vainness, and the frailties, and the foolishness of men! When they are learned they think they are wise, and they hearken not unto the counsel of God, for they set it aside, supposing they know of themselves, wherefore, their wisdom is foolishness and it profiteth them not. And they shall perish.

29 But to be learned is good if they hearken unto the counsels of God.

30 But wo unto the rich, who are rich as to the things of the world. For because they are rich they despise the poor, and they persecute the meek, and their hearts are upon their treasures; wherefore, their treasure is their god. And behold, their treasure shall perish with them also.

31 And wo unto the deaf that will not hear; for they shall perish.

32 Wo unto the blind that will not see; for they shall perish also.

33 Wo unto the uncircumcised of heart, for a knowledge of their iniquities shall smite them at the last day.

34 Wo unto the liar, for he shall be thrust down to hell.

35 Wo unto the murderer who deliberately killeth, for he shall die.

36 Wo unto them who commit whoredoms, for they shall be thrust down to hell.

37 Yea, wo unto those that worship idols, for the devil of all devils delighteth in them.

38 And, in fine, wo unto all those who die in their sins; for they shall return to God, and behold his face, and remain in their sins.

> *39 O, my beloved brethren, remember the awfulness in transgressing against that Holy God, and also the awfulness of yielding to the enticings of that cunning one. Remember, to be carnally-minded is death, and to be spiritually-minded is life eternal.*

Questions to Ponder: What blessings come to the righteous? What do these verses teach us about the plan of salvation? About God? The Atonement? The gospel? What parts stood out to you? Why do you think that is? What can we learn from these verses?

The Way For Man Is Narrow

> 2 Nephi 9:41-42 - 41...Behold, the way for man is narrow, but it lieth in a straight course before him, and the keeper of the gate is the Holy One of Israel; and he employs no servant there; and there is none other way save it be by the gate; for he cannot be deceived, for the Lord God is his name.

> 42 And whoso knocketh, to him he will open; and the wise, and the learned, and they that are rich, who are puffed up because of their learning, and their wisdom, and their riches—yea, they are they whom he despiseth; and save they shall cast these things away, and consider themselves fools before God, and come down into the depths of humility, he will not open unto them.

Feels like a lot to unpack in two short verses. Look at all of the principles laid out here: the way is narrow / Christ is the keeper of the gate / that's the only way / knock & he'll open / the prideful are despised / the importance of humility.

This is a great verse to turn to when things feel...off. It's a firm reminder of how this all works. That yes, it's hard. It's strict. There are rules and laws and commandments and that obedience is important. That we have to have the right motivations, and they need to be on the humble end of the spectrum, not the prideful end.

Ever just feel stuck? I know I've been there. What do we need to DO when we feel stuck? Take a breath, sit, try to get some perspective.

Questions to Ponder: Are we doing things that would put us in the wrong side of the line in these verses? How can we humble ourselves and focus on Christ and the plan of salvation and the gospel?

Daily Challenge: Mark this verse, whether on your phone, or in your scriptures, or flag/star/save this email. We'll all get stuck at some point, and you'll want to have this readily available when that time comes.

I Will Be Their King

> 2 Nephi 10:14 - *For he that raiseth up a king against me shall perish, for I, the Lord, the king of heaven, will be their king, and I will be a light unto them forever, that hear my words.*

There's a promise in there, but what does this verse mean? Jacob is talking about America, and how it is meant to be. In verse 11 he says:

And this land shall be a land of liberty unto the Gentiles, and there shall be no kings upon the land, who shall raise up unto the Gentiles.

I'm not sure why the "no kings" rule, but it's there in plain site. He does say in verse 12 that he will fortify this land against all other nations, my assumption is that if we were to break the "no kings" rule that it would be harder for him to fortify the land.

Look at the opposite though. We have the Lord as our king, a light unto us forever, that hear his words. Sounds much better than a King.

I think this verse mainly gives me something to focus on. No matter what is going on politically, who is leading the country, what war we're fighting or not fighting, etc, this verse just puts it all into perspective. To me it means that none of that matters, because in the end we'll be lead and governed by the Lord and his laws - heavens laws. Eternal laws that are good, and people are going to want to follow them.

Questions to Ponder: What does that mean now? What should we do about this verse? How does it change how we look at the world, and specifically at politics or similar matters?

Daily Challenge: Spend some time thinking about how we interact with others about topics like religion and politics and other things that can be divisive. How can we start to be more inclusive? Think about how our choices and our actions can reflect our broader perspective.

They Who Are Not For Me Are Against Me

> 2 Nephi 10:16 - Wherefore, he that fighteth against Zion, both Jew and Gentile, both bond and free, both male and female, shall perish; for they are they who are the whore of all the earth; for they who are not for me are against me, saith our God.

The part that really hits me is the bluntness of the last part of the verse - they who are not for me are against me. We've come out of a lesson just in the last week about how there is opposition in all things - well that applies here as well.

It's binary. There's no middle ground. Either you're for him or against, fighting for Zion or fighting against it. We know what happens to those that fight against...

The point is that there's a choice that has to be made, and the actions that follow that choice determine where we stand.

Questions to Ponder: How are your actions now reinforcing your stance? What can we do better? How can we fight for Zion in our daily lives, in the decisions we make throughout the day? In how we spend our time? In what we choose to talk about?

Daily Challenge: Find one opportunity today to "fight for Zion". If Zion is the pure in heart, the ultimate destination for the saints, make an action or decision today that is in alignment with that.

For They Shall Perish

> 2 Nephi 13:10-11 - 10 Say unto the righteous that it is well with them; for they shall eat the fruit of their doings. 11 Wo unto the wicked, for they shall perish; for the reward of their hands shall be upon them.

So much talk of perishing in the scriptures. It's not a word that I ever use, but I counted over 40 scriptures that mentioned the word or the concept. It's typically used in an if/then (or wo unto/for) manner, as a consequence laid out for those that choose wickedness over righteousness, sin over obedience.

To perish means to suffer death, complete ruin, or destruction.

Dang.

If we're using these scriptures to broaden our perspective of the principles of the gospel contained in The Book of Mormon (I hope we are) then this is one concept to spend a lot of time thinking about. Another email I subscribe to about Stoicism recently pushed out a series of emails on the phrase "Memento Mori", or the practice of reflecting on our own mortality. I feel like the scriptures our teaching us to "memento perish" (no, I don't know latin), that there are consequences of our actions, both for good and for bad. It should help us realize that we need to make conscious decisions, to take our agency seriously, and to live the gospel with as much discipline as we can.

Questions to Ponder: How can we "memento perish", and use it in a way that helps us to better live the gospel? Why would the prophets use this principle and this word so frequently in the scriptures? What's the modern version of the word that we can use to apply to our own lives and the decisions we make?

Daily Challenge: Spend some time pondering / meditating on the word and concept "perish". Try to expand your perspective on it and why the prophets would harp on it so much as a punishment for sin and unrighteousness.

Wo Unto Them

> 2 Nephi 15:20 - Wo unto them that call evil good, and good evil, that put darkness for light, and light for darkness, that put bitter for sweet, and sweet for bitter.

This verse has been on my mind for a few months now. At the beginning of the year my business partner and I started an online political show called Zion Politics. While diving head first into the arena of news, politics, current events, and so on, I quickly realized the responsibility placed upon those that speak to a group of people.

I feel it even more now that I write these emails every day. With a platform comes the responsibility to be truthful, honest, and forthright, while also being vigilant in not distorting facts or principles to your own ends.

Yet, it seems that there are plenty of people that profit off of this very concept. There's certainly money to be made in the realm of calling evil good and good evil. While I'm not here to tell you which news outlets fall under which category, what I do want to say is that it is important to check the sources, to be lead by the spirit, to make sure that we are learning about the world from people with the proper motivations.

There are so many inputs in our lives today compared to even a generation ago. How many different 24 hour news networks are there? Not to mention the different websites, social media channels and profiles, plus numerous other platforms all vying for our attention. If we are not aware, if we are not careful, this is one of the many ways that Satan can deceive us and lead us astray. Believing that evil is good and good evil is literally an alternate reality, and the choices that come from living in that distorted version of the world can't be good, because they aren't of God.

It's a topic I try to take very seriously, and I hope you'll do the same.

Questions to Ponder: What sources do you turn to to get your news and to learn what is going on in the world? How do we know if they are reputable, trustworthy, and "of good report"? What can we do to test that we are calling good good, and evil evil?

Daily Challenge: Perform an audit of your social media feeds and news sources. Are there any extreme voices that you're consuming on a regular basis that could be culled or removed?

We Labor Diligently To Write

> *2 Nephi 25:23 - For we labor diligently to write, to persuade our children, and also our brethren, to believe in Christ, and to be reconciled to God; for we know that it is by grace that we are saved, after all we can do.*

I love this verse, and have since my seminary days back in California. There's something extra special about The Book of Mormon, how it was written, preserved, translated - every step of the way there were hardships and obstacles. Satan really didn't want this book to get into our hands. But look at the fruit of their labors now, these brave men and women that helped this book to come forth. We can literally access it any time we want, anywhere we want. It's practically ubiquitous.

They labored diligently to write. I know that's not the promise part of the verse, but I love that. It reminds me that the prophets that wrote this book saw our day and knew how important these words would be for us in this time.

Then, the principle: It is by grace that we are saved after all we can do. As I've been working on the book, one of the recurring themes when it comes to the atonement of our Savior is that it's not just a free pass. It requires effort on our part - our faith, our diligence, our obedience to the commandments. It is there, available for all of us, but we have to choose it. We do that through our actions. Salvation wouldn't be possible without the atonement of our Savior, but we must do all we can as well.

Questions to Ponder: When you think of the phrase "all we can do", what comes to mind? What more could we be doing? How important must these scriptures be if so many individuals labored diligently to write, preserve, and translate it for us to have?

Daily Challenge: Offer a prayer of gratitude. Don't ask for anything, just think and pray with thanks for the atoning sacrifice of our Savior, Jesus Christ, and all that he has done for us. For the plan of salvation. For the scriptures. For the Holy Ghost that guides and comforts us. Then spend some extra time listening to the promptings of the Spirit testifying and teaching you.

Ye Must Bow Down Before Him

> *2 Nephi 25:28-29 - 28 ...And the words which I have spoken shall stand as a testimony against you; for they are sufficient to teach any man the right way; for the right way is to believe in Christ and deny him not; for by denying him ye also deny the prophets and the law.*

> *29 And now behold, I say unto you that the right way is to believe in Christ, and deny him not; and Christ is the Holy One of Israel; wherefore ye must bow down before him, and worship him with all your might, mind, and strength, and your whole soul; and if ye do this ye shall in nowise be cast out.*

First, some context. In this chapter Nephi is summarizing all of the words of Isaiah he had just quoted, and tells everyone that he "glories in plainness" (v. 4). He then goes on to prophesy (v. 7) about the scriptures, how they will be understood in the last days. He prophesies about how the Jews will return from Babylon, crucify the Messiah, and be scattered and scourged, that they will be restored when they believe in the Messiah. He says Christ will first come six hundred years after they left Jerusalem. (These all came true, by the way...)

Then, toward the end of the chapter, two other verses emphasizing the importance of the scriptures:

> *23 For we labor diligently to write, to persuade our children, and also our brethren, to believe in Christ, and to be reconciled to God; for we know that it is by grace that we are saved, after all we can do.*

> *26 And we talk of Christ, we rejoice in Christ, we preach of Christ, we prophesy of Christ, and we write according to our prophecies, that our children may know to what source they may look for a remission of their sins.*

These scriptures are incredibly important to Nephi. You can feel the fervor in his words, they're extra emotional, filled with so much determination, like he's willing them into our hearts somehow. I know that's not how it works, but you kinda feel like Nephi wish he could just give his testimony directly to us.

Then the promise in verses 28-29. "These words will stand against you, for they are sufficient to teach any man the right way". How often do we turn to self-help books or gurus or coaches for guidance in our lives? Why??? The scriptures are sufficient! Once I read those words I've tried extra hard to trade my non-fiction reading for scripture reading, and it's incredible the change that has happened in my life. So much more clarity, guidance, direction - all from one little change.

It's about believing in Christ, and being humble about it. We don't know everything, and we're not going to find answers to many of life's problems out in the world or on the internet. The principles are all right her, right in this book of scripture. For free. Any time, anywhere. It doesn't mean it's easy - it requires all our might, mind and strength, and our whole soul. But look at the blessings that come from that sort of worship, that level of faith in Christ.

Questions to Ponder: What questions do you have or struggle with when it comes to the gospel? To your life? What answers are you looking for on Google or YouTube? What self help books are you reading? Could those answers be found in the scriptures instead?

Daily Challenge: Read through your scriptures for the next week with one question in mind. The question that you haven't yet found an answer to - could be about your relationship, your business, your finances, your health - and challenge these scriptural promises. Put it to the test. Ask God to help you find answers, and look for them in the scriptures.

Then Cometh Speedy Destruction

> *2 Nephi 26:11 - For the Spirit of the Lord will not always strive with man. And when the Spirit ceaseth to strive with man then cometh speedy destruction...*

In this chapter, Nephi is still prophesying of the coming of the Savior, his resurrection, and his ministry to the Nephites. He also sees the destruction of his people and is taking it pretty hard. In this moment he gives this warning, that the Spirit of the Lord will not always strive with man.

He warns of those that become prideful and disobedient. That they aren't entitled to the Spirit just because at one point they were converted and baptized and received the gift of the Holy Ghost. No, rather the Spirit is something we have to qualify ourselves for constantly. We have to be living the gospel and humbling ourselves constantly to have that real connection with the Spirit. Once we start making exceptions for a little sin here and a little pride there, we're heading in the wrong direction.

When the Spirit stops striving with man then comes speedy destruction. I've seen that in my own life and the life of loved ones. It's a sharp decline and can happen even to the best of us. Let this verse serve as a reminder of the importance to be obedient and to be humble. To repent and to diligently search the scriptures and to be led by the Spirit in all things.

Questions to Ponder: How is your relationship with the Holy Ghost? Are you familiar with his "voice" - how he communicates with you personally? How often do you communicate? Do you feel like you're being led on a daily basis by the promptings of the Spirit? How can we improve that relationship and have it become one of our most important relationships in our lives?

Daily Challenge: President Lorenzo Snow once spoke of the Holy Ghost as our "friend". When I read that chapter I was floored - I'd never heard the Holy Ghost described that way. Spend some time today having a "friendly" conversation with the Holy Ghost. Share what's on your mind, ask for help with the things you need help with, just as you'd text or call your best friend with the same problems.

He Worketh Not In Darkness

> *2 Nephi 26:23-24 - 23 For behold, my beloved brethren, I say unto you that the Lord God worketh not in darkness. 24 He doth not anything save it be for the benefit of the world; for he liveth the world, even that he layeth down his own life that he may draw all men unto him...*

How comforting are these words? Sometimes we need that sort of black and white, line in the sand delineation in our lives. The Lord doesn't work in darkness, so anything that is categorized as "darkness" comes from the devil. Simple right?

His motivations are solely for the benefit of the world, to the extent of laying down his life. If we ever find ourselves doubting the existence of our Savior or our Heavenly Father, their love for us, or the things that are happening in our lives, we can turn to scriptures like this to be reminded about their infinite love for us.

Questions to Ponder: How can we use the concept of light and darkness to direct the choices in our lives? How can we use this perspective of Christ's motivation to feel comfort and love from our Savior?

Daily Challenge: Find a place in your life where there might possibly some darkness. The media we consume? The time we spend on social media? The people we spend time engaging with? How can we remove that darkness and replace it with light?

I Am The Same Yesterday, Today, and Forever

> *2 Nephi 27:23 - For behold, I am God; and I am a God of miracles; and I will show unto the world that I am the same yesterday, today, and forever; and I work not among the children of men save it be according to their faith.*

When I started out I was hesitant to repeat verses that had similar phrases or even similar concepts. "The readers will get bored of it if it's so repetitive..." I thought. Then I read through again a bunch of the verses for a chapter of the book I'm working on, and realized that the frequency of certain topics or certain principles meant something in and of itself.

I had separated all of these verses by keywords, and one of the keywords I chose was "Attributes of Christ". By the end, after I had entered in every single one of the more than 300 verses that I had found in The Book of Mormon, I clicked sort by keyword.

What I found is that the most used keyword was, you guessed it, "Attributes of Christ".

If there's any doubt that this book of scripture is truly "Another Testament of Jesus Christ", I hope this help puts that doubt to rest.

The book teaches us SO MUCH about the attributes, character, life and mission of our Savior. Two that come up frequently are included in this verse - that he is eternally the same, and that the Atonement is in some ways dependent on our faith.

Questions to Ponder: Why is it so important that The Book of Mormon be "another testament of Jesus Christ"? Why do we need another one? Why does the plan os salvation depend on our own faith, our own obedience, our own agency? What is the importance or significance of our Savior being the same "yesterday, today, and forever"?

Daily Challenge: Do a search on your device or online in the scriptures for "yesterday, today, and forever" and see how many verses show up, and what books they're in. Then if you want to go deeper start looking at the reference scriptures connected to those verses. Do a little scripture chase. Try to further understand the importance of this attribute of our Savior.

If the Inhabitants of the Earth Shall Repent

> 2 Nephi 28:15-17 - 15 O the wise, and the learned, and the rich, that are puffed up in the pride of their hearts, and all those who preach false doctrines, and all those who commit whoredoms, and pervert the right way of the Lord, wo, wo, wo be unto them, saith the Lord God Almighty, for they shall be thrust down to hell!

> 16 Wo unto them that turn aside the just for a thing of naught and revile against that which is good, and say that it is of no worth! For the day shall come that the Lord God will speedily visit the inhabitants of the earth; and in that day that they are fully ripe in iniquity they shall perish.

> 17 But behold, if the inhabitants of the earth shall repent of their wickedness and abominations they shall not be destroyed, saith the Lord of Hosts.

Quite the warning.

It's worth reading these verses again, but taking each phrase or sentence and trying to translate them into a more modern language. Imagine Elder Scott saying this over the pulpit, staring down the barrel of the camera right into your soul. (It can't be just me that feels that way, right?)

I love how these verses work together. There's an incredible warning in the first two verses, ending with "they shall be thrust down to hell" and "they shall perish". I feel like they included these verses because they knew how hard things would get in our day. How many temptations, how much pressure, how much noise we'd have to deal with that could lead us away from the gospel. How many of us have friends today that are currently "reviling against that which is good", friends that at one point had an incredibly strong testimony?

It could happen to anyone.

Yet, after all that even, the promise remains. If they repent of their wickedness and abominations they shall not be destroyed. That is the power of the atonement and of repentance. That is the love our Heavenly Father and our Savior have for us.

That is the message of these verses.

Questions to Ponder: How often do we repent? Should we do it more often? What would the Lord have us do?

Daily Challenge: See if there is anything in your life that could be seen as prideful, or "reviling against that which is good". Find a way to remove it from your life, either cold turkey or over a period of time. Use the opportunity to be introspective and humble, and see how it changes your life. I'm going through that right now - it's hard at times, but the blessings (at least for me) have come immediately. It's rather incredible, and it strengthens my testimony in the gospel and atonement of Christ.

We Have Enough

> *2 Nephi 28:30 - For behold, thus saith the Lord God: I will give unto the children of men line upon line, precept upon precept, here a little and there a little; and blessed are those who hearken unto my precepts, and lend an ear unto my counsel, for they shall learn wisdom; for unto him that receiveth I will give more; and from them that shall say, We have enough, from them shall be taken away even that which they have.*

I figured the subject for this email would be "line upon line" or "hearken unto my precepts", but for some reason "We Have Enough" stood out.

On my mission in Washington, D.C. I had a bishop in one of our wards who was extremely well read, as was his wife. At dinners at their house we would talk in depth about different aspects of the gospel that we didn't get to talk about that often. His wife taught the gospel principles class, and I was always impressed at how she could teach in a way that would be interesting to an investigator as well as us missionaries in the room.

But then, something changed. I was only in the area for about three months, but I could tell something was off. She started mentioning our Heavenly Mother in gospel principles class, you know, the class for new converts and investigators? Some of the deep doctrine started seeping into her classes, as well as over the pulpit from the bishop.

A few months later, after being transferred out of that area, I learned from another set of missionaries that the couple had left the church in pursuit of that deeper doctrine, which they felt could not be found in the gospel.

What they had failed to realize is encapsulated in today's verse. The promise is for those who hearken unto the Lord's precepts, and lend an ear to his counsel - those that are humble and teachable enough to listen. The promise is that they will learn wisdom, and that that person will learn more.

How did they miss this simple principle? How do WE miss simple principles of the gospel? Look at how one misunderstanding, one small failure to understand the gospel lead to the apostasy of this incredible couple. Opposite of this example, they were searching for "more", whatever that meant to them at the time, rather than saying "they had enough", yet the result was the same - the had everything they had taken away.

I hope reading this verse today can help us understand the principle of how the Lord teaches us and how we can truly learn wisdom.

Questions to Ponder: How is wisdom different than knowledge? Why would you want one over the other, or both in equal measure? Have we ever told ourselves that "we've had enough"? Are we aware of the consequence of that type of pride in our lives?

Daily Challenge: Do a deep dive on one of your favorite gospel topics. Humility. Light. The Atonement. Repentance. Start with your favorite verse, chase the footnotes and see where they lead. Search the church website for conference talks on the subject. See how you feel at the end, and what new ideas and inspiration comes as you do so.

My Arm Is Lengthened

> 2 Nephi 28:32 - ..I will be merciful unto them, saith the Lord God, if they will repent and come unto me; for mine arm is lengthened out all the day long, saith the Lord of Hosts.

This is your weekly reminder that The Book of Mormon teaches us the importance of repentance, second only in frequency to how often the prophets taught about Christ. I love the imagery in this verse, that the Lord's arm is lengthened all the day long. It reminds me of the outstretched arms of the father of the prodigal son, anxious to embrace his son upon his return.

We all make mistakes. We all are imperfect. We have weaknesses, and we have the tendencies of "the natural man". Yet we also have repentance. The Lord's promise is of mercy and love for those that repent and come unto him. Let's take advantage of that promise and that blessing, and repent often so that we can feel that love and that mercy provided through the atonement of Christ.

Questions to Ponder: Can you imagine the Lord's face, his arms outstretched, his infinite love for you? How does it make you feel? How often do you repent? Can we repent more?

Daily Challenge: This one's easy. Take the opportunity to repent. Find something you wish you hadn't done, a mistake you made, a weakness that got the better of you, a sin you committed. Strive to be better. Ask for forgiveness then really try to eliminate that from your life going forward. Don't worry, I'm not perfect either, so I'll be doing the same :)

My Work Is Not Yet Finished

> *2 Nephi 29:9 - And I do this that I may prove unto many that I am the same yesterday, today, and forever; and that I speak forth my words according to mine own pleasure. And because that I have spoken one word ye need not suppose that I cannot speak another; for my work is not yet finished; neither shall it be until the end of man, neither from that time henceforth and forever.*

We've heard this statement before - that He is the same yesterday, today, and forever - but I love the extra context here. How great is it to have the knowledge that God lives, that he speaks to us today through a modern prophet, that we are able to receive new revelation and guidance from him both as a church and individually and for our families.

I can't tell you how many times I've been struggling, and went to the temple to inquire of the Lord what I needed to do, and received answers. It happened today, in fact. Last night was brutal - I have been bottling up some stress for probably 8 months now, and it kind of all came out last night. It was rough, but I asked my family for some extra prayers, and this morning I did a session at the Provo City Center Temple before work.

Today was incredible. There was this extra clarity, this uplifting feeling like everything was lighter. I had some serendipitous things occur, I met some good people that are sure to be quick friends, and made some progress on some of the projects I'm working on. This same thing has happened on a number of occasions, and I am so incredibly grateful for the reality of the Spirit, and for the revelation that comes through him.

Questions to Ponder: How does this verse make you feel? What stands out the most? What does it mean to you? Given that, what should you do about it?

Daily Challenge: Revisit a favorite conference talk. See what ideas and thoughts it sparks, and what the Spirit teaches you as you study those words from our modern prophets.

Out Of The Books Which Shall Be Written

> *2 Nephi 29:11 - ...for out of the books which shall be written I will judge the world, every man according to their works, according to that which is written.*

I may have mentioned this before, but I spend an inordinate amount of time reading self-help and non-fiction books. I'm always searching for new business principles or life hacks or diet tips...it's not a great way to live because you always feel like you're missing some secret, rather than doing the best with what you have. That statement was for me...not necessarily for you ;)

But then I look at the scriptures, and verses like this, and realize that THIS is what it's really all about. We'll be judged not on how much money our business makes, or what our body fat percentage is, or how tidy our closets are.

We'll be judged according to our knowledge and our actions as they pertain to the gospel of Jesus Christ. Were we repentant? Were we righteous? Did we serve with charity and love? Did we help "bring to pass the immortality and eternal life of man"? And did we keep our covenants?

It's a nice nudge to be able to reframe how we look at our life and what is important. It's one of my favorite aspects of studying the scriptures - the perspective that comes from learning and living the gospel.

Questions to Ponder: How much consumption of other media do you consume in a day? Facebook, TV, podcasts, books... is it possible that we could trade 10 or 20 or even 30 minutes a day of that time to consume the scriptures? To study the gospel just a little more each day?

Daily Challenge: It goes along with the questions to ponder. Find some time in your day, even if you have to wake up a half hour early, to add in time for daily scripture study. Start with just 5 minutes - maybe just these emails. Then add a minute more, and a minute more, and a minute more until it becomes a daily habit.

The Lord Coveneteth With None...

> *2 Nephi 30:1-2 - 1 ...For behold, except ye shall keep the commandments of God ye shall all likewise perish.*

> *2 For behold, I say unto you that as many of the Gentiles as will repent are the covenant people of the Lord; and as many of the Jews as will not repent shall be cast off; for the Lord covenanteth with none save it be with them that repent and believe in his Son, who is the Holy One of Israel.*

Here, again, another emphasis on the importance of repentance, in very clear language. Repentance qualifies us - those that repent are the covenant people of the Lord. If we don't repent and have faith in Christ, we're not living up to our end of the covenant.

If you look at the incredible blessings that come from living the gospel, it's curious why we fail to repent at times. Sometimes out of pride, sometimes because we're not thinking about it... but based purely on the number of times it's mentioned in the scriptures, and how many prophets were called, specifically, to preach repentance and faith on the Lord Jesus Christ, we should be able to learn this very important lesson: that it's imperative that we repent.

Questions to Ponder: What is it about repentance that is so important that it comes up so often in the scriptures? How does repentance relate to, or what role does it play in the atonement of our Savior?

Daily Challenge: You know where we're headed with this. Repent today, for anything. Being impatient with a family member. Not doing something you should have. Doing something you shouldn't have. None of us are perfect, and we're definitely not going to get any better if we don't repent.

The Lord Giveth Light

> 2 Nephi 31:3 - *For my soul delighted in plainness; for after this manner doth the Lord God work among the children of men. For the Lord God giveth light unto the understanding; for he speaketh unto men according to their language, unto their understanding.*

I. Love. This. Scripture.

It's so perfect, so well worded, so powerful, so illuminating and enlightening. (Do those mean the same thing? Sorry for the redundancy...)

The gospel of Jesus Christ is simple, it's intended to be easy to understand. The promise is that as we seek to learn and understand, the Lord gives us light/truth/knowledge/wisdom/understanding. We all "hear" a little differently, and there are a ton of conference talks about how the still small voice works for different people.

The reason I connect so much with this verse is it is how I learn. When I'm studying, or praying, or seeking answers, the Lord speaks to me in clarity. What that means is that one choice out of the many options feels like it makes sense, where the others feel confusing or unclear. Put another way, it's almost as if the correct path is illuminated.

Isn't it just incredible that we have this ability to speak with our Heavenly Father and his Son through prayer, and receive answers this way? That we can learn literally anything if we just ask? I don't think I'll ever get over the wonderment, and how comforting it is to know that when all around us it seems at times like the light is diminishing from the lives of so many.

Questions to Ponder: How does it feel when you read this verse? Which part stands out? How does the Holy

Ghost communicate with you? When was the last time that happened? What do you need help with or understanding of now?

Daily Challenge: Re-read today's verse again. Then take some time after a prayer today to sit and listen. Think on the different options around the thing you're trying to understand or make a decision about. Think back to this verse - which option is plain, or simple, or feels illuminated? Which one has the most clarity around that course of action?

Endure To The End

2 Nephi 31:12-17 - 12 And also, the voice of the Son came unto me, saying: He that is baptized in my name, to him will the Father give the Holy Ghost, like unto me; wherefore, follow me, and do the things which ye have seen me do.

13 Wherefore, my beloved brethren, I know that if ye shall follow the Son, with full purpose of heart, acting no hypocrisy and no deception before God, but with real intent, repenting of your sins, witnessing unto the Father that ye are willing to take upon you the name of Christ, by baptism—yea, by following your Lord and your Savior down into the water, according to his word, behold, then shall ye receive the Holy Ghost; yea, then cometh the baptism of fire and of the Holy Ghost; and then can ye speak with the tongue of angels, and shout praises unto the Holy One of Israel.

14 But, behold, my beloved brethren, thus came the voice of the Son unto me, saying: After ye have repented of your sins, and witnessed unto the Father that ye are willing to keep my commandments, by the baptism of water, and have received the baptism of fire and of the Holy Ghost, and can speak with a new tongue, yea, even with the tongue of angels, and after this should deny me, it would have been better for you that ye had not known me.

15 And I heard a voice from the Father, saying: Yea, the words of my Beloved are true and faithful. He that endureth to the end, the same shall be saved.

16 And now, my beloved brethren, I know by this that unless a man shall endure to the end, in following the example of the Son of the living God, he cannot be saved.

17 Wherefore, do the things which I have told you I have seen that your Lord and your Redeemer should do; for, for this cause have they been shown unto me, that ye might know the gate by which ye should enter. For the gate by which ye should enter is repentance and baptism by water; and then cometh a remission of your sins by fire and by the Holy Ghost.

Faith. Repentance. Baptism. Receiving the Holy Ghost. Enduring to the End.

The gospel is laid out pretty concisely in these six verses. I've always been intrigued by the order that these principles and ordinances come in. It makes sense though - faith is requisite for everything that follows. Repentance brings humility, which we need in order to be baptized and to listen to the promptings of the Spirit. Enduring to the end is the part that takes the longest, so we need all of the things that come before it to be able to actually endure.

Then that one warning there in the middle: if you deny me, it would have been better for you that you had not known me.

Yikes.

Doesn't that apply to all of us? Those of us lucky enough to be a part of the true, restored church, to have the fulness of the gospel, to have a knowledge of our Savior and Heavenly Father? How many of us have friends or family members who have left the church and ultimately denied the existence of God?

The warning is a serious one, and we should heed it with the gravity it deserves.

Questions to Ponder: Why the importance of each of the different steps, the principles and ordinances of the gospel? What can we do to strengthen our will, our faith, our ability to endure to the end? What can we do for those that have left the church, let their testimonies wither away, and who deny the existence of God and Christ?

Daily Challenge: Offer a prayer for a friend or loved one who is struggling. Could be anyone, but especially those who have left the church must be really dealing with a lot in these extreme times we live in. Think of ways you can serve them and bring some of the light of Christ back into their lives.

Ye Shall Have Eternal Life

> 2 Nephi 31:20 - *Wherefore, ye must press forward with a steadfastness in Christ, having a perfect brightness of hope, and a love of God and of all men. Wherefore, if ye shall press forward, feasting upon the word of Christ, and endure to the end, behold, thus saith the Father: Ye shall have eternal life.*

Scripture mastery anyone?

The awesome reminder that this whole "living the gospel" thing is a lot of work. But guess what, there's a pretty incredible blessing at the end of all that work: eternal life.

Anyone interested?

I'm sorry for my tone on this one, but it just seems so straightforward. Work hard, has hope and charity for everyone. Study the scriptures and keep at it, all of it, and the promise from our Father in Heaven is Eternal Life!?! I mean, come on. We're seriously getting the better end of that deal.

Questions to Ponder: How often do you think about the gospel? About how you live it? About what is asked of us? How much does the promise of eternal life motivate you in the decisions you make on a daily basis?

Daily Challenge: Perspective. Find a way, whether through study, meditation, prayer, or otherwise, to give some more perspective to this scripture. Find out how to make Eternal Life with our Father in Heaven and our families a driving force in your life.

Feast Upon The Words Of Christ

> 2 Nephi 32:3 - ...Wherefore, I say unto you, feast upon the words of Christ; for behold, the words of Christ will tell you all things what ye should do.

I've tried to keep this verse in my mind throughout the last year and a half or so since we came across it in Gospel Doctrine in early 2016. I had been reading so many non-fiction, self help, business type books and getting nowhere, and every time that I'd turn to the scriptures and prayer instead the answers would come.

Amazing, right?

The promises in The Book of Mormon are real. I've experienced them in my own life, and yet I still fail to remember them sometimes. You'd think after enough reinforcement that it would sink in and I'd do a better job of remembering, but I'm still human. That's what I hope that this daily email does though, is help us to remember these incredible promises and blessings that we have because of the gospel.

Questions to Ponder: What's tough right now? What is something that you could use some direction and guidance on? How can we learn to turn to the scriptures in times of need, rather than the internet or self-help books?

Daily Challenge: Find some time today to feast on the words of Christ. Start and end it with prayer, and give yourself some time to receive the answers you're looking for. They may not come today, but they definitely won't come if you don't seek them out.

All Things

> 2 Nephi 32:5 - For behold, again I say unto you that if ye will enter in by the way, and receive the Holy Ghost, it will show unto you all things what ye should do.

This may be the biggest takeaway from my study of The Book of Mormon over the last year or two - the power of the Holy Ghost and the things that it can do for us. Teach us all things. Show us all things that we should do. The list goes on... (I'm sure we'll revisit this topic soon.)

It's worth doing a deep dive into the subject if it interests you, but I just want you to know how real the Holy Ghost is, and how incredible a resource he is in our lives if we're living in a way where we're listening and humble enough to act on what we're taught.

Question to Ponder: What can we do to strengthen our relationship with the Holy Ghost?

Daily Challenge: Pray. Listen. Act. Test the promises of the scriptures. See if they work. It's pretty amazing.

Ye Must Pray

> *2 Nephi 32:8-9 - 8 ...For if ye would hearken unto the Spirit which teacheth a man to pray, ye would know that ye must pray; for the evil spirit teacheth not a man to pray, but teacheth him that he must not pray.*

> *9 But behold, I say unto you that ye must pray always, and not faint; that ye must not perform any thing unto the Lord save in the first place ye shall pray unto the Father in the name of Christ, that he will consecrate thy performance unto thee, that thy performance may be for the welfare of thy soul.*

When I was around fourteen or fifteen, we had a stake youth conference that lasted two days up in the mountains of northern California. There was a sister from the stake that gave an incredible lesson on prayer, and it was one of the foundational pieces of what became my testimony of God, Christ, the scriptures, and the gospel.

I remember her reading from the Bible Dictionary about prayer. It's still highlighted in my scriptures today:

> *As soon as we learn the true relationship in which we stand toward God (namely, God is our Father, and we are His children), then at once prayer becomes natural and instinctive on our part (Matt. 7:7-11). Many of the so-called difficulties about prayer arise from forgetting this relationship. Prayer is the act by which the will of the Father and the will of the child are brought into correspondence with each other. The object of prayer is not to change the will of God but to secure for ourselves and for others blessings that God is already willing to grant but that are made conditional on our asking for them. Blessings require some work or effort on our part before we can obtain them. Prayer is a form of work and is an appointed means for obtaining the highest of all blessings.*

> *...We pray in Christ's name when our mind is the mind of Christ, and our wishes the wishes of Christ—when His words abide in us (John 15:7). We then ask for things it is possible for God to grant. Many prayers remain unanswered because they are not in Christ's name at all; they in no way represent His mind but spring out of the selfishness of man's heart.*

It was after that lesson on prayer that I took the opportunity to go out into the woods on my own to pray and ask about the truthfulness of the gospel and the scriptures. I had never to that point had such a strong desire to know. I read some more scriptures, and pondered on the things I had just learned. I felt like it would take me forever to understand the depths of the doctrine of prayer, but I wanted to try. I wanted to test it to see what would happen.

I remember praying and asking the words "please help me know that this is true. I want to know."

At that moment the still breeze became a warm gust that rushed toward me. I felt embraced by it. I even opened my eyes to look to see if anything had changed, and I watched as the wind raced through the trees pulling the branches along with it. There was the most incredible feeling of comfort and clarity and knowledge that I don't know how else to describe, other than in that moment I had everything that the things I had read about happen. I felt one with my Heavenly Father, like my will was aligned and that this blessing of knowledge came and filled my mind and heart.

It was undeniably a direct answer to this sincere prayer. I know that we have a Father in Heaven who knows us, personally, and intimately, and who has blessings in store for us if we will only align ourselves with the gospel and ask for them through prayer.

I know that Joseph Smith was a prophet of God who saw our Heavenly Father and Jesus Christ, who translated this incredible book of scripture and brought about the restoration of the gospel. I know the gospel is true, and that it centers on Christ. I know that he lived, and died for us. I know that through him we can have true happiness and eternal joy.

I hope that if you feel in any way that you are alone, or that no one understands what you're going through, that you'll remember that we have a way to communicate directly with our Heavenly Father, and feel his love for us.

Questions to Ponder: How do you feel? What thoughts are in your mind? What actions are you inspired to take? What should you do about it?

Daily Challenge: Act on whatever thoughts or inspirations come to mind. Write them down, remember them, act on them.

DAILY MORMON

The Holy Ghost

> *2 Nephi 33:1 - ...for when a man speaketh by the power of the Holy Ghost the power of the Holy Ghost carrieth it unto the hearts of the children of men.*

For any of us that have served a mission we can probably testify of the truthfulness of this. But honestly, I've felt it even in writing these emails. The response has been incredible, and it's a testament to the reality of the Holy Ghost and the power that it has to teach us, to testify of Christ, to remind us and guide us.

The question, then, is how do we speak by the power of the Holy Ghost more often?

Questions to Ponder: How DO we speak by the power of the Holy Ghost? What does that mean? How can we do it more often to help more people who may need it and the truths it can testify of in their lives?

Daily Challenge: Go on a scripture hunt. Starting with 2 Nephi 33:1, tap on or follow the footnotes for Speaketh, and see where it leads you.

JACOB

The Intent To Do Good

> Jacob 2:18-19 - 18 But before ye seek for riches, seek ye for the kingdom of God.

> 19 And after ye have obtained a hope in Christ ye shall obtain riches, if ye seek them; and ye will seek them for the intent to do good—to clothe the naked, and to feed the hungry, and to liberate the captive, and administer relief to the sick and the afflicted.

I'm going to fight the urge to get political here, because that's not what this platform is for. I will point to this verse as a core tenet of what it means to be a Christian and a follower of Christ - to use what we have with the intent to do good. We make this promise in the temple as well through the law of consecration.

I love the simplicity of this verse - before ye seek for riches seek the kingdom of God. Again, it gives us focus and perspective, helping us to make choices that will lead us toward our Heavenly Father, not become a stumbling block or an obstacle.

Questions to Ponder: What is the Kingdom of God that we should seek? If we're blessed in this life with "riches" (of any kind), what can we do to use them with the intent to do good? Who should we target with our giving and our aid?

Daily Challenge: We just experienced one of the worst floods in the United States in recent history. Is there something you can do to support those in need in the Houston area?

This People Shall Keep My Commandments

> Jacob 2:29 - *Wherefore, this people shall keep my commandments, saith the Lord of Hosts, or cursed be the land for their sakes.*

I often wonder how the Lord groups people together, and who qualifies for statements like this? Is it a neighborhood of ~200 people? A city of a hundred thousand or more? A state? A nation?

Then I realized the question is beyond the point, isn't it? We can't control the people around us, especially as we expand the radius of who those people are. What we can control is ourselves, our own actions, our own agency. We can focus on our faith, and our belief that keeping the commandments is not only important, but that we are part of communities, and cities, and states and nations, and that our actions matter.

Sometimes the Lord gives us specific instructions - keep the commandments because no unclean thing can dwell with God - and sometimes it's more broad like this verse, but the principle is the same: keep the commandments.

Questions to Ponder: Is there something in your life that can be removed, some sin, some addiction, some bad habit? What can you do to take steps to do that?

Daily Challenge: Ponder on the importance of keeping the commandments. The principle comes up over and over again in various ways throughout the scriptures. It must be important, no?

Look Unto God

> *Jacob 3:1 - ...Look unto God with firmness of mind, and pray unto him with exceeding faith, and he will console you in your afflictions, and he will plead your cause, and send down justice upon those who seek your destruction.*

Oh man, if there was eve a comforting verse in times of trial. There's something about the way this verse is written that you really get into the relationship our Savior has with us. Console. Plead. This isn't just some acquaintance. This is someone who loves us dearly and would do anything for us...as proven by the actions he took while here on earth on our behalf.

But there's another part of this verse. We have to look to him with a firmness of mind, and pray with exceeding faith. This isn't some lackadaisical offering. No. Look again at the words used. Firmness. Exceeding. This verse helps describe the relationship we should be striving for with our Savior, and puts into the proper perspective how we should go about our day and our lives in order to be able to receive these incredible blessings that come through that relationship.

Questions to Ponder: What does firmness of mind and exceeding faith mean to you? How would that be different than what you currently do when it comes to your faith and your prayers?

Daily Challenge: Go over these questions again. Try to carry them with you throughout the day, and really ponder on what we can do differently to strengthen our relationship with our Savior.

All These Witnesses

> *Jacob 4:6-7 - 6 Wherefore, we search the prophets, and we have many revelations and the spirit of prophecy; and having all these witnesses we obtain a hope, and our faith becometh unshaken, insomuch that we truly can command in the name of Jesus the very trees obey us, or the mountains, or the waves of the sea.*

> *7 Nevertheless, the Lord God showeth us our weakness that we may know that it is by his grace, and his great condescensions unto the children of men, that we have power to do these things.*

I wasn't sure which part of today's scripture to focus on, but reading over it again this part (the title/subject of this email) stood out. Now, the promise or statement is that humility gives us power, because it gives us perspective and the knowledge to depend on him and his power, and through that process we too can have power to do incredible things. That alone is incredible.

However, what stood out to me was when Jacob wrote: "having all these witnesses". How often do we feel like faith is hard. How many of us have friends that have let their faith "dwindle in unbelief" to the point that they go inactive or leave the church. How many of us have gone through that.

So often we refer to faith in a way that seems blind. You "just do it", you just "have faith". Well, not always. Sometimes, yes, faith does work that way, in that we have to believe before seeing, like Adam or others. But look at what Jacob says. He already has some faith, but because of all of the prophets, their writings, their witnesses, they obtain a hope, and their faith becomes unshaken.

I feel like this is actually how faith works. We look at what faith we have, see where we are lacking - see where we have weaknesses or can improve. We study and search diligently to strengthen that faith. We find witnesses that can help us with their words, their lives, their testimonies, and use their faith to strengthen our own.

Questions to Ponder: Who's testimony do you admire, whether it's a friend or a prophet from the scriptures? How can we use their witness to strengthen our own testimony?

Daily Challenge: Find someone you admire and have a conversation with them about the gospel. If you're struggling, ask them about how they got their faith and testimony in that principle. If you feel like you're not struggling, try and find someone who is, and see if you can find a way to share your testimony with them and help strengthen their faith.

Seek Not To Counsel The Lord

> *Jacob 4:10-11 - 10 Wherefore, brethren, seek not to counsel the Lord, but to take counsel from his hand. For behold, ye yourselves know that he counseleth in wisdom, and in justice, and in great mercy, over all his works.*

> *11 Wherefore, beloved brethren, be reconciled unto him through the atonement of Christ, his Only Begotten Son, and ye may obtain a resurrection, according to the power of the resurrection which is in Christ, and be presented as the first fruits of Christ unto God, having faith, and obtained a good hope of glory in him before he manifested himself in the flesh.*

Ok, maybe it's inevitable. It may just be that the nature of the scriptures are that they can be so aptly applied to our modern day political climate that it's impossible to not be political. My personal stance and opinions aside, I think these verses can be directly applied to recent events.

The point is not to focus on the events themselves, but the counsel that these verses give for when these things happen. A new policy, a new revelation, a change in the direction, whatever it may be - if it comes from a prophet of God it comes from the Lord.

We are told directly to seek not to counsel the Lord, but take counsel from his hand, but to be reconciled unto him through the atonement. There is no better advice that I could give, so I'm not going to try. What I will say is that the course we are to take has been laid out by Jacob over 2500 years ago. Anything that has proven to be true for that long...well, that plus Jacob was a prophet...must be true.

Whether you get this in September, March, June or December, there's another general conference in just a few months. There may be changes. There may be things you don't understand or things you disagree with. That doesn't make them wrong. Seek not to counsel the Lord. Be reconciled through the atonement, and focus on the facts that we have modern prophets, modern revelation, a direct link to communicate with our Heavenly Father and have his will revealed to us.

Questions to Ponder: What is a time that you've attempted to counsel the Lord? Or claim to know better? Or have stepped out in front of the church on any subject? How did that go? What does it mean to take counsel from the Lord's hand? How can we do that better when these situations arise?

Daily Challenge: Go back to a point of doctrine or a statement or anything from the church that you may have found or still find difficult. Seek counsel from the Lord. How would he have you act? What is his will for you?

The Spirit Speaketh The Truth

> *Jacob 4:13 - ...for the Spirit speaketh the truth and lieth not. Wherefore, it speaketh of things as they really are, and of things as they really will be; wherefore, these things are manifested unto us plainly, for the salvation of our souls. But behold, we are not witnesses alone in these things; for God also spake them unto the prophets of old.*

More perspective and information about the Spirit and Truth. If you did the "deep dive" on the attributes of the Holy Ghost from a few emails back, you may have already stumbled across this verse. You've undoubtedly seen it before. Yet, in the context of this daily email, it seems to give even more comfort, doesn't it?

Whenever we receive impressions from the Spirit, or personal revelation, or when the Spirit is testifying of a truth to us, we can know that he "speaketh the truth, and lieth not". With so much uncertainty in our day to day lives - are carbs good for you, or bad for you? - how great is it to know that our Heavenly Father has given us this incredible gift. It also reinforces the fact that at times, and sometimes very often, life is hard. It's not necessarily meant to be easy. Yet, knowing that, our Heavenly Father gave us a true north, a way to know the truth, things as they really are and really will be, and they are easy to see if we look and seek it out.

Questions to Ponder: What do you feel when you read this verse? What sticks out to you? Why? What should we do about it?

Daily Challenge: Think about something you're struggling with, or an area in your life where you could use some help. Seek out the guidance of the Holy Ghost and find the truth about what you should do and the choices and actions you should take.

As Many As Will Not Harden Their Hearts

> *Jacob 6:4 - ...but as many as will not harden their hearts shall be saved in the kingdom of God.*

It's about as simple as a statement you'll get from this email series. Consider it the "my father dwelt in a tent" scripture. Hardening of hearts is a symptom of pride, and the antidote is humility. We have to be humble, and teachable, and willing to obey the will of the Lord if we want to be saved in the kingdom of God.

If you want it, the way is clearly laid out for you. The actions you take each and every day are what show the Lord that you do, actually want it.

Questions to Ponder: Why is pride such a stumbling block? Why is it discussed so often in the scriptures? Why would nearly every prophet find an opportunity to speak about pride and humility when it comes to salvation?

Daily Challenge: Dig deep. You are incredible bunch of people, but we need to find ways we can be better. What is something where are hearts can be softened, either individually or as a group? Find something you can do today to work on becoming more humble and teachable about it.

Harden Not Your Hearts

> *Jacob 6:6 - ...but as many as will not harden their hearts shall be saved in the kingdom of God.*

It's about as simple as a statement you'll get from this email series. Consider it the "my father dwelt in a tent" scripture. Hardening of hearts is a symptom of pride, and the antidote is humility. We have to be humble, and teachable, and willing to obey the will of the Lord if we want to be saved in the kingdom of God.

If you want it, the way is clearly laid out for you. The actions you take each and every day are what show the Lord that you do, actually want it.

Questions to Ponder: Why is pride such a stumbling block? Why is it discussed so often in the scriptures? Why would nearly every prophet find an opportunity to speak about pride and humility when it comes to salvation?

Daily Challenge: Dig deep. You are incredible bunch of people, but we need to find ways we can be better. What is something where are hearts can be softened, either individually or as a group? Find something you can do today to work on becoming more humble and teachable about it.

What Can I Say More?

> *Jacob 6:11-12 - 11 O then, my beloved brethren, repent ye, and enter in at the strait gate, and continue in the way which is narrow, until ye shall obtain eternal life.*

> *12 O be wise; what can I say more?*

Again, Jacob with the simple plainness in his writing. I really do love the way he says things. Repent. Be Baptized. Be obedient. Be wise.

I think a lot of the frustration in our lives is caused by our being to focused on one small thing - having "tunnel" vision - and not having enough perspective. So many little decisions that end up causing us the most grief, the most stress, the most problems could be avoided if we spent the time to be "wise" when making the decision.

That eternal perspective could fix a lot of what we struggle with in our lives. Is it easy? No. Is it a cure-all? Absolutely not. There is much more nuance to this life and how it's lived than that, but it is such a simple and important principle to try and live by: be wise.

Questions to Ponder: How is wisdom different than knowledge? How is it different from faith or belief? Why chose wisdom in this case over any other word? Are there any other conditions besides obedience and baptism to obtain eternal life?

Daily Challenge: Find a way to incorporate more wisdom, or a broader perspective into your life. That could mean taking longer to make certain decisions, giving you time to think about them and weigh them out. Where could you benefit most from more wisdom? Financially? Spiritually? Physically? There are so many ways it could be applied, find one small area of your life and give it a shot.

Save They Have Spoken Concerning This Christ

> *Jacob 7:9-11 - 9 And I said unto him: Deniest though the Christ who shall come? And he said: If there should be a Christ, I would not deny him; but I know that there is no Christ, neither has there been or ever will be.*

> *10 And I said unto him: Believes thou the scriptures? And he said, Yea.*

> *11 And I said unto him: Then ye do not understand them: for they truly testify of Christ. Behold, I say unto you that none of the prophets have written, nor prophesied, save they have spoken concerning this Christ.*

Hope you'll allow two extra verses for context today. The principle lies in the last verse, that none of the prophets have written, prophesied, or spoken, save it were concerning Christ.

This is a powerful principle. It helps us realize how we should approach the things that they teach us, whether in general conference, the ensign, or in official declarations like the family proclamation.

Sometimes the things they say will be hard to understand, or we won't know the full context, or we may even disagree. Yet, here it is in principle. It's up to us to go to the Lord and ask for clarity, for understanding, and for the spirit to confirm it and comfort us if we're struggling with it.

The church is a living church, and the gospel a living gospel. There will be more revelations, there will be more things for us to learn and adjust to.

Questions to Ponder: How would you have responded if you were around during past revelations? How would you react now? What process can we put in place for when the next change occurs so that it doesn't disrupt our faith, or prevent us from fully living the gospel?

Daily Challenge: Take something to the Lord in prayer. Listen for an answer, or comfort, or confirmation. Practice that communication with the Lord and learn how to better hear the responses.

ENOS

Ye Shall Receive It

> *Enos 1:15 - ...Whatsoever thing ye shall ask in faith, believing that ye shall receive in the name of Christ, ye shall receive it.*

This is the one right here, guys. This one has helped me so many times. It's such a simple, straightforward promise, with never-ending possibilities. Whatever we need help with, whatever we're struggling with, the Lord has provided a way. In this incredible plan of happiness, there's a support function built in. If things get too hard, we can ask for help, and receive help. We can receive guidance, and comfort, and knowledge, and anything else we need if we just ask in faith and believe.

The answers may not come in the way we expect, but the fact that we can receive answers is sometimes all we need - to know that we have a Father in Heaven who listens, who loves us, and who wants to help us.

Questions to Ponder: What does prayer mean to you? What is possible with prayer? What experiences in the past have you had with prayer that have helped you have a testimony of it?

Daily Challenge: I've received a number of emails from you all, the readers of this book, and it seems like there are many that are struggling with their faith. I'd urge you to pray, sincerely. It probably won't all magically change overnight, but I can promise you that if you work on making prayer a habit, on regularly communicating with your Heavenly Father and strengthening that relationship, that it will help you immensely as you seek to strengthen your testimony and to live the gospel. So start there - a single prayer today. Then another tomorrow. Soon it will become a habit, and you'll learn what the Lord needs of you and how you can find the things you are after.

JAROM

As Many As Are Not Stiffnecked

> Jarom 1:4 - ...And as many as are not stiff-necked and have faith, have communion with the Holy Spirit, which maketh manifest unto the children of men, according to their faith.

We've discussed a few times about the Holy Ghost and everything he can do for us in our lives. This verse informs that relationship a little more - that we need to make sure we are not being stiff necked, and that faith is requisite.

Stiffneckedness is a symptom of pride, and it prevents us from being willing to listen to the promptings of the Spirit. Just think of it visually - how hard would it be to try and speak to someone who isn't willing to turn to listen to you while you were talking? It would get old pretty quickly.

Let's not be that way. Seek out the Spirit through humility and faith.

Questions to Ponder: What is communion with the Holy Spirit? Why should you seek it? Why would faith be an important part of your relationship with the Holy Ghost?

Daily Challenge: Find a way to identify ways that you are stiff-necked or lacking in faith. What can you do to become more humble and faithful?

OMNI

Come Unto God, The Holy One Of Israel

> Omni 1:25-26 - 25 ...wherefore, I shall deliver up these plates unto him, exhorting all men to come unto God, the Holy One of Israel, and believe in prophesying, and in revelations, and in the ministering of angels, and in the gift of speaking with tongues, and in the gift of interpreting languages, and in all things which are good; for there is nothing which is good save it comes from the Lord: and that which is evil cometh from the devil.

> 26 And now, my beloved brethren, I would that ye should come unto Christ, who is the Holy One of Israel, and partake of his salvation, and the power of his redemption. Yea, come unto him, and offer your whole souls as an offering unto him, and continue in fasting and praying, and endure to the end; and as the Lord liveth ye will be saved.

Pretty great gospel lesson right here in these two verses. I'm writing this on a Saturday night, looking forward to heading into the sabbath day. Too many times I go into Sundays unprepared, but look at the exhortation here - believe in prophesying, and in revelations, and in all things which are good...partake of his salvation, and the power of his redemption. I immediately started thinking about the sabbath day and its purpose.

Feels like this sums up the sabbath pretty well.

Beyond that, though, it's how we should live our lives - with faith, with the proper perspective, focusing on Christ and the atonement, and enduring to the end.

Questions to Ponder: How can you embody these verses? How can you apply the principles, even just one principle, into your daily life?

Daily Challenge: Sit and ponder these verses. Take the time to think, to ponder, to meditate. See what comes to mind, what actions feel appropriate, and how to become better at coming unto Christ and partaking of his salvation.

MOSIAH

We Must Have Suffered In Ignorance

> Mosiah 1:3 - ...I would that ye should remember that were it not for these plates, which contain these records and these commandments, we must have suffered in ignorance, even at this present time, not knowing the mysteries of God.

I always get a little excited when I get to the book of Mosiah. It contains some of my favorite chapters in The Book Of Mormon, from some of my favorite people.

This verse gives us a good setup for what we're about to get into over the next few chapters of scriptures. The prophets knew the importance of the plates - but do we?

Questions to Ponder: What are the consequences if we ignore the scriptures, and neglect them? What if we didn't have them at all? What are we able to know because of them?

Daily Challenge: Find a favorite statement or promise in The Book of Mormon, and see how it can bless your life.

These Records Are True

> Mosiah 1:6 - ...I would that ye should remember that these sayings are true, and also that these records are true.

It's scriptures like this that were a big part of the impetus for me writing this book. I had been spending so much time reading "worldly" books - granted, from some very smart and well-meaning people - but I was neglecting the principles in The Book of Mormon. The ones from actual prophets.

If we can seek to remind ourselves of the truthfulness of this scriptural record and the teachings it contains, imagine how incredibly our lives would change for the better.

Questions to Ponder: How often do you turn to the scriptures when you need help? What other places are you turning instead? Why? How can you make the scriptures a larger part of your life?

Daily Challenge: The next time you go and search for a youtube video or a non-fiction book, turn to the scriptures with a prayer in your heart. See what different answers come because of that faith.

Search Them Diligently

> *Mosiah 1:7 - And now, my sons, I would that ye should remember to search them diligently, that ye may profit thereby; and I would that ye should keep the commandments of God, that ye may prosper in the land according to the promises which the Lord made unto our fathers.*

How many of us have goals we're striving for? How many of us want to be better?

The scriptures are there for us to do so. By searching them diligently, we can profit from the teachings and principles they contain. Combined with righteous living and keeping the commandments, we have a promise that we will prosper in the land. What that means specifically is different for each of us, but it brings me an incredible amount of comfort when times get rough, or things aren't working out exactly as planned.

Our Heavenly Father has a plan for us, and part of that plan is joy and happiness. He wants us to be happy, to get the righteous desires of our hearts, and ultimately to have the incredible joy of returning to live with him again.

Questions to Ponder: Why would the prophets spend so many verses talking about the importance of the scriptures? How did their actions support their beliefs and their teachings? How can your actions support the things you believe when it comes to the scriptures, especially The Book of Mormon?

Daily Challenge: Find a favorite scripture and read over it a few times. Study the context - read the chapter heading, look at the footnotes. Think about why it's a favorite scripture and what you should do about it. What is the Spirit teaching you or testifying to you?

This Highly Favored People

> Mosiah 1:13 - ...if this highly favored people of the Lord should fall into transgression, and become a wicked and an adulterous people, that the Lord will deliver them up, that thereby they become weak like unto their brethren; and he will no more preserve them by his matchless and marvelous power, as he has hitherto preserved our fathers.

Just a few chapters ago I posed the question of how the Lord reacts when an entire group of people stop living the gospel and turn wicked. Here's our answer. Look at the consequences of the transgressions of an entire group of people. They're serious.

A group of people, historically, typically doesn't make the switch overnight. It happens one person at a time, one sin at a time, on choice at a time. The individuals in the group are still responsible for their own choices. It's their agency compounded with the agency of their peers that ends up bringing on these consequences.

No matter what is going on around us, it's essential that we maintain our righteousness and our relationship with the Lord, that we endure to the end and do everything we can to live the gospel to its fullest.

Questions to Ponder: What, if anything, in the world today would qualify as a highly favored people falling into transgression? What are some historical examples? What are the signs? How can you prevent it from happening to you?

Daily Challenge: Take inventory of the different groups, both online and off, that may need some auditing. Are there people we're associating with that need some repentance, that could be pulling us down? Think about how to deal with those possibilities to maintain or improve our standing with God.

The Service Of Your God

> Mosiah 2:17 - ...when ye are in the service of your fellow beings ye are only in the service of your God.

Why is that? We all know this scripture. W've probably had it memorized since our teens if we grew up in the church. Have we ever dug into why this scripture is true? How it works?

On the surface at least, it's because God needs us to be his hands, his voice, when it comes to the direct, physical service of his children, since he has chosen to remain behind the veil except for very specific moments, such as the first vision with Joseph Smith.

He easily could have had angels translate The Book of Mormon and hand it off to Joseph Smith fully completed. Think of how much more scripture we would have, and how much easier it would have been for Joseph, Oliver, and the early saints who devoted their lives to bringing this book into the world.

Rather, the Lord gives people the opportunity to serve. While we haven't been called to translate an entire new book of scripture, or restore the gospel and the priesthood to the earth, the things we have been called to do are also important.

It's not about the big things that we or others are called to do. It's about all of the small things - ministering, preparing a lesson in church and prayerfully thinking about the needs of the people in the class, treating everyone we meet with respect and looking for small ways to serve them. That's what it's about.

At scale - with all of us, MILLIONS of us doing small things every day - the effect is massive. That's how we serve God, by serving our brothers and sisters on earth as often as we can find opportunities to do so.

Questions to Ponder: How have you been directly called to serve in the Church? What about indirectly? How can you do more, serve more often, change your paradigm to be thinking about service all the time?

Daily Challenge: Pray for an opportunity to serve, then be aware of all the opportunities that cross your path throughout the day. Be active. Do more than you normally do to serve others.

Unprofitable Servants

> Mosiah 2:20-21 - 20 ...if you should render all the thanks and praise which your whole soul has power to possess, to that God who has created you, and has kept and preserved you, and has caused that ye should rejoice, and has granted that ye should live in peace one with another—

> 21 I say unto you that if ye should serve him who has created you from the beginning, and is preserving you from day to day, by lending you breath, that ye may live and move and do according to your own will, and even supporting you from one moment to another—I say, if ye should serve him with all your whole souls yet ye would be unprofitable servants.

One of the biggest lessons I learned on my mission was the importance of humility. If memory serves me I spent over a month during the time I was training a new missionary studying the topic of humility in the extra hour of study we had every morning. I learned so much. I only wish that I had actually become more humble at the same rate as I was learning how important it was.

These verses, spoken by King Benjamin as he was addressing his people, sum up the concept perfectly - we would yet be unprofitable servants.

The real question though is: knowing the importance of humility in our lives, what should we do about it? How should that translate into our daily lives?

The more humble we are, the more teachable we are. The more we will listen to and heed the promptings of the Spirit. The more we will be willing to go to our Heavenly Father in prayer. The more we will be willing to listen to the prophets, to new revelations, to changes that may come. Remaining humble prepares us for heaven.

Questions to Ponder: Besides those already posed, what should YOU do about it? Are you striving to be humble? How can you be better? What would having more humility do for your life?

Daily Challenge: How important is humility to you? Ponder that question and find some things you can implement into your daily life, starting today.

He Never Doth Vary

> Mosiah 2:22 - ...he never doth vary from that which he hath said; therefore, if ye do keep his commandments he doth bless you and prosper you.

This verse also helped inform my reasons for seeking out the "statement" or "principle" verses in The Book of Mormon, and writing this book. If these words are true, what does it mean for us? What should we do about it? How would that effect how we live our lives, the decisions we make, what we focus on, and countless other things?

Beyond that, how comforting is it to know that we have a Savior whose words never vary, whose promises are eternal and unchanging? Doesn't that help us with our faith? It sure makes it easier for me to commit to following Him throughout my life, especially when things are hard.

"If ye keep his commandments he doth bless you and prosper you." That's the gospel right there, isn't it? Listen to what He says, be obedient, and reap the blessings.

Questions to Ponder: How does it make YOU feel to know that the Lord never varies from what he has said? What does that mean? How does that play into your life?

Daily Challenge: Are there ways that you can be more obedient, better at keeping the commandments? Think about that for a little today and see if there's a way that you can be better. Seek out inspiration from the Lord through the Holy Ghost, as perfect as you may already be, I'm sure there are still ways we can all be better.

The Evil Spirit

> Mosiah 2:32-33 - 32 But, O my people, beware lest there shall arise contentions among you, and ye list to obey the evil spirit, which was spoken of by my father Mosiah.
>
> 33 For behold, there is a wo pronounced upon him who listeth to obey that spirit; for if he listeth to obey him, and remaineth and dieth in his sins, the same drinketh damnation to his own soul; for he receiveth for his wages an everlasting punishment, having transgressed the law of God contrary to his own knowledge.

King Benjamin warns the people of the things that he sees as the biggest threats to their prosperity. I can imagine King Benjamin, without the benefit of technology, or loudspeakers, or any real way to reach all of his people in real time - so he chose his words carefully, limiting them to the most important things that he felt they needed to hear at that time.

After speaking about service and other principles for a while, he follows with this. A warning against contentions, and being obedient to the devil rather than to the Lord, followed by the consequences.

If you look at the world around us, do you see any contentions? See anyone "obeying the evil spirit"?

It's important that we strive to have charity and love, rather than be contentious.

Questions to Ponder: Are you prone to contention? Do you ever take offense, or find yourself arguing with others as the first reaction? What should you do about it?

Daily Challenge: Have a "no contention" day, or week, or month. Challenge yourself based on where you're at. Focus on eliminating contention from your life and allowing the Spirit to fill that space instead.

Ye Have Known And Been Taught These Things

> *Mosiah 2:36-39 - 36 And now, I say unto you, my brethren, that after ye have known and have been taught all these things, if ye should transgress and go contrary to that which has been spoken, that ye do withdraw yourselves from the Spirit of the Lord, that it may have no place in you to guide you in wisdom's paths that ye may be blessed, prospered, and preserved—*

> *37 I say unto you, that the man that doeth this, the same cometh out in open rebellion against God; therefore he listeth to obey the evil spirit, and becometh an enemy to all righteousness; therefore, the Lord has no place in him, for he dwelleth not in unholy temples.*

> *38 Therefore if that man repenteth not, and remaineth and dieth an enemy to God, the demands of divine justice do awaken his immortal soul to a lively sense of his own guilt, which doth cause him to shrink from the presence of the Lord, and doth fill his breast with guilt, and pain, and anguish, which is like an unquenchable fire, whose flame ascendeth up forever and ever.*

> *39 And now I say unto you, that mercy hath no claim on that man; therefore his final doom is to endure a never-ending torment.*

The takeaway for me from these verses, as dark a picture as they paint, is that King Benjamin was speaking to each person on an individual level, despite this being essentially a general conference of the church. He's also talking to us, those that know and have been taught these things.

It's our personal responsibility to maintain our faith, to nurture it, to care for it. It takes time and effort and sometimes sacrifice, but look at the alternative.

Questions to Ponder: What can you do better? Where are you weak and open to the temptations of the devil? How can you "patch up" those weak spots and become stronger disciples of Christ?

Daily Challenge: Pick one thing you want to get better at, and commit to doing it perfectly for one week. Reading scriptures every day, praying every day, not swearing, not committing a certain sin, whatever it may be, do it.

Blessed And Happy State

> *Mosiah 2:41 - ...I would desire that ye should consider on the blessed and happy state of those that keep the commandments of God. For behold, they are blessed in all things, both temporal and spiritual; and if they hold out faithful to the end they are received into heaven, that thereby they may dwell with God in a state of never-ending happiness. O remember, remember that these things are true; for the Lord God hath spoken it.*

Here's another reminder of the importance and blessings of obedience and keeping the commandments. King Benjamin's perspective amazes me. He knows what his people need to hear, he knows how to teach them, while at the same time teaching us hundreds of years later.

Let's all take time to consider the blessed and happy state of those that keep the commandments of God.

Questions to Ponder: Who are the happiest people you know? What do they have in common? How has keeping the commandments brought you blessings in the past?

Daily Challenge: Get in touch with someone whose happiness and/or obedience you respect, and have a conversation about the gospel. Ask them about their perspective on obedience, humility, the gospel, anything that comes to mind.

Wo Unto Him Who Knoweth

> *Mosiah 3:12 - But wo, wo unto him who knoweth that he rebelleth against God. For salvation cometh to none such except it be through repentance and faith on the Lord Jesus Christ.*

In order to be repentant and faithful, we first need to be humble. The opposite of that, obviously, is being prideful - prideful enough to knowingly rebel against God and still think that one could be saved in those circumstances.

Humility is in so many gospel principles, especially these first principles of repentance, faith, and baptism. We can't feel the promptings of the spirit if we aren't humble. We can't progress without humility. But is it so hard? I imagine the more prideful we become the harder it is to be humble, but in general, what does it take to be humble? A little perspective? King Benjamin gave that to us in the last chapter. Here it is again:

> *20 ...if you should render all the thanks and praise which your whole soul has power to possess, to that God who has created you, and has kept and preserved you, and has caused that ye should rejoice, and has granted that ye should live in peace one with another—*

> *21 I say unto you that if ye should serve him who has created you from the beginning, and is preserving you from day to day, by lending you breath, that ye may live and move and do according to your own will, and even supporting you from one moment to another—I say, if ye should serve him with all your whole souls yet ye would be unprofitable servants.*

That perspective is what allows us to be humble. To see the world for what it is. To realize the power of the atonement of our Savior on our behalf. To submit to the will of the Lord no matter what the outcome may be. It may be one of the most important things we can strive to learn here on earth.

Questions to Ponder: What other statements on humility are in The Book of Mormon? How can you become more humble? What can you do on a daily basis to become better?

Daily Challenge: Pray, asking for help to become more humble, to gain perspective where you need it, to actively work on eliminating pride.

No Other Name Given

> Mosiah 3:17 - And moreover, I say unto you, that there shall be no other name given nor any other way nor means whereby salvation can come unto the children of men, only in and through the name of Christ, the Lord Omnipotent.

Perspective. So much perspective in these chapters. King Benjamin really had a way of understanding and communicating the gospel to his people. It's the chapters in The Book of Mormon that I turn to the most when I just need some answers. Even though the answers aren't direct, I often find answers in these words because of the perspective that it gives. It forces me to take a step back and remember what's important, and what it is that I'm truly after - salvation, returning to live with my Father in Heaven and my Savior again, and happiness in the process, if I can.

In church this last Sunday we read a talk from the April 2017 conference, where President Nelson had spoken about how the Atonement should always be referenced along with our Savior. So we don't just say "the atonement," but rather "the atonement of Jesus Christ," or, "the atoning sacrifice of our Savior." This verse in Mosiah reflects that, because there truly is no other way nor means but through Christ. That perspective is important. Just *today* a friend of mine wrote about her process of leaving the church, ending with the statement: "Enter Zion - not by church but by passion."

While I don't claim to fully understand her reasoning or her sentiments here, both options are incomplete. Without a focus on our Savior and His atonement, we cannot be saved. We cannot have any of the blessings of the gospel if we don't focus on Christ and His sacrifice, then humble ourselves enough to follow Him, to be obedient to the gospel, to have faith, to repent, and to live as He would have us live.

I'm so grateful for the reality of our Savior and His atonement on our behalf. I'm grateful for it, and for the knowledge I have of His life and His teachings. I hope that we can all strive to maintain that perspective as we go through our lives, the ups and downs, the good times and the bad, and turn to him for comfort and strength when we need it, and for the perspective that immediately brings joy.

Questions to Ponder: What can you do without a focus on the Savior? (Not much, but it has helped me in the past to ask that question, and then come to realize that, "yeah, the Atonement of Jesus Christ is pretty important.) What do you risk if you try to take your salvation into our own hands?

Daily Challenge: Study the atonement. Find a conference talk on lds.org, or read the account in the new testament. Find what stands out and ponder on it - why is it standing out now? What perspective is there to gain?

A Bright Testimony Against This People

> *Mosiah 3:24-27 - 24 And thus saith the Lord: They shall stand as a bright testimony against this people, at the judgment day; whereof they shall be judged, every man according to his works, whether they be good, or whether they be evil.*

> *25 And if they be evil they are consigned to an awful view of their own guilt and abominations, which doth cause them to shrink from the presence of the Lord into a state of misery and endless torment, from whence they can no more return; therefore they have drunk damnation to their own souls.*

> *26 Therefore, they have drunk out of the cup of the wrath of God, which justice could no more deny unto them than it could deny that Adam should fall because of his partaking of the forbidden fruit; therefore, mercy could have claim on them no more forever.*

> *27 And their torment is as a lake of fire and brimstone, whose flames are unquenchable, and whose smoke ascendeth up forever and ever. Thus hath the Lord commanded me. Amen.*

The verse before this section states that King Benjamin "[had] spoken the words which the Lord hath commanded [him]," and that's what stands as a bright testimony against the people, the fact that they had heard the words. They knew the gospel, they knew how it all worked, and they knew the consequences.

Remind you of anyone you know?

We're judged according to our works, but also in regards to the amount of knowledge and testimony we gain here on earth. I write this email tonight at the end of the first day of General Conference in October 2017, and as I was scrolling through social media in between (ok, and sometimes during...) sessions, I was incredibly saddened by the number of people I consider close friends who were speaking out, on today of all days, about their reasons for leaving the church. This, after a full day of incredible insights and powerful talks from our leaders, as well as an incredible outpouring of the Spirit testifying of the truth of their words.

And I was sad, because of these verses and others like them. These words stand as a bright testimony against them. And it reminds me, again, that no one is immune from this. Even Elder Holland today talked about the need for humility, for repentance, for the atonement of our Savior, even for him! We all need the gospel, whether we choose to believe that or not.

The consequences are serious and sad, and I wouldn't wish them on my worst enemy. So when my friends come out against the church, having left behind a testimony and a truth they once held dear, I wonder what should I do? What CAN I do to help them? My prayer tonight is that we all can find someone who may be off the path a bit and help them return, whether it be through service, through prayer, through our example, or through our direct influence on their lives. I hope we can all live in a way where the Spirit is always with us because of our faith and our obedience to the gospel. Let us all be a light in the darkness that is so pervasive in our world today. The world needs us, our friends and loved ones need us, and the Lord needs us.

Questions to Ponder: Why do you think the Lord, through King Benjamin, would use such strong language in these verses? What can you do to live a life of good works rather than evil ones? How can you help others do the same?

Daily Challenge: Pray for a friend who is struggling, who has left the church or has concerns about it. Find out how the Lord can use you to help them come back, to help with their testimony and help them feel the spirit in their lives.

None Other Salvation

> *Mosiah 4:8-10 - 8 And this is the means whereby salvation cometh. And there is none other salvation save this which hath been spoken of; neither are there any conditions whereby man can be saved except the conditions which I have told you.*

> *9 Believe in God; believe that he is, and that he created all things, both in heaven and in earth; believe that he has all wisdom, and all power, both in heaven and in earth; believe that man doth not comprehend all the things which the Lord can comprehend.*

> *10 And again, believe that ye must repent of your sins and forsake them, and humble yourselves before God; and ask in sincerity of heart that he would forgive you; and now, if you believe all these things see that ye do them.*

Continuing on the discussion from the last chapter, I've come back to these verses a few times when thinking about friends who have left the church. "This is the means..." There is only one way for salvation, and it's through Christ. So many people that have that knowledge have wandered off the path, let go of the iron rod, and are wandering in darkness. There is literally no other way than through Christ.

Questions to Ponder: What does it mean for you though? What is your responsibility with these verses? How can you help others?

Daily Challenge: Find a way to serve a friend in need. Pray for them, reach out to them, reconnect. Find ways to enter into their lives and share the light of Christ with them.

If Ye Do This Ye Shall Always Rejoice

> *Mosiah 4:11-12 - 11 ...I would that ye should remember, and always retain in remembrance, the greatness of God, and your own nothingness, and his goodness and long-suffering towards you, unworthy creatures, and humble yourselves even in the depths of humility, calling on the name of the Lord daily, and standing steadfastly in the faith of that which is to come, which was spoken by the mouth of the angel.*

> *12 And behold, I say unto you that if ye do this ye shall always rejoice, and be filled with the love of God, and always retain a remission of your sins; and ye shall grow in the knowledge of the glory of him that created you, or in the knowledge of that which is just and true.*

Perspective. Humility. Prayer. Diligence in keeping the commandments and honoring your covenants. These are the things that lead to happiness, a remission of sins, and knowledge of God.

These recurring themes can add some perspective on how we approach the gospel and living our lives in accordance with it. There are principles and truths that are eternal, and it's important for us to remember them. It's easy to forget. It's natural to be prideful and selfish. It's easy to fall asleep without saying a prayer, or waking up late and not having time.

Yet, the truth is still the truth, independent of whether we believe it or not or if we take the time to apply that truth to our lives. These topics were echoed in the October 2017, general conference. We have to remain humble. We have to pray. We need to be diligent in keeping the commandments.

Questions to Ponder: Why is it so hard at times to keep the necessary perspective? What things get in the way? What changes can you make to make prayer and repentance and obedience more habitual, and easier to remember?

Daily Challenge: Grab a sheet of paper or a page in your journal, if you keep one, and write a page or two without stopping or editing or thinking - just write about how these verses make you feel. Write whatever comes to your mind. Think about the principles of perspective, humility, prayer, and diligence. Then review it afterward and see what came through and what you may be able to learn from it. I do this every morning, and it's been an incredible way to keep focused on the things that matter.

According To Their Wants

> Mosiah 4:26 - ...I would that ye should impart of your substance to the poor, every man according to that which he hath, such as feeding the hungry, clothing the naked, visiting the sick and administering to their relief, both spiritually and temporally, according to their wants.

I'm fighting every urge to get political here. Why is that? Shouldn't the gospel inform our political positions? How we treat others? What policies we support and which ones we fight against? How we spend our money, what leaders we elect, and how we live our lives? Aren't politics a large part of our lives, from how we make money, to the roads we drive on, etc. etc.?

That's the conversation I'd rather have. Not "why I think you should vote for X candidate or belong to X political party (or no political party...)," but rather, "how does your faith inform your politics?"

The thing is that I feel my faith absolutely informs my political opinions. I don't think Christ intended his life to only be an example for how we spend our sabbaths, or how we interact with others within certain boundaries. No, rather I think his life was extremely political, and that there is much to learn from the way he interacted with those in power.

The important thing from this verse, however, is how we treat the poor, the hungry, the naked, the sick. "According to their wants" is an interesting phrase. It's definitely not "according to our wants," is it? The verse is pretty straightforward, and fits the rest of this chapter in Mosiah which teaches us about how to live a Christlike life. How we treat others less fortunate than us is a large part of that.

Questions to Ponder: What difference can this attitude (or quality) make in your life? What events in the world today would benefit from this sort of attitude from our leaders? How would the world be different if we treated others this way? How can you practice these actions?

Daily Challenge: Do an audit - ask yourself if you have political beliefs that aren't in line with what these verses in Mosiah teach. What should you do about them? Personally, I think I'm much too focused on providing for my own family and my own needs, rather than looking at how I can help others. I'm by no means "rich" or even "well off," and I think I use that as an excuse to do less, to give less, to think about others less than I could.

Watch Yourselves

> Mosiah 4:30 - ...if ye do not watch yourselves, and your thoughts, and your words, and your deeds, and observe the commandments of God, and continue in the faith of what ye have heard concerning the coming of our Lord, even unto the end of your lives, ye must perish. And now, O man, remember, and perish not.

Lots of these sort of statements from King Benjamin. He truly had a lot of concern for the welfare of his people. Luckily for us, we get to learn these principles directly from him through The Book of Mormon.

This idea of being mindful, watching ourselves, our thoughts, words and deeds, I've been thinking about a lot. I started a morning journaling practice a year or so ago, but it wasn't until just a few weeks ago where I made a connection. This year in Sunday School we've been studying the stories of the pioneers, and I realized that because these stories were written down and preserved, then studied and turned into lessons, we're able to go back and read them, learn from them, and change our lives based on the things these stories teach us.

Our journaling is just that - writing down the stories of our lives so that we can go back and learn from them and make the necessary changes. This, to me, has been an incredible practice. It certainly isn't easy, to observe our thoughts and our actions and to diagnose them and try to make changes based on what went right and what went wrong, mainly because there's - in my case, at least - a lot of things I do wrong.

This practice of watching ourselves and being mindful leads us to salvation. It prevents us from perishing, which doesn't sound fun at all.

Questions to Ponder: How can you watch your thoughts words and actions? What comes to mind when you ponder that question? What do you need to work on?

Daily Challenge: Try a journal page - write down the things that happened today or yesterday, what went right and what went wrong, and pair that journal entry with prayer and pondering about how to be better today and tomorrow.

Turn To The Lord

> Mosiah 7:33 - But if ye will turn to the Lord with the full purpose of heart, and put your trust in him, and serve him with all diligence of mind, if ye do this, he will, according to his own will and pleasure, deliver you out of bondage.

For the last - this is embarrassing - TWO years, my business has been struggling. It honestly has felt like I was on a path and then ran into a dead end, but rather than turning around or looking for other options, I just kept walking into the rock wall at the end of that dead end. Over and over again, not learning, not changing.

My business wasn't working. I was lying to myself, I was stuck, I was, well, it might be what damnation or bondage feels like.

Then, this summer, things got even worse. We had clients bail on their projects. No new work was coming in. On top of feeling stuck, I felt like a failure, and by all measurements I really was one.

So, finally, I turned to the Lord. I knelt down in prayer and asked for help, because I didn't know what else to do.

That moment, that exact moment, with NO hesitation whatsoever, the Spirit started sending inspiration after inspiration, idea after idea. That's where this book idea came from.

Along with the idea for another book. And a new web series. And a new screenplay. And a new approach to networking and relationship building. And countless other lessons and perspective.

It felt like the Lord came up behind me, still walking into that dead end, and gently took my shoulders, turned me around, and pointed toward a path that was perfectly paved, well lit, and had way finding signage, water and snacks along the way, and the destination in plain sight.

It felt, and continues to feel, amazing.

Here's the verse, again:

> But if ye will turn to the Lord with the full purpose of heart, and put your trust in him, and serve him with all diligence of mind, if ye do this, he will, according to his own will and pleasure, deliver you out of bondage.

It's true. I can tell you, this promise is true.

Questions to Ponder: Where are you stuck? Spiritually? Financially? What options haven't you tried? What might the Lord be able to help you with, if you'll just ask?

Daily Challenge: Whatever thing you just thought of, wherever you're stuck, take a moment to find some humility, and ask the Lord for help. I don't know what the answer will be, or when it will come, but I know that the Lord is aware and anxious to give you what you need.

Things Which Are To Come

> Mosiah 8:16-18 - 16 And Ammon said that a seer is a revelator and a prophet also; and a gift which is greater can no man have, except he should possess the power of God, which no man can; yet a man may have great power given him from God.

> 17 But a seer can know of things which are past, and also of things which are to come, and by them shall all things be revealed, or, rather, shall secret things be made manifest, and hidden things shall come to light, and things which are not known shall be made known by them, and also things shall be made known by them which otherwise could not be known.

> 18 Thus God has provided a means that man, through faith, might work mighty miracles; therefore he becometh a great benefit to his fellow beings.

How many of us have friends that have left the Church for reasons surrounding church policy, or church culture, or something someone said over the pulpit? This isn't a new phenomenon. Early saints left the Church over things like misspelling a name, and not sharing milk and cream in the expected amount.

Yet when my friends have left, they tend to be fairly vocal about it. One friend just took the opportunity, on her "one year mark" of not attending meetings, to write about it on her popular blog. So many people resonated with her comments and help solidify the stance she's taken, yet, she's forgetting simple principles like this one in these verses about our prophets.

It seems so short sighted to walk away from the truth, from the gospel, from the ordinances and blessings of full fellowship in the Church over something so small in the eternal scheme of things. Couple that with the fact that prophets and seers can see much more than we can, so their perspective is different from ours. Wouldn't we benefit from listening to them, given that knowledge?

This is the way God has provided us: to be led by a prophet to salvation in the eternities with Him and our loved ones.

Questions to Ponder: Are there topics or policies that are hard for you? How should you go about resolving them? What other perspective can you try and gain to help see a bigger picture? How can you humble yourself and listen to the guidance of your leaders?

Daily Challenge: If there's something you're struggling with, work on it. Talk with someone whose testimony you admire. Pray about it and ask the Lord for help. Seek guidance through studying the scriptures, past conference talks, and other words of the apostles.

How Long He Doth Suffer With His People

> Mosiah 8:20-21 - 20 O how marvelous are the works of the Lord, and how long doth he suffer with his people; yea, and how blind and impenetrable are the understandings of the children of men; for they will not seek wisdom, neither do they desire that she should rule over them!
>
> 21 Yea, they are as a wild flock which fleeth from the shepherd, and scattereth, and are driven, and are devoured by the beasts of the forest.

The contrast between the nature of the Lord and His people here is pretty stark. I want to focus on our Savior though, especially how He, figuratively as the shepherd, suffers with His people, His flock.

As if it weren't enough that he sacrificed his life for us and atoned for our sins, he's also incredibly patient with us as our short-sightedness, pride, ignorance, or any number of things prevent us from keeping the proper perspective and reverence for what he has done for us.

I have a brother-in-law who truly believes he has done too many bad things to ever be redeemed. We all know how untrue that is, but he can't forgive himself, and continues to punish himself both physically and emotionally. If only he could humble himself enough to remember his Savior, the gospel truths that he was raised with, and the reality of repentance and forgiveness, for the mercy that he can receive through the Savior...how different his life would be.

We all have times like this, where we're being too hard on ourselves, and feel unworthy or lacking. Yet, the truth is that our Savior suffers with us, despite our diminished understanding and the things we do that draw our focus away from him. If the October 2017 conference was any indication, MANY of us feel this way, as there were many talks trying to help us understand that being hard on ourselves isn't part of the gospel.

I hope you'll read these verses and take some extra comfort in our loving Savior and his sacrifice on our behalf.

Questions to Ponder: Is there anything that would disqualify us from the love and patience of our Savior and our Father in Heaven? What are the implications of that answer?

Daily Challenge: Forgive yourself, then humble yourself, then ask for forgiveness and move forward. Focus on and rely on the Savior, and see the blessings come, the weight lifted.

Except They Repent

> *Mosiah 11:20-21 - 20 ...Wo be unto this people, for I have seen their abominations, and their wickedness, and their whoredoms; and except they repent I will visit them in mine anger.*

> *21 And except they repent and turn to the Lord their God, behold, I will deliver them into the hands of their enemies; yea and they shall be brought into bondage; and they shall be afflicted by the hand of their enemies.*

In Sunday school today as I was teaching the lesson, the topic of faith came up, and we discussed how integral faith is to the entire gospel. Literally, without faith, the gospel doesn't really work. It's an action verb, and requires us to do more than just believe or have the knowledge of our Savior's atonement, of the commandments, and of the plan of happiness. We have to actually act in faith.

Second to that principle is the principle of repentance. While the language in these verses may seem severe, I feel like that's the proper perspective we need to have when it comes to repentance. It's such an incredible gift to be able to repent of our sins, to be forgiven, and to ultimately be washed clean through baptism, and then later through repentance and the atonement of Christ.

Let's not be like the people that Abinadi is speaking of here. Let's be the saints that repent often, that are humble in the way we live our lives, and let us live with faith

Questions to Ponder: Why is it that prophets are sent to preach repentance? Why is repentance so powerful? What else can you do in your life to deepen your understanding of the doctrine of repentance, and have the faith to repent often?

Daily Challenge: Repent! It feels so incredible to repent and to search for ways to improve. Rather than feeling guilty or ashamed, we should see repentance as an opportunity for growth, for forgiveness, for peace and love. So do it! Repent today, strive to be better, and strengthen your relationship with your Savior by acting in faith.

Except They Repent...

> Mosiah 11:25 - And except they repent in sackcloth and ashes, and cry mightily to the Lord their God, I will not hear their prayers, neither will I deliver them out of their afflictions; and thus saith the Lord, and thus hath he commanded me.

It's really on us. The blessings are there waiting for us, but it requires faith and ACTION on our part. We have to repent. We have to pray. Otherwise, we're telling the Lord, "nah, I'm good, I got this, I don't need your help."

How prideful can we be???

Sadly, this was me for a few months this summer. I was beating my head against a wall trying to figure out - on my own - what was wrong with my business, where I was failing, what I wasn't doing right. It wasn't until I repented and knelt down in prayer that the answers started coming. And boy, they came. It's like the blessings were right there waiting for me to humble myself and ask.

The Lord already did his part. It's up to us.

Questions to Ponder: What are you "afflicted" by right now? Are you getting in your own way? Are there answers waiting for you if you'll just ask?

Daily Challenge: Get some extra humility and go to the Lord in prayer and ask for help. It's there, waiting for you.

Were It Not For The Atonement

> Mosiah 13:28 - And moreover, I say unto you, that salvation doth not come by the law alone; and were it not for the atonement, which God himself shall make for the sins and iniquities of his people, that they must unavoidably perish, notwithstanding the law of Moses.

That word *unavoidably* hit me really hard when revisiting this verse. I've had my own testimony reaffirmed time and time again when it comes to the reality and importance of the atonement of Christ. It's important that we remember the state we would end up in were it not for the atonement of Christ.

Questions to Ponder: How does salvation work? What would life be like were it not for the Atonement? How would your life be different without the ability to take the sacrament, to repent of your sins, to be baptized, to become like God and return and live with him and your family again?

Daily Challenge: Write down some of your thoughts in your journal or wherever you keep your thoughts. Refer to them often so that you can keep that perspective of why the Savior and his atonement are important to you.

These Are They For Whom He Has Died

> Mosiah 15:11-12 - 11 Behold I say unto you, that whosoever has heard the words of the prophets, yea, all the holy prophets who have prophesied concerning the coming of the Lord—I say unto you, that all those who have hearkened unto their words, and believed that the Lord would redeem his people, and have looked forward to that day for a remission of their sins, I say unto you, that these are his seed, or they are the heirs of the kingdom of God.

> 12 For these are they whose sins he has borne; these are they for whom he has died, to redeem them from their transgressions. And now, are they not his seed?

You know that saying "you can't win 'em all"?

I don't want to seem insensitive, but that's the first thing that came to mind for me. The Lord, though incredibly loving and caring to the point of sacrificing His life for every single one of us, realizes that He can't save us all. He can only do everything He can do, which He has. He has taken upon Him all of our sins and transgressions, and made it possible for us to be redeemed and to live with Him again someday.

We are His seed.

Yet there are some, because of the nature of the plan and the presence of agency, that will choose not to listen to the prophets, the testimonies, the words that have been written. There will be some with the knowledge of God and his plan who will choose something else, a different ending, a different way.

They will choose to not be saved.

There's nothing Christ can do to save them beyond what He's already done. The difference between someone who chooses to follow Christ and someone who doesn't comes down to agency. It's up to us. The work has been done. The atonement of our Savior has occurred and the gospel restored to the earth to teach us the principles and ordinances we need to adhere to in order to be saved.

So no matter what happens, no matter what our friends or family are doing, no matter what the world says, we have a choice. We can follow Christ, or we can follow our own way, our own pride, and be led by Satan to a place other than eternal life with our eternal families.

It's our choice.

DAILY MORMON

Questions to Ponder: What do these verses teach you about your relationship with Christ? What does that mean to you? What should you do about it?

Daily Challenge: Turn to Mosiah 15 in your scriptures, then go down to verse 10 and find the footnote for the word seed. Do a little scripture chase. See what the scriptures teach you about this relationship between Christ and His seed.

There Is A Resurrection

> Mosiah 16:8-12 - 8 But there is a resurrection, therefore the grave hath no victory, and the sting of death is swallowed up in Christ.

> 9 He is the light and the life of the world; yea, a light that is endless, that can never be darkened; yea, and also a life which is endless, that there can be no more death.

> 10 Even this mortal shall put on immortality, and this corruption shall put on incorruption, and shall be brought to stand before the bar of God, to be judged of him according to their works whether they be good or whether they be evil—

> 11 If they be good, to the resurrection of endless life and happiness; and if they be evil, to the resurrection of endless damnation, being delivered up to the devil, who hath subjected them, which is damnation—

> 12 Having gone according to their own carnal wills and desires; having never called upon the Lord while the arms of mercy were extended towards them; for the arms of mercy were extended towards them, and they would not; they being warned of their iniquities and yet they would not depart from them; and they were commanded to repent and yet they would not repent.

In gospel doctrine class, I often end the lesson wondering if I had done enough as a teacher/leader of the discussion to get across the magnitude of what we just studied. I feel that same way with these verses - I'm not sure how to reinforce or give any extra weight. But there is a resurrection. This is an incredible statement, one that should dictate everything we do throughout our lives. Our Savior, as the light of the world, should be our "north star" with every big decision, every principle we live by, everything.

Yet, we go through our lives and make mistakes. We forget. We lose focus.

Sometimes it sucks being a "natural man." Wouldn't it be great to just be perfect for a few days?

Questions to Ponder: What do you think of when you hear the word "resurrection"? What does it mean that Christ is the light and life of the world? Why is it important? How should it impact your life?

Daily Challenge: Studying "light" is/has been one of my favorites of all time. Start in the Bible Dictionary, then look into the Topical Guide and let the footnotes lead you. It's a seemingly never-ending topic of study.

Look Forward

> Mosiah 18:21 - And he commanded them that there should be no contention one with another, but that they should look forward with one eye, having one faith and one baptism, having their hearts knit together in unity and in love one towards another.

First, some context. Verse 1 of chapter 18 reads:

> 1 And now, it came to pass that Alma, who had fled from the servants of king Noah, repented of his sins and iniquities, and went about privately among the people, and began to teach the words of Abinadi—

In verse 3 we learn that Alma would teach anyone that would listen, and that after a while there were "a goodly number of people gathered together" (v7). He taught them the gospel, and about baptism, then baptized many present (v16).

Alma established the church over the next few verses, and called it The Church of Christ. He ordained priests, and taught them the gospel. It's at this point that we get to verse 21, and it stood out to me because this is one of the first things Alma teaches this new congregation of saints:

"There should be no contention one with another."

It's not hard to guess why he felt this was so important. The entirety of The Book Of Mormon hinges on the contentions of Laman against Nephi, and later their descendants against one another.

If Alma were speaking to us today in General Conference, it wouldn't be too hard to imagine him saying the exact same words. Avoid contention. Have one faith, and have unity and love one toward another.

I also keep thinking about the song "Imagine" by John Lennon, and other similar sentiments. How many sitcoms have we watched where some character yells "can't we all just get along!?!" It seems like this is a universally accepted principle, to love one another, and to avoid contention. Yet, it's one of the first things Satan uses to distract us from our faith. If he can get us to stop loving one another, to think inward, to focus on our pride, and then get us to contend with each other, that's the easiest way to get us to become divided. Look at the world today.

Look at our country! It's hard to miss the contention that's seemingly growing every single day.

Questions to Ponder: Why is "avoiding contention" such an important principle to follow? How does it apply to faith? What can you do better to be less contentious and more loving and charitable?

Daily Challenge: Is there someone that you've been contentious with, even in the slightest way? Take the opportunity to make it right, to apologize with all the humility you can, and mend that relationship. The other day I got really upset with my four year old, and I could tell that it was affecting him all day. It took me way too long to humble myself (why do I have to apologize to a little kid?), but when I did it was a beautiful conversation, one that I knew he needed. So don't rob yourself of that chance.

Not Expedient That Ye Should Have A King

> *Mosiah 23:7-8 - 7 ...Ye shall not esteem one flesh above another, or one man shall not think himself above another; therefore I say unto you it is not expedient that ye should have a king. 8 Nevertheless, if it were possible that ye could always have just men to be your kings it would be well with you to have a king.*

Over the last few weeks, even today actually, I come across political conversations online that seem to pull out scriptures to defend their argument. That's not really what the scriptures are for though. The scriptures aren't meant to be cherry-picked to support your political diatribes, or taken out of context to justify your stance.

Really, they're meant to teach us principles and, as Joseph Smith said, have us govern ourselves based on what we know and what the prophets teach and what the spirit leads us to do. We should change our views and stances to align with the doctrines of the gospel, not the other way around.

The important principle for me here is that we shouldn't esteem one flesh above another. That could be according to race, or gender, or age, or education, or any number of things. We should treat all of our brothers and sisters with charity and love and find ways to serve them and bring them unto Christ. We also shouldn't strive to be "above" another ourselves. History is rife with examples where men did that very thing and terrible things came of it.

Questions to Ponder: How could these verses be interpreted for today's political climate? What are the things you take away from these verses? How should you change the way you handle politics and the people we choose to represent you?

Daily Challenge: If you see a political conversation/argument online, find a way to inject some perspective, or see the other person's side and find common ground.

Trust No One

> *Mosiah 23:13-14 - 13 ...stand fast in this liberty wherewith ye have been made free, and that ye trust no man to be a king over you.*

> *14 And also trust no one to be your teacher nor your minister, except he be a man of God, walking in his ways and keeping his commandments.*

Follow up from the last chapter, in a way. At least on the "kings" concept. In a similar manner, verse 14 is a poignant principle. It encapsulates why I started on this search for principles in The Book of Mormon.

I'm sure I've written about this before, but I have read so many non-fiction books, trying to "crack the code" on the secret to success in my business, my finances, etc. I got to a point where I started wondering if I was looking in the wrong place. Answer: duh!

There are such better answers in The Book Of Mormon, and the practice of figuring out how to apply the teachings in this incredible book to our own lives is part of what makes it so amazing. We have to diligently search, use our faith, and ponder and pray about the answers we get. All of this make us more in tune with the Holy Ghost, the ultimate conduit to pure knowledge from our Heavenly Father.

Whatever it is you're struggling with, I urge you to read The Book of Mormon to find your answers. It reminds me of this story from The Teachings Of President Hinckley:

> *Let me tell you [another] story about the Book of Mormon. I heard a man who was a banker in California tell this story. He said his secretary smoked, constantly smoked. She was addicted to smoking. She could not set it aside. She said to him one day, "How can I stop smoking?"*

> *He reached down in his desk and took out a copy of the Book of Mormon and handed it to her. He said, "Now, you read this."*

> *She said, "All right, I'll read it."*

> *She came back a couple of days later and said, "I've read 200 pages, and I didn't see the word smoking anywhere. I didn't see the word tobacco anywhere. I saw nothing that referred to it."*

> *He said, "Keep reading."*

> *So she came back another couple of days later and said, "I've read 200 more pages—no mention of smoking, no mention of nicotine, no mention of anything associated with tobacco."*

> *He said, "Keep reading."*

> *She came back three or four days later. She said, "I've read the entire book. I didn't see tobacco anywhere; I didn't see smoking anywhere. But," she said, "there has come into my heart as a result of reading that book some influence, some power, that has taken from me the desire to smoke, and it is wonderful."*

Questions to Ponder: What is it about the Book of Mormon that makes it so powerful? How is it that we can receive answers to things not even mentioned in the book? What makes prophets such great teachers?

Daily Challenge: Ponder this story from President Hinckley and see if you can apply it to anything in your own life.

He Trieth Their Patience And Their Faith

> *Mosiah 23:21-22 - 21 Nevertheless the Lord seeth fit to chasten his people; yea, he trieth their patience and their faith.*

> *22 Nevertheless—whosoever putteth his trust in him the same shall be lifted up at the last day. Yea, and thus it was with this people.*

As weird as it may sound, I find this principle extremely comforting. So many of these struggles that we deal with in our lives - the financial stress, the relationship issues, the social problems of our times - many of them are specific for us and for our growth. They exist, in some part, to try our patience and our faith.

I love the part where it says "the Lord seeth fit." This isn't a coincidence. It's not happenstance. The Lord has a purpose for this type of chastening and these trials. Why? Because He needs strong people.

Where would the Church be without the strength of the early saints? The handcart companies that came across the plains? Those that were kicked out of their homes, hunted, and even killed? I don't think the Church would be as strong if not for that foundation the early saints laid for us. The Lord put them through an incredible amount of chastening in order to sculpt them into the people he needed to move his work forward.

One of my favorite talks of all time is from Elder Hugh B. Brown. It's a talk I'd listen to over and over again on my mission, called God is the Gardener. You may remember it as the story of the currant bush, where throughout the story we are reminded that God is the gardener here. It's an incredible speech. I highly recommend looking it up and giving it a watch or a listen.

Questions to Ponder: Why do you need your patience and faith tested? What is the benefit of going through chastening? What blessings come to those that endure to the end?

Daily Challenge: Read the speech or watch the video/audio version. (It's incredible!)

Because Of Their Unbelief

> Mosiah 26:3 - And now because of their unbelief they could not understand the word of God; and their hearts were hardened.

There are many paths that lead toward "unbelief," and I'm sure that term has a different meaning for each of us as well. The warning here is clear though: from our unbelief comes the inability to understand the word of God and a hardening of our hearts.

We're talking about those saints that were children at the time of King Benjamin's speech (v1), and have, since that time, let their faith weaken and stopped maintaining their faith and their belief. It's clear that these consequences are on them.

Each day that we don't do something to strengthen our testimonies is a day that could lead to another, and another, and another. We've been told countless times over our lives the importance of tending to our testimonies. How sad to let it get to the point that we can no longer understand the word of God, to miss out on the things He wants to teach us.

The Book Of Mormon teaches us time and time again that good people can falter, and that those that have wandered off the path can return. Wherever you are in your journey, I think it's important to realize those two realities, take an assessment of where we are, where we want to be, and where we're going.

Questions to Ponder: What would you do without the word of God in your life? Without the ability to understand his word?

Daily Challenge: Take the time to do a quick (or a longer, deeper) assessment. Where are you on the path? Where do you want to be? Which way are you currently headed?

Forgive One Another

> *Mosiah 26:29-31 - 29 Therefore I say unto you, Go; and whosoever transgresseth against me, him shall ye judge according to the sins which he has committed; and if he confess his sins before thee and me, and repenteth in the sincerity of his heart, him shall ye forgive, and I will forgive him also.*

> *30 Yea, and as often as my people repent will I forgive them their trespasses against me.*

> *31 And ye shall also forgive one another your trespasses; for verily I say unto you, he that forgiveth not his neighbor's trespasses when he says that he repents, the same hath brought himself under condemnation.*

There was a really great post I read just the other day that I recommend called Why People Leave The Church And Never Come Back. It talks about how when people sin, or transgress, it's effects are amplified because of the guilt and shame that's often heaped on them from others.

If the Lord is willing to forgive as often as people repent, shouldn't we also? Especially if the sins or transgressions of others don't even affect our lives?

In Elders' Quorum on Sunday a comment was made that there are members who tell their children that they are forbidden from playing with non-member friends and neighbors. How are we supposed to share the light of Christ with them if we aren't ever around them? How will they ever feel our happiness and joy if we put up a wall because they "aren't worthy"?

We're commanded here to forgive one another or face condemnation. It's as clear a statement as any other we've covered in the scriptures so far.

Questions to Ponder: Are there those you've walled ourselves off from because of your unwillingness to forgive? Is there anyone that God is unwilling to forgive? A limit to how many times forgiveness is given? Why should we be any different?

Daily Challenge: If you have a relationship that is in disrepair because of a transgression, or because you or someone else was wronged, think about it. Ponder it. Ask the Lord for the strength and help you need to forgive and to reconcile with that person. I promise you that blessings will come into your life for doing so.

Unless They Do This

> Mosiah 27:25-26 - 25 ...Marvel not that all mankind, yea, men and women, all nations, kindreds, tongues and people, must be born again; yea, born of God, changed from their carnal and fallen state, to a state of righteousness, being redeemed of God, becoming his sons and daughters.

> 26 And thus they become new creatures; and unless they do this, they can in nowise inherit the kingdom of God.

Everything about these verses is pretty boiler-plate Mormon doctrine, right? Then you hit the "unless they do this" and it hits you: oh, this is serious.

There are laws. There are rules. Sometimes they're categorized as commandments, other times they're less codified like this statement in verse 26. How they're organized or presented doesn't change the principle or the reality of it.

It is up to us during our time on earth to become new creatures, to change our state, to shrug off the natural man and be redeemed of God.

Sounds hard, right?

YES! And in that process, that hard process, we become new, we become His sons and daughters. It's the story of the rocks in the river, how they are smoothed over time with the persistence of the river rolling against them constantly, day after day, for years. We can be like that, but we have to be diligent in living the gospel day in and day out for our entire lives.

That's why there's always a blessing attached. God doesn't command us to live these laws and obey these commandments for no reason. The promise is that we can, through doing this, inherit the kingdom of God. If that's not enough reason to try, what is?

Questions to Ponder: What's hard about living the gospel? Which commandments are harder to follow? What perspective could be gained to help with that principle and give you the desire to work at it and change?

Daily Challenge: Take some time to ponder where you can improve, where you could be more diligent. NOT because you have to be perfect, NOT because you're not doing enough already, and NOT to add stress to your life. No, rather it's to bring more blessings into your life through living the gospel to a fuller extent.

He Will Visit You With Great Destruction

> *Mosiah 29:27 - And if the time comes that the voice of the people doth choose iniquity, then is the time that the judgments of God will come upon you; yea, then is the time he will visit you with great destruction even as he has hitherto visited this land.*

Oh man this verse has been on my mind a lot lately. I'll be the first to admit that I may be looking at the world today through a very narrow lens and that this has happened before, but it feels like this past year saw a lot more destruction and devastation than recent history. It's mid-October as I write this, and we've just had months of hurricanes and flooding, earthquakes, the worst wildfire California has ever seen, the worst mass shooting that the US has ever experienced, and countless other events across the world that seem to have "The Worst..." tagged onto the front of each headline.

Is our world more wicked? Are we being punished for our iniquity? Are these the judgments of God coming down on us?

Then I remember that A) it's not an answer that I'm going to receive. My personal belief is that is the role of the prophet and the apostles. We also just had General Conference, and there were no warnings, there were no wide-sweeping calls to repentance. The watchmen of the tower gave us no cause for alarm there. And B) it's not a fruitful exercise to think about these things. Whether or not these are the judgments of God doesn't affect how I should be living my life every day.

What we *can* do is use these events to gain more perspective and more empathy for others. To prepare our homes and our lives with the things we need were we to be caught in a tragedy or a natural disaster. To repent of our sins and try to be better people each and every day, filled with more humility and more charity for our brothers and sisters here on earth.

Questions to Ponder: What do these events mean to you? What should you do about them? What changes should you implement into your life as a result of them?

Daily Challenge: Think through the basic things we've been taught about preparedness and planning, and ways that you can improve. Do you have enough food and water to get through a natural disaster? Do you have emergency kits that are stocked and easily accessible? Do you have a plan in place in case something happens?

ALMA

It Would Prove Their Entire Destruction

> *Alma 1:12 - ...and were priestcraft to be enforced among this people it would prove their entire destruction.*

Some context: Nehor shows up and starts preaching his own doctrine to the people, and explains that preachers like himself should be supported by the people. He starts taking their money, and establishes a church, which constitutes priestcraft.

He stumbles upon Gideon who contends with him (verbally) to the point that Nehor slays him by the sword. He is brought before Alma, who utters the words of this scripture.

> *12 But Alma said unto him: Behold, this is the first time that priestcraft has been introduced among this people. And behold, thou art not only guilty of priestcraft, but hast endeavored to enforce it by the sword; and were priestcraft to be enforced among this people it would prove their entire destruction.*

I always found it an interesting way to make a living - preaching a gospel you believe is true. Sure, I and many others paid money to go and preach the gospel, but we knew that it wasn't financially feasible to do it for longer than those two years. We also didn't get paid for it.

So, yes, my situation is a bit different, but still: how do people feel that this is ok? That it's ok to take money from people and pay yourself a salary for preaching the word of God.

I guess it kind of goes without saying - if someone is supporting themselves on their preaching, they may not be called of God. We sustain one prophet at a time, who leads and guides the church. If you're being misled by someone other than that prophet, be warned that following and allowing that sort of priestcraft leads to destruction. Worse even than that, as it states in D&C 121, any priesthood holders using their authority to mislead others are also guilty of priestcraft. So we that hold the priesthood must be especially vigilant when it comes to the scriptures, the priesthood, and our use of both of them.

Questions to Ponder: What other forms does priestcraft come in? What would be considered priestcraft today? How should you respond when confronted with it?

Daily Challenge: Think a little bit longer about the other forms of priestcraft. This recent conference talk that talks a little more about it: He Trusts Us, by Stanley G. Ellis, from the October 2006 General Conference.

Every Man That Is Cursed

> *Alma 3:19 - Now I would that ye should see that they brought upon themselves the curse; and even so doth every man that is cursed bring upon himself his own condemnation.*

I've got three little boys, ages 6, 4, and 3 at the moment, and one of the lessons we've tried to teach them throughout their short time on earth so far is that actions have consequences. That's the principle stated here as well.

Now, this doesn't mean that everything bad that happens to us is our fault. We need to pay close attention to the words used in this verse. "Cursed" and "Condemnation" is very different from "every man going through hard times brought it on himself."

The point is, actions have consequences. Agency is one of the greatest gifts we've been afforded here on earth, all because of our Savior Jesus Christ and His willingness to act as a Savior for us. So what we do with that agency matters. It matters what choices we make. It matters how we live our faith. It matters how we act on the knowledge we've been blessed with. It matters so much that there are consequences for bad decisions, put in place to help nudge us back to the path we need to be on.

Let's use our agency wisely and do the best we can to live in a way that helps others, rather than condemns ourselves.

Questions to Ponder: What curse did the Amlicites bring upon themselves in this chapter? What is a modern day version of someone bringing a similar curse upon themselves? What can you do if you find yourself facing the consequences of your own actions? (What did the Lamanites ultimately do in The Book of Mormon?)

Daily Challenge: Ponder the gravity, the weight of the trust that's been placed in us with free agency. Our Savior gave His life so we could have it. What should you do with that knowledge and perspective?

There Can No Man Be Saved

> *Alma 5:21 - ...for there can no man be saved except his garments are washed white; yea, his garments must be purified until they are cleansed from all stain, through the blood of him of whom it has been spoken by our fathers, who should come to redeem this people from their sins.*

I love how things line up like this, over and over again as I write this book. This past Sunday, in Elder's Quorum, our teacher - who's a psychiatrist - had us do an exercise where we tried to create the equivalent of Maslow's Hierarchy Of Needs but for our faith, the ultimate goal being Charity and Salvation. He spoke to us about how, with Maslow's hierarchy, you need to take care of the most basic needs first, like psychological and safety needs, before working on the higher tier needs like esteem and self-actualization.

So, what did we come up with? Granted, we only had about 30 minutes to figure it all out, much less time - I assume - than Maslow spent on his theory.

At the very bottom we had humility and a desire to know God, up until the very end of the lesson when we all realized that without God, without a Savior, without an Atonement, without a Plan of Happiness, there is no foundation. None at all.

Without Christ, we cannot be saved. There is no salvation. There is no such thing as faith. There is no reason for obedience to the laws because there would be no laws. Everything rests on our Savior doing what He did on our behalf.

It's incredible that He would do that for us, to make such an incredible sacrifice so that we can be made clean, and ultimately return to live with our Heavenly Father and our loved ones again.

Questions to Ponder: Do you agree? Is the existence of God the foundation of your spiritual hierarchy of needs? Where do other attributes and needs fall for you? What is your ultimate goal? Are there parallels you can find that line up with the different tiers in the hierarchy, such as the ultimate goal of self-actualization?

Daily Challenge: If it helps, decide what five or six attributes or needs you'd put in your own spiritual hierarchy of needs.

An Invitation Unto All Men

> *Alma 5:33-36 - 33 Behold, he sendeth an invitation unto all men, for the arms of mercy are extended towards them, and he saith: Repent, and I will receive you.*

> *34 Yea, he saith: Come unto me and ye shall partake of the fruit of the tree of life; yea, ye shall eat and drink of the bread and the waters of life freely;*

> *35 Yea, come unto me and bring forth works of righteousness, and ye shall not be hewn down and cast into the fire—*

> *36 For behold, the time is at hand that whosoever bringeth forth not good fruit, or whosoever doeth not the works of righteousness, the same have cause to wail and mourn.*

Ever feel like you messed up so bad that you can't go to church, or talk to the bishop, or pray? I've been there.

Verses like these, however, teach us the opposite principle: that if we repent, the Lord will receive us. If we are diligent in repenting and turning from our sins, and living the gospel to as full an extent as possible, the blessings are incredible - partaking of the fruit of the tree of life, drinking the waters of life, having eternal life.

We're all going to mess up. We're going to feel the pain of those mistakes, but that's how we learn how important the gospel is in our lives, and how essential it is to our salvation. That pain is an incredible teacher. Look at Paul, at Alma, at so many that have had incredibly painful experiences surrounding their repentance, only to feel incredible joy and happiness on the other side of that transformation.

If we don't repent, if we don't turn back to the Lord and learn from our mistakes, we miss out on the blessings and the experience of going through that pain. So don't turn away from it. Don't fear it. Repent, and humbly learn what you need to learn and then continue on in living the gospel.

Questions to Ponder: How is the tree of life described in the scriptures? What are the bread and water of life? Are they desirable? Should you have these as goals? Why?

Daily Challenge: Repent! Do it! It may not be today or tomorrow, but the next time you feel too far gone to repent, don't cheat yourself of the opportunity to learn and grow from your mistakes. Repent!

The Good Shepherd Doth Call You

> *Alma 5:38 - Behold, I say unto you, that the good shepherd doth call you; yea and in his own name he doth call you, which is the name of Christ; and if ye will not hearken unto the voice of the good shepherd, to the name by which ye are called, behold, ye are not the sheep of the good shepherd.*

Pretty clear statement here. We have to listen, to "hearken unto the voice." Any time that we spend on things that make us less likely to listen to the voice of the Savior puts us in a situation where we cannot be led and guided by him. How often have the prophets talked about the type of media we consume, or the things we put into our bodies, or what we spend our time doing and who we do it with? All of these, to me, go back to this principle that those who listen are the sheep, and those who do not are not the sheep.

Every day that we use our agency to grow closer to our Savior, we will be blessed. The opposite is also true.

Questions to Ponder: What does listening or hearkening mean to you? What does that look like in your day to day actions? How can you listen better?

Daily Challenge: Give up one thing, one thing that keeps you from being able to listen. It may be a TV show, a habit, a small transgression that pops up here or there. Give it up for a week. Then another. Then a month. See what changes. See how much closer you get to your Savior by showing him through your actions that you want to listen and be numbered among his sheep.

Whatsoever Is Good

> Alma 5:40-41 - 40 For I say unto you that whatsoever is good cometh from God, and whatsoever is evil cometh from the devil.

> 41 Therefore, if a man bringeth forth good works he hearkeneth unto the voice of the good shepherd, and he doth follow him; but whosoever bringeth forth evil works, the same becometh a child of the devil, for he hearkeneth unto his voice, and doth follow him.

Such a fundamental scripture here. Almost everything in the gospel can be traced back to this principle. Every decision we make, every person we choose to learn from or follow, the people we interface with on a daily basis... we can always look to the actions of those people, whether they're good or evil (or somewhere along that spectrum) and make choices accordingly.

It has been a helpful exercise when I'm faced with a tough decision to weigh the options in this context. Is one "more good"? Does one option have more Godliness associated with it? That's the way to go.

It also helps when we look at our daily actions, the way we live our lives, the way we interact with others, the words we choose to use, and what we believe. Are we kind to others? Or are we quick to anger? Do we partner with and work with good people with good ethics? Do we vote for men and women with standards and integrity?

It's important to listen to "the voice of the good shepherd" and "follow him." Let's choose to do that as often as possible.

Questions to Ponder: What are the definitions of Good and Evil in this context? How broad are those definitions? What are the good and evil things that are parts of your life? What should you do about it?

Daily Challenge: Find something - a belief, a habit, an action - that would fall into the evil side of the good-evil spectrum, and let it go. Abandon the belief, shirk the habit, and avoid that action in the future.

Repent!

> *Alma 5:51 - —Repent, for except ye repent ye can in nowise inherit the kingdom of heaven.*

Here's your weekly reminder to repent, everyone!

I'm not sure how many of the prophets in The Book of Mormon spoke of/wrote of repentance, but my first guess would be: most of them. There has to be a reason that it is so often mentioned in the scriptures, by so many different people.

Repentance is hard. I think that's part of it. It requires humility, a desire to change things that we're doing, to admit mistakes and to become better. None of that is easy. It requires emotional as well as physical fortitude, and is a process that takes time where we may mess up again.

Yet, the blessings are even greater than the hard things we have to go through to get them. The kingdom of heaven, to name one.

Whenever we find ourselves in need of repentance, it always helps to put it into perspective. Are we going to let one weakness, one sin, one mistake prevent us from the kingdom of heaven? Well, when you put it that way, it seems foolish to say yes, doesn't it?

Questions to Ponder: Why do YOU think repentance is mentioned so often in The Book of Mormon? Is there anything in your life you need to repent of? Anything that's preventing you from becoming your best self? What blessings have you received from repenting in the past?

Daily Challenge: Say it with me now: Repent! R E P E N T! Let's do it. I'll do it, you'll do it, we'll all do it together. And tomorrow, we'll feel even better and be better versions of ourselves.

Walk In His Paths

> *Alma 7:9 - —Repent ye, and prepare the way of the Lord, and walk in his paths, which are straight; for behold, the kingdom of heaven is at hand, and the Son of God cometh upon the face of the earth.*

I feel like I need to spend a lot more time thinking about and searching for more context and info about this verse, especially the "walk in his paths" part. There's no footnote there, for walk or paths, and nothing in the topical guide on the matter. Also nothing in any of my Book of Mormon study manuals... but for some reason the phrase stood out to me tonight.

A different place to start from might be in Doctrine and Covenants 19:23:

> *Learn of me, and listen to my words; walk in the meekness of my Spirit, and you shall have peace in me.*

The footnote for *walk* in that verse leads to Moroni 7 and talks about being a follower of Christ and a good member of the church.

So what do you think? The Spirit told Alma to cry unto the people these words, and these words were also intended for us.

Questions to Ponder: What does it mean to prepare the way of the Lord? To walk in his paths?

Daily Challenge: Ponder what it means to you to walk in His paths.

Lay Aside Every Sin

> Alma 7:14-16 - 14 Now I say unto you that ye must repent, and be born again; for the Spirit saith if ye are not born again ye cannot inherit the kingdom of heaven; therefore come and be baptized unto repentance, that ye may be washed from your sins, that ye may have faith on the Lamb of God, who taketh away the sins of the world, who is mighty to save and to cleanse from all unrighteousness.

> 15 Yea, I say unto you come and fear not, and lay aside every sin, which easily doth beset you, which doth bind you down to destruction, yea, come and go forth, and show unto your God that ye are willing to repent of your sins and enter into a covenant with him to keep his commandments, and witness it unto him this day by going into the waters of baptism.

> 16 And whosoever doeth this, and keepeth the commandments of God from thenceforth, the same will remember that I say unto him, yea, he will remember that I have said unto him, he shall have eternal life, according to the testimony of the Holy Spirit, which testifieth in me.

Alma really liked to talk to people about repentance. Given his own conversion experience, it's easy to see why.

The process of repentance isn't just for those who are becoming converted and preparing to enter the waters of baptism. No, it's for everyone. Look in verse 16 - *"whosoever doeth this, AND keepeth the commandments of God from thenceforth..."*

Alma teaches that we have to repent, be baptized, AND continue in righteousness by keeping the commandments. Unfortunately, we're going to fail at least once. None of us has been or will be perfect at keeping the commandments. Fortunately, we have a Savior, Jesus Christ, who atoned for our sins and made it possible for us to repent.

I feel like there is so much more to repentance that I'm not getting, because it keeps coming up, and I just keep thinking "yeah, I get it, repentance is important," but that feels like a surface level understanding of repentance. I know there are more scriptures coming with this topic, as it was the second or third most referenced topic as I was going through these verses and categorizing them. Hopefully we'll all learn together from the Spirit the things we need to know to deepen our understanding of this incredible gift we've been given.

Questions to Ponder: Why does repentance keep coming up? Why do the prophets teach it so often to so many different people? What do you need to do about that? Are you repenting enough? Can you do it more often?

Daily Challenge: If you feel, like I do, that there is more to learn about this topic, say a prayer and ask God to help open your mind to more knowledge and understanding.

One Eternal Round

> *Alma 7:20-21 - 20 ...he cannot walk in crooked paths; neither doth he vary from that which he hath said; neither hath he a shadow of turning from the right to the left, or from that which is right to that which is wrong; therefore his course is one eternal round.*

> *21 And he doth not dwell in unholy temples; neither can filthiness or anything which is unclean be received into the kingdom of God; therefore I say unto you the time shall come, yea, and it shall be at the last day, that he who is filthy shall remain in his filthiness.*

I love the scriptures that give us insight into the characteristics and attributes of God. Not only does it help me understand Him better, but it gives me guidance and direction on how to live my own life. Each of these statements are things we can strive to live up to and would benefit from.

> *- Don't walk in crooked paths : stay true to your faith and be diligent in keeping the commandments*

> - Don't vary from that which you have said : be true to your word

> - Don't turn from right to left : don't be a hypocrite

> - Don't dwell in unholy temples : who you choose to be around and where you spend your time matters and has influence on your life

Because of these things "his course is one eternal round." Think about how incongruent it would be were He not to abide by these principles. Then think about how much our lives would be blessed if we were to live them as He did.

Questions to Ponder: What part of these verses stands out to you the most? Which seems like one to try and work on in your own life? What would be the benefit if you tried?

Daily Challenge: Try to be a little more Christ-like today. No hypocrisy. Be true to your word. Be faithful and diligent in keeping the commandments. Audit who you spend your time with and where you spend it.

Then Ye Will Always Abound In Good Works

> Alma 7:23-24 - 23 And now I would that ye should be humble, and be submissive and gentle; easy to be entreated; full of patience and long-suffering; being temperate in all things; being diligent in keeping the commandments of God at all times; asking for whatsoever things ye stand in need, both spiritual and temporal; always returning thanks unto God for whatsoever things ye do receive.

> 24 And see that ye have faith, hope, and charity, and then ye will always abound in good works.

These verses could be turned into a manifesto of what it means to be a disciple of Christ, or a Latter-day Saint. Any time you're struggling, or having a hard time dealing with others, or feel like things aren't working out, you can turn back to these verses and see where something is amiss. Could you be more humble? More patient or temperate? More diligent in keeping the commandments?

If someone asked you to describe the ideal version of yourself, I imagine these are the characteristics you would list off.

I can't think of anyone that wouldn't benefit from striving to gain more of these qualities. The real question though is how. How do we improve. At times it can feel overwhelming, like there is too much being asked of us, and we fall too short when we try. How can we have faith AND hope AND charity AND humility AND AND AND...

For me it comes down to working on one at a time. Start with faith. Then add humility. Then work on charity. Then patience. One at a time, one day at a time. One step at a time. Some modern psychologists and thought leaders have prescribed a 1% improvement each day. If you can improve just 1%, the thinking goes, then in 100 days you won't have just increased by 100%, because of the math. You'll have improved much more than that because of that constant effort and constant progress. Just as a mountain can be moved one shovelful at a time, so can we improve our Christlike attributes one day at a time.

Questions to Ponder: Which characteristics do you want to increase? Which seem like you'd have the most enjoyment of fulfillment working on and gaining more of? How can you start making small improvements each day for the next 30 or 100 days? What do you have to lose if you try?

Daily Challenge: Pick one attribute you'd like to work on. Think up a game plan. Write out things you can do to improve, like studying the topic in the scriptures, finding an opportunity each day to practice that quality, etc. Then do it! Commit to doing it for a week or a month or 100 days straight, and do it!

I Will Visit This People In Mine Anger

> Alma 8:29 - —Repent ye, for thus saith the Lord, except ye repent I will visit this people in mine anger; yea and I will not turn my fierce anger away.

We often talk about the blessings of repentance, and how wonderful a gift it is that we are able to repent. However, there's the flip side: what happens when we don't repent? What happens when we continue on in our sins, fully aware of what we're doing? This verse teaches us that the Lord can get angry, upset; fiercely so.

Growing up, one of the greatest motivations for me to "live right" was because I knew how much my parents loved me, and how sad it would make them if I were to make any serious mistakes. Don't get me wrong, I was nowhere close to perfect, but I lived a pretty straightforward mormon life.

I think it's similar for us - we know how much our Heavenly Father and our Savior Jesus Christ love us. It's not only taught to us time and time again in the scriptures, but look at the actions they took to show us the extent of that love for us. We also know, from verses like this one, that there are consequences to our sins and transgressions, to our pride, to our abandoning the truth and knowledge that we have and for not repenting.

If we need yet another reason to repent, let this be it.

Questions to Ponder: Can you imagine the Lord being fiercely angry about your choice to not repent? Is He talking about an individual or a group of saints? What should you do about this verse.

Daily Challenge: Repent! You can't repent too much or too often, so find something that you can repent of and do it.

He Commandeth You To Repent

> *Alma 9:12-13 - 12 Behold, now I say unto you that he commandeth you to repent; and except ye repent, ye can in nowise inherit the kingdom of God. But behold, this is not all—he has commanded you to repent, or he will utterly destroy you from off the face of the earth; yea, he will visit you in his anger, and in his fierce anger he will not turn away.*

> *13 Behold, do ye not remember the words which he spake unto Lehi, saying that: Inasmuch as ye shall keep my commandments, ye shall prosper in the land? And again it is said that: Inasmuch as ye will not keep my commandments ye shall be cut off from the presence of the Lord.*

Repentance. Again. There's a lot of talk about repentance in the book of Alma. By this point, Alma has met up with Amulek after returning to preach to the people in Ammonihah. The people in Ammonihah were not members of the church (Alma 8:11), and we're told that "Satan had gotten great hold upon the hearts of the people in the city" (Alma 8:9).

One of the first things he teaches the people there, non-members, who are wicked and following the path Satan would have them follow, the FIRST thing he teaches is repentance. Why? Because an angel told him so! Alma 8:16:

> *16 And behold, I am sent to command thee that thou return to the city of Ammonihah, and preach again unto the people of the city; yea, preach unto them. Yea, say unto them, except they repent the Lord God will destroy them.*

Repentance provides the foundation for the gospel to take place in the hearts of people, wicked or faithful. It forces us to be humble, to be teachable, to learn the true state that we are in, and that we need the help of our Savior and His atonement.

And it's not a singular event, as proven by how often it is taught in The Book of Mormon. We all need to repent often and receive the blessings that come from it.

Questions to Ponder: Why do you think that repentance is the first thing that prophets are told to preach to their people? Why is repentance such an important principle? What are the benefits you've seen in your life from repenting?

Daily Challenge: Dig a little deeper. Study repentance in the Bible Dictionary, or the Topical Guide. See where it takes you.

It Shall Be More Tolerable For Them

> *Alma 9:15 - Nevertheless I say unto you, that it shall be more tolerable for them in the day of judgment than for you, if ye remain in your sins, yea, and even more tolerable for them in this life than for you, except ye repent.*

More tolerable for whom? The Lamanites, who had not kept the commandments and had been cut off from the presence of the Lord. Alma teaches here that it will be better for those that broke the commandments than those who live in their sin and fail to repent.

That's us, guys. We're the ones who have made covenants, who have been baptized and have committed to keep the commandments. If we chose to forgo our faith and live in sin, without repenting, well, the consequences are bad.

I don't think Alma would have talked this way to a group of faithful saints, but it is helpful, at times, to have some perspective when it comes to the seriousness of keeping the commandments and living the gospel. We should never be motivated by fear when it comes to living righteously, because fear is the opposite of faith. But we have to have a reason for that faith, a desire to nurture it into knowledge and conviction and everything else we need in order to live the gospel out of our own agency.

Sometimes a little perspective helps.

Questions to Ponder: Do you know anyone living in sin in this way? Unrepentant and no desire to change? How can you help that person? What do they need? (Love, charity, compassion, understanding, empathy?)

Daily Challenge: It may be hard, but see if there's some way to reach out to that person you just thought of. Let them know you're thinking of them, that you love them, that you care, and that you're here. No judgment, no criticism, just charity and love.

Nigh At Hand

> Alma 9:25 - ...Repent ye, for the kingdom of heaven is nigh at hand.

More repentance. The word "nigh" means near, or almost. These words were written over 2000 years ago, and even then the prophets, like Alma, were warning the people of the importance of repentance, with the reason that the kingdom of heaven is almost here.

I think that could mean a number of things. One - we don't know when we'll die, so the idea that we will be able to repent on our death bed may not be the best strategy. The other one that comes to mind is that no one knows the timing of the second coming. We need to constantly be repenting and keeping ourselves as clean as possible because we don't know when that event will occur.

Questions to Ponder: With the knowledge of this scripture, how important do you find repentance? What should you do about it?

Daily Challenge: Repent! It's fun, and by now, it should be almost a habit.

Through Faith On His Name

> *Alma 9:27-28 - 27 And behold, he cometh to redeem those who will be baptized unto repentance, through faith on his name.*

> *28 Therefore, prepare ye the way of the Lord, for the time is at hand that all men shall reap a reward of their works, according to that which they have been—if they have been righteous they shall reap the salvation of their souls, according to the power and deliverance of Jesus Christ; and if they have been evil they shall reap the damnation of their souls, according to the power and captivation of the devil.*

While I take some comfort in the statement that those who have been evil and done evil things in their lives on this earth will reap damnation of their souls (I'm thinking of mass murderers and the like), the more poignant part of these verses for me are the importance of our works and our actions and our faith.

We were given agency for a reason.

We have to have faith and live accordingly. Those are the requirements the Lord has asked of us, time and time again. Have faith, be obedient, repent when it doesn't go perfectly (it won't), and endure to the end. These are all choices.

We will "reap a reward of our works, according to that which they have been." Our works do more than just show people we're Mormon or Christian or "good." They are what qualify us for redemption and eternal life with our Heavenly Father and our Savior.

Questions to Ponder: What else stands out to you in these verses? What should you do about it? What is it that the Lord asks of us when it comes to the gospel and our agency?

Daily Challenge: Spend some time thinking and pondering on these verses. See what the Lord wants to teach you through the Spirit. Pray for guidance, for inspiration, to know what his will is for you at this time in your life.

The Voice Of This People

> Alma 10:19 - ...if the time should come that the voice of this people should choose iniquity, that is, if the time should come that this people should fall into transgression, they would be ripe for destruction.

I take this verse to show the importance of being involved in our communities, our neighborhoods, our country. To be involved in elections both local and national. To do what is necessary to ensure that good people with integrity are voted into office and given authority to represent the interests of their constituents, whether that be a school board, a congressional district, or other position.

There is a weird aspect of US politics that less than half of the electorate votes in elections. In Provo where I live, despite thousands of people living in the area, there are often less than 10,000 votes counted. If we don't engage in keeping our officials honest and electing people with integrity and morals, well, we see the consequences here and throughout the recorded history of The Book of Mormon.

I'm sure there are other ways to interpret this scripture, but in this country we have been given the privilege of being able to vote in elections, to have the "voice of the people" be heard through these elections. Let's make sure we're doing our part to participate and to prevent the voice of the people from choosing iniquity.

Questions to Ponder: Are you a voter? Why/why not? What would the effect be if more people voted? What are the consequences of watching from the sidelines and not participating?

Daily Challenge: With elections occurring every year, make a decision to get involved, be educated on the candidates and the policies up for a vote, and participate in the process.

The Kingdom Of Heaven

> *Alma 11:37 - And I say unto you again that he cannot save them in their sins; for I cannot deny his word, and he hath said that no unclean thing can inherit the kingdom of heaven; therefore, how can ye be saved, except ye inherit the kingdom of heaven? Therefore, ye cannot be saved in your sins.*

I love these super logical, rational verses. The prophets posing questions this way just shows the truthfulness of the gospel. "Go ahead, try and poke holes in this. You can't. The gospel is true. *Mic Drop*"

What do we need to learn from this verse? We cannot be saved in our sins, for one. But we all sin! All the time! So what do we do about it? (What have the last 100 or so chapters been about?) Repent! Awesome. Next.

Inherit the kingdom of heaven. This is more of a perspective thing for me, in that it's not something we can do, today, right now. But it's the big picture, the long term goal. It's what we should think about when we're making our daily decisions and choices - will this decision I'm about to make right now help me or hurt me when it comes to inheriting the kingdom of heaven?

The perspective is huge for me. We have to have internal reasons for making the choices we make, for living the gospel, for being obedient. Without it, we're left with the external influences that change depending on who we're with, where we're at, and what we're doing. We don't want to be left with only external pressures when it comes to our salvation, so we need to have a proper perspective on the kingdom of heaven as a worthwhile pursuit.

Questions to Ponder: What do you think about when you think of the kingdom of heaven? What does it look like? Feel like? Who's with you? Is it a place you want to go to?

Daily Challenge: Make one resolution today to give up something that is preventing you from potentially entering the kingdom of heaven. Find something that helps you be 1% better. Start there, start small, and make progress every day.

Salvation Cometh To None Else

> *Alma 11:40-41 - 40 And he shall come into the world to redeem his people; and he shall take upon him the transgressions of those who believe on his name; and these are they that shall have eternal life, and salvation cometh to none else.*

> *41 Therefore the wicked remain as though there had been no redemption made, except it be the loosing of the bands of death; for behold, the day cometh that all shall rise from the dead and stand before God, and be judged according to their works.*

I'm interested by the division in these verses. In 41 it says that all shall rise from the dead to stand before God. There's no qualifying there, nothing we need to do to be eligible for resurrection.

Yet, there is a separation between those who believe and those who are wicked. The righteous who believe in Jesus Christ and His atonement will have eternal life and salvation, while the wicked remain. Belief and obedience are what qualify us for salvation, to be able to receive the kingdom of heaven and live with our eternal families.

I feel like we don't talk about these qualifiers enough. I don't remember them being a big part of Sunday school lessons. Yet there it is, plain as can be right in The Book of Mormon.

Questions to Ponder: What should you do with this information? How does it change your perspective on living the gospel and your faith in Christ?

Daily Challenge: Ponder these scriptures. Try and expand your perspective on what is asked of us regarding salvation and eternal life.

The Mysteries of God

> *Alma 12:9-11 - 9 And now Alma began to expound these things unto him, saying: It is given unto many to know the mysteries of God; nevertheless they are laid under a strict command that they shall not impart only according to the portion of his word which he doth grant unto the children of men, according to the heed and diligence which they give unto him.*

> *10 And therefore, he that will harden his heart, the same receiveth the lesser portion of the word; and he that will not harden his heart, to him is given the greater portion of the word, until it is given unto him to know the mysteries of God until he know them in full.*

> *11 And they that will harden their hearts, to them is given the lesser portion of the word until they know nothing concerning his mysteries; and then they are taken captive by the devil, and led by his will down to destruction. Now this is what is meant by the chains of hell.*

What we're really talking about here is pride an humility. I know it's a really tough call to choose between the two (I'm being facetious) but let's run down the outcome from each approach.

Pride: Hardening of one's heart, receiving a lesser portion of the word until they know nothing about the mysteries of God; being taken captive by the devil and led to destruction. Fun, right?

Humility: Not hardening one's heart; receiving a greater portion of the word until they know the mysteries of God in full.

How incredible to know ALL of the mysteries of God. To have a FULLness of knowledge. The benefits are so incredible, and more than just dangling them out in front of us, the prophets give us a clear path to receiving these blessings: have humility, and give heed and diligence to the knowledge that you receive. Listen. Work hard to learn more. Show the Lord through your actions that you value the knowledge that you've been given, and you'll get more!

This is especially encouraging for the younger readers of this book. It's been so cool to hear that some parents are reading this every day with their teenagers, and that it's been a helpful resource. This chapter feels important for you young people in particular.

I remember when I was thirteen and fourteen and hadn't yet had that "huge event" that everyone seemed to talk about where I received my testimony. What I learned from a teacher at a youth conference though is the same principle taught here, and the same one you've likely heard before. "Line upon line. Precept on precept. Here a little there a little."

This is how gaining a testimony works. Even for Joseph Smith, who had the most incredible experience seeing our Heavenly Father and Jesus Christ in person - he had been diligently searching, asking questions, reading and studying the scriptures, seeking knowledge. Our path is the same. We have questions. All of us do. But the questions don't come if we don't search for them, and they especially don't come if we harden our hearts. As soon as we close ourselves off to the possibility that there are answers, we've already prevented them from ever reaching us in the first place.

I hope that you've had some moments of clarity and understanding through the book so far. It's over 4 months of daily scripture study and questions to ponder. If you're still at the point where you feel like you haven't "got it" yet, don't feel discouraged. It may be tonight or tomorrow, it may be a few more months or years. I can promise you that if you continue searching that the answers and knowledge will come. That's what a testimony is - a knowledge of things that is hard to describe any other way than "I just know."

If you're reading this as someone who's struggled with your faith and/or your testimony, know that you're not the only one, and you're not a bad person for going through this. We've all been there. I'VE been there. We're going to have ups and downs in life, but what I can testify of is that our Heavenly Father loves us and knows us intimately. If we seek Him out and try to know Him better, He will reciprocate.

I know these things are true, and that if we apply them and try to live our lives the way the scriptures teach us to, we will be so incredibly blessed we'll wonder how we ever lived any other way. God is real. Our Savior truly lived and died for us so that we can return and be with them again one day. All of us. Each one, a brother or a sister, a son or a daughter of God, together again one day.

Questions to Ponder: The feelings of clarity, of enlightenment, of happiness and joy, or courage, or understanding - those are all ways and feelings that the Spirit uses to teach and communicate with us. All good things come from God, remember? So what feelings do you have right now? How is the Spirit speaking to you? What does it want to teach you right now? Is there a place - a notebook or a journal or an app - that you can write down your thoughts and the promptings you're getting?

Daily Challenge: Do that now - find somewhere to write, and do it for as long as there is inspiration and promptings coming your way. Don't worry about spelling and grammar or if anyone is going to read it later. This is just for you. Seek out that knowledge and understanding, write it down, and then act on it. "Give heed."

Whosoever Dieth In His Sins

> Alma 12:16-18 - 16 And now behold, I say unto you then cometh a death, even a second death, which is a spiritual death; then is a time that whosoever dieth in his sins, as to a temporal death, shall also die a spiritual death; yea, he shall die as to things pertaining unto righteousness.

> 17 Then is the time when their torments shall be as a lake of fire and brimstone, whose flame ascendeth up forever and ever; and then is the time that they shall be chained down to an everlasting destruction, according to the power and captivity of Satan, he having subjected them according to his will.

> 18 Then, I say unto you, they shall be as though there had been no redemption made; for they cannot be redeemed according to God's justice; and they cannot die, seeing there is no more corruption.

After spending a number of chapters talking about repentance, we now get these verses with a warning for those who "die in their sins," meaning those who committed sins and were unrepentant. The outcome isn't great. I mean, any time there's mention of "fire and brimstone," "flames," and being "chained down to an everlasting destruction," that's enough reason for me to do whatever it is the prophet is telling us to do.

Questions to Ponder: What - if anything - is something you haven't repented for? Something that you've been hanging on to for a while? What are the consequences? What's the reason you haven't taken care of it yet?

Daily Challenge: Don't stress yourself out or anything, but think if there's anything you haven't repented for from your past, that you could clear up with God or even your bishop if necessary. If not, see if there is someone you can forgive, or reconcile with, or reach out to who might be in need of your friendship.

A Time To Prepare To Meet God

> *Alma 12:24-25 - 24 And we see that death comes upon mankind, yea, the death which has been spoken of by Amulek, which is the temporal death; nevertheless there was a space granted unto man in which he might repent; therefore this life became a probationary state; a time to prepare to meet God; a time to prepare for that endless state which has been spoken of by us, which is after the resurrection of the dead.*

> *25 Now, if it had not been for the plan of redemption, which was laid from the foundation of the world, there could have been no resurrection of the dead; but there was a plan of redemption laid, which shall bring to pass the resurrection of the dead, of which has been spoken.*

So much comfort from these verses. How many of us here on earth struggle with questions like "what am I here for?" "Why do bad things happen to good people?" "Is there a God?" All of these questions center around the core need for certainty and understanding our purpose here, and that's what these verses give us.

This life is a probationary state, a time to prepare to meet God. So this life has a purpose, and there IS a God. There is a heaven, and a plan put in place to redeem us from our fallen state here on earth to be reunited with him and our families after we die.

Just think about those truths. These are HUGE revelations from thousands of years ago, answering some of the biggest questions that people continue to have to this day. I'm sure you could think of dozens of people who would benefit greatly from these revelations. How different would their lives be if they knew these things, if they had a testimony of them, if they had answers to the questions that keep them from being truly happy or fully aware of their purpose here on the earth?

We all have a fundamental need to feel certainty about our lives, and to feel like there is some purpose, some significance. And there is. These verses give that to us.

Questions to Ponder: How do these verses change your perspective about your purpose here on earth? Why are you here? What happens when you die? What effect would this knowledge have on others who don't have these truths in their lives?

Daily Challenge: Think of someone you know who could benefit from the truths of the gospel. Reach out to them, reconnect, and start a conversation about the gospel. If you need a prompt, think about these verses in a non gospel context - "have you ever wondered why we're here? if there's a purpose to all of this?" or "what do you think happens to us when we die?" Ask a question or two, listen to their answer, what it says about their beliefs, and find a way to share your testimony with them if the situation allows for it.

God Did Call On Men

> *Alma 12:33-36 - 33 But God did call on men, in the name of his Son, (this being the plan of redemption which was laid) saying: If ye will repent, and harden not your hearts, then will I have mercy upon you, through mine Only Begotten Son;*

> *34 Therefore, whosoever repenteth, and hardeneth not his heart, he shall have claim on mercy through mine Only Begotten Son, unto a remission of his sins; and these shall enter into my rest.*

> *35 And whosoever will harden his heart and will do iniquity, behold, I swear in my wrath that he shall not enter into my rest. 36 And now, my brethren, behold I say unto you, that if ye will harden your hearts ye shall not enter into the rest of the Lord; therefore your iniquity provoketh him that he sendeth down his wrath upon you as in the first provocation, yea, according to his word in the last provocation as well as the first, to the everlasting destruction of your souls; therefore, according to his word, unto the last death, as well as the first.*

Whoa.

I've always had a hard time imagining God's "wrath" because I don't know that I've ever really experienced it in my life. That said, it doesn't sound pleasant. Again we are given a serious warning to not harden our hearts, but to stay humble and repent.

I also love the little aside - "this being the plan of redemption which was laid" - reminding us that this is all part of a plan. It's not happenstance or coincidence. There is a reason we are here on earth. We have a purpose. There was a perfect plan that required a perfect Savior, and because that Savior provided an atonement for us we are able to repent and return to live with God again. That's not something that just *happens*. If you ever find yourself wondering why you're here, what you're here for, if any of this means anything, just think back to verses like this one. It's too perfect to have happened any other way.

Questions to Ponder: How important is humility? How damning is pride, or the hardening of our hearts? What do these verses teach about the plan of salvation? How does that make you feel?

Daily Challenge: Have a conversation with a friend or loved one about the plan of salvation. You can use these verses as a kick-off point, but just take some time to talk and share with each other how you feel and some things that you know are true, ask questions, and listen. Strengthen each other through that conversation.

Humble Yourselves Before The Lord

> *Alma 13:27-29 - 27 And now, my brethren, I wish from the inmost part of my heart, yea, with great anxiety even unto pain, that ye would hearken unto my words, and cast off your sins, and not procrastinate the day of your repentance;*

> *28 But that ye would humble yourselves before the Lord, and call on his holy name, and watch and pray continually, that ye may not be tempted above that which ye can bear, and thus be led by the Holy Spirit, becoming humble, meek, submissive, patient, full of love and all long-suffering;*

> *29 Having faith on the Lord; having a hope that ye shall receive eternal life; having the love of God always in your hearts, that ye may be lifted up at the last day and enter into his rest.*

Do we want eternal life? To be lifted up at the last day and enter into the Lord's rest?

If we truly do, the only way to show that is through our actions. It starts with a desire, then hearkening unto the words in the scriptures and from the prophets. The rest of the steps are right there, laid out for us, one after another. Humility. Prayer. Obedience. More humility, probably.

The gospel is simple. That doesn't mean that it's easy. It's often very difficult to live the gospel because of the temptations we are faced with, or the circumstances we find ourselves in. A friend just this morning emailed me to tell me about his marriage, how it's crumbling, how he's losing his faith. This is for him and for all of you. We're told to pray, to be led by the Holy Spirit, to be humble and submissive, meaning willing to listen and to act based on what the Lord tells us.

Our perspective is so small compared to His, why wouldn't we listen?

Questions to Ponder: How can you get more humility? What are things you can do on a daily basis to help cultivate that quality in your life?

Daily Challenge: Ponder that first question - do you want eternal life? Do something today to show that you do - pray, repent, read, study, serve.

The Blood Of The Innocent

> Alma 14:11 - ...and he doth suffer that they may do this thing, or that the people may do this thing unto them, according to the hardness of their hearts, that the judgments which he shall exercise upon them in his wrath may be just; and the blood of the innocent shall stand as a witness against them, yea, and cry mightily against them at the last day.

This one has helped me a ton when certain tragedies happen. We've seen some of the worst shootings in the history of our country in just the last two months as I write this, and it's easy to wonder why a loving God would allow things like this to happen.

First, we all have agency, and that includes the agency to hurt another person if that's what we choose to do with our lives. But this verse teaches us that He allows these things to happen so that His judgements which He shall exercise upon them in His wrath may be just. The blood of the innocent, as tragic and sad as it is, will stand as a witness against them at the last day. These cowards that kill other people and then take their own life think they are escaping justice, but boy do they have something coming. I know I wouldn't want to face the Lord's wrath.

It's interesting that much of this is caused by the hardness of their hearts as well. We don't grow up with a desire to hurt others. We have to harden our hearts over time to get to a point where we would inflict harm on another one of God's children. Yet another reason for us to remain humble and teachable, open to the whisperings of the Holy Ghost, obedient, faithful, and prayerful.

Questions to Ponder: Does this verse help at all? Why/Why Not? What perspective does it add to this life? What should you do about it in your own life?

Daily Challenge: The next time something tragic happens, where someone uses their agency to harm another person, remember to go back to this verse, and try that perspective on for size. It won't make the situation change, but it will certainly help the way you see things.

My Arm Is Extended

> *Alma 19:36 - ...and we see that his arm is extended to all people who will repent and believe on his name.*

If this were at the end of all of the verses about repentance, it would be a perfect summation. But it's not at the end. There are many more verses about repentance.

It's still valuable to remember that He's there for us no matter what, all we need to do is have faith and repent. The visual of Christ extending His arm on our behalf brings so much comfort and strength as I set out each day to not only live my life, but to live the gospel as well.

Questions to Ponder: Where are you weak in your faith? How can you strengthen it? What's something you can do on a daily basis to strengthen your faith and your relationship with God?

Daily Challenge: It's been a few days, so, Repent! And find something you can do today to strengthen your faith and your relationship with our Savior.

Repent!

> *Alma 22:6 - —If ye will repent ye shall be saved, and if ye will not repent, ye shall be cast off at the last day*

Salvation isn't something that just happens to us. We have to participate in the plan. It requires faith in our Savior, enough that we go through the process of repenting of our sins and becoming better for it. "If" is the operative word, and it happens over and over again. If we repent we will be saved. If not... well, being cast off doesn't sound pleasant at all.

Questions to Ponder: Why do the prophets spend so much time preaching repentance? Is there anyone exempt from this commandment? Are you repenting enough?

Daily Challenge: Repent! (You saw that one coming, didn't you?)

Receive The Hope Which Thou Desirest

> Alma 22:16 - ...yea, if thou wilt repent of all thy sins, and will bow down before God, and call on his name in faith, believing that ye shall receive, then shalt thou receive the hope which thou desirest.

It's notable how often the concepts of faith/belief and prayer are associated with repentance. They obviously go hand in hand - you can't really have repentance without prayer or faith. This verse also gives us some perspective on why we would want to repent:

To receive the hope which you desire.

It's part of a process we go through to receive something we want. What do we want? To be happy. To be fulfilled. To be loved. To be with people we love. How do we get those things? Repentance, faith, and prayer is a good place to start.

Questions to Ponder: What are the things that you desire? What are you really after? What do your actions suggest that you're after? And do those actions align with the real things you want?

Daily Challenge: If you journal you can do this there, or you can just spend some time pondering, but there's power in taking a really detailed look at our actions compared to our desires. If we say that we want to start a business and leave our job, but never actually make any progress on the business and spend you weekends binging the new season of your favorite tv show, your actions and stated desires aren't in alignment. The same goes for the desires of our hearts. Do we want to live with God and our families for eternity? And do our actions align with and support that desire? Take some time to write down the things you want out of life, and then assess if your actions are revealing those desires, or others.

The Salvation of His People

> *Alma 24:27 - 25 And it came to pass that they threw down their weapons of war, and they would not take them again, for they were stung for the murders which they had committed; and they came down even as their brethren, relying upon the mercies of those whose arms were lifted to slay them.*

> *26 And it came to pass that the people of God were joined that day by more than the number who had been slain; and those who had been slain were righteous people, therefore we have no reason to doubt but what they were saved.*

> *27 And there was not a wicked man slain among them; but there were more than a thousand brought to the knowledge of the truth; thus we see that the Lord worketh in many ways to the salvation of his people.*

I wonder why I don't talk about the gospel more. It seems that outside of writing the Daily Mormon emails and this book, and then teaching my gospel doctrine classes, I don't mention the Savior much, or have gospel or doctrinal based conversations other than with my children. Yet, here is our Savior, working in many ways to the salvation of his people. He dedicated his life for mine, the least I could do is spend more time thinking about and talking about him...

Questions to Ponder: How does it feel to know that the Savior has and is working for your salvation and the salvation of your loved ones? How should that affect your daily life? What should you do with that information?

Daily Challenge: Find someone today, a family member or friend, or even a non-member or a co-worker, and have a gospel conversation. Ask them their favorite part of the gospel, or their feelings about their savior, or what the gospel means in their life.

Their State Becomes Worse

> *Alma 24:30 - And thus we can plainly discern, that after a people have been once enlightened by the Spirit of God, and have had great knowledge of things pertaining to righteousness, and then have fallen away into sin and transgression, they become more hardened, and thus their state becomes worse than though they had never known these things.*

It's a pretty incredible statement, and puts us in a position of great responsibility. I have a number of friends who have fallen away from or left the Church, some that served missions, some that held callings, even a Bishop and his wife from my mission. We've read before how there really isn't anyone who isn't susceptible to the temptations of the devil, whose whole goal is to lead us away and make us as miserable as he is.

Yet, whether they know it or believe it or not, those that leave after having had a testimony of the gospel will have to face the consequences that come with that decision. That doesn't give us an excuse to chastise them or anything, they're dealing with enough already. Rather, it should motivate us that still remain faithful to the gospel to reach out to them with love and empathy to try to bring the light of Christ back into their lives so that they can be touched by the Spirit again. We know the consequences. We need to try and help them return to a place where they can feel that as well.

Questions to Ponder: Do you know anyone who has fallen away from the church or turned their back on the testimony they once held? What should you do about it? How can you help those that have fallen away return to the faith? What are some ways that you can show empathy and charity to them in a way that helps them rather than pushes them further away?

Daily Challenge: Pray for an opportunity to help a friend or loved one. Ask the Lord to provide a way to help or to serve, or to have a conversation with them.

There Is None That Knoweth These Things

> Alma 26:21-22 - 21 And now behold, my brethren, what natural man is there that knoweth these things? I say unto you, there is none that knoweth these things, save it be the penitent.

> 22 Yea, he that repenteth and exerciseth faith, and bringeth forth good works, and prayeth continually without ceasing—unto such it is given to know the mysteries of God; yea, unto such it shall be given to reveal things which never have been revealed; yea, and it shall be given unto such to bring thousands of souls to repentance, even as it has been given unto us to bring these our brethren to repentance.

Enough gloom and doom, lets get to the good stuff.

Anyone else here want to know the mysteries of God? Guess what? There's a formula for that, and it's laid out, right here in the scriptures.

There are such incredible blessings that come into our lives that we can't even imagine if we'll just do the things the Lord asks us to do. Pray, repent, have faith, be obedient, and do good things. Keep it up and you're promised the ability to know the mysteries of God, to reveal things that have never been revealed, and to bring souls unto repentance. I can't think of a more worthwhile pursuit in our lives.

Questions to Ponder: Do you want this more than you want to binge the latest Netflix show? Do you want it more than you want other worldly pursuits? How badly do you want these promised blessings? How can you make changes to your life to show that you actually want them?

Daily Challenge: Find one thing you can do better from this scripture and commit to doing it for at least a week. See how it goes. See how your life changes from trying to come closer to God.

He Is A Merciful Being

> *Alma 26:35 - ...for he has all power, all wisdom, and all understanding; he comprehendeth all things, and he is a merciful Being, even unto salvation, to those who will repent and believe on his name.*

For some reason I love reading about the attributes of our Heavenly Father and Jesus Christ. There's so much comfort in knowing they have all power, all wisdom, and all understanding, comprehending all things.

Growing up my main motivation for making good choices was knowing that my parents loved me and wanted good things for me. That was enough for me to stay obedient, hang around good people, and get through my high school years pretty unscathed. It's the same with our Heavenly Father. We can rely on the knowledge that he loves us, and wants us to return home, and use it to motivate us to stay obedient, repent, and cultivate and grow our faith.

Questions to Ponder: What other attributes do our Heavenly Father and Jesus Christ share? Which ones stand out to you? Which ones do you enjoy the most? Why?

Daily Challenge: If you have a moment, will you shoot me an email, let me know what you think of the book, what you like, what you don't like, etc? I'd love the feedback if you have any. My address is info@dailymormon.email

Thanks for reading!

God Is Mindful Of Every People

> *Alma 26:37 - Now my brethren, we see that God is mindful of every people, whatsoever land they may be in; yea, he numbereth his people, and his bowels of mercy are over all the earth...*

I can't imagine how hard the judgement day would be if God didn't have an intimate knowledge of who we were, the challenges we faced in our lives, and the choices we made. How unfair do we feel it is when a cop pulls us over for a speeding ticket when we KNOW we weren't going THAT much over, and that we had a good reason for it? Imagine that extrapolated out millions of times over millions of decisions. We'd likely come away from whatever judgement we received feeling like we got a bum deal.

No, our Heavenly Father and Jesus Christ know us so intimately that they know us better than we know ourselves. I take comfort in that, and it's one of the foundational beliefs I have that allows me to have faith enough to pray, to repent, to ask for help, and to believe in the gospel. If this statement weren't true, the gospel wouldn't work the way it does.

Questions to Ponder: How do your intimate relationships differ from your other relationships? What are the qualities that differentiate between them? How does knowing that God knows you so well, and has such mercy for you, make you feel?

Daily Challenge: Say a prayer. Have a conversation with your Heavenly Father. Ask him what it is He wants you to know, to do, to understand. Ask Him for the things that you need.

To Him It Is Given According To His Desires

> Alma 29:4-5 - 4 ... for I know that he granted unto men according to their desire, whether it be unto death or unto life; yea, I know that he allotted unto men, yea, decreeth unto them decrees which are unalterable, according to their wills, whether they be unto salvation or unto destruction.

> 5 Yea, and I know that good and evil have come before all men; he that knoweth not good from evil is blameless; but he that knoweth good and evil, to him it is given according to his desires, whether he desireth good or evil, life or death, joy or remorse of conscience.

Ooh. This one stings a little.

It's all on us guys. If you're reading this, you know. You've read the scriptures, studied the gospel, you probably have or have had a testimony of the truthfulness of it at some point. We're in the "he that knoweth" group.

So what does that mean? "It is given according to his desires." So, what do we want? How does that manifest itself?

Our actions reveal our values - the things we desire, the things we care about, the things we want. You can't say you want to inherit the kingdom of heaven and then go out and break the law of chastity all the time. It doesn't work that way. Knowingly committing sin and then repenting of it as a "loophole" isn't actually a loophole, it's just sinning.

Good and evil have come before all men. We all have choices, opposition, and temptation around us at all times. It's how we choose to live our life that reveals our desires, and the Lord has promised that we receive accordingly. Let's all commit, or recommit, to make choices that align with our eternal desires.

Questions to Ponder: How would it feel to have joy of conscience? How do you obtain that? What other blessings come from living according to the gospel and the commitments and covenants you've made with God?

Daily Challenge: Think of one thing you'd like to change or improve. It could be something you give up, or something to start doing. When do you want to start? How long will you commit to it?

❖ ❖ ❖

Counsel In Wisdom

> Alma 29:7 - ...the Lord doth counsel in wisdom, according to that which is just and true.

Ever get bad life advice?

Ever have someone say something incredibly mean to you, embarrass you, shame you?

Someone ever lie about something you did or didn't do or say?

Yeah. Me too.

I was thinking through this verse, and was trying to find something that the Lord wouldn't be able to help me with. I mean, I have a pretty specific situation, right? There wasn't such thing as a "film producer" in Christ's day. He never had to go and find clients to pay the bills, did he?

Despite my best efforts, the whisperings of the Spirit kept nudging me - "Come on Daren, this is fruitless. You can stop now."

He's right. Whether I believe it or not, or more likely, whether I'm humble enough to listen, the Lord is able to counsel us in wisdom, meaning that out of everyone we could possibly turn to - our wives or husbands, our children or parents, our friends, or books specific to the problems we're dealing with - there is no other counsel we could receive that will be as personal, as wise, as just and true, as that which comes from God.

It's such a comforting thought, yet my instinct is to constantly seek out the next best seller on the topic. I think it's because I get answers more quickly that way. I can search my Kindle app and find exactly what I think I'm looking for, whereas with God, it takes so much more effort. Sometimes I don't know how to define what I need. I doubt my worthiness to receive answers. I question my faith in being able to act upon the answers that come. So rather, I default to the "philosophies of men." The times that I have gone to the Lord to ask for help, I've been surprised at how often and quickly and clearly the answers come, that as I sit and type this I wonder why I don't do it more often.

The Lord is there. God loves us, and wants to help us if we'll only go to Him in prayer and seek out His counsel.

DAILY MORMON

Questions to Ponder: What does counsel in wisdom mean to you? How would you describe it to someone else? What is the benefit of having a God who can do so?

Daily Challenge: Take a problem or struggle to God and seek out His counsel. I feel like I have a list of things I could go to Him with after writing this chapter. But know that if you're humble and faithful that the answers will come. You are worthy, and He loves you. I hope you get the answers you seek.

By Thy Lying And By Thy Flattering Words

> *Alma 30:47 - ...it is better that thy soul should be lost than that thou shouldst be the means of bringing many souls down to destruction, by thy lying and by thy flattering words; therefore if thou shalt deny again, behold God shall smite thee, that thou shalt never open thy mouth any more, that thou shalt not deceive this people any more.*

One of my favorite parts of finding all of the verses for this project was how black and white many of them are. In this chapter, Alma is going back and forth with Korihor about the existence of God, among many other things. Korihor asks for a sign, and Alma says he's had "signs enough." Korihor tempts him one more time, at which point Alma says the above words.

Korihor wasn't a believer, someone who had a testimony of God. Rather he was an atheist, leading the people away from the truth. Combine this thought from Alma with an earlier scripture about how much worse it would be for those that had a testimony, and that starts to get pretty serious for us in the Church if we ever choose to leave.

In my last ward, and for the first time ever in my life, the Bishop got up one Sunday to announce that a member of the ward had been excommunicated for apostasy. The silence in the chapel that day was intense. The member had gone inactive before we moved in so I didn't know who he was, but the thought that came to mind was that this could happen to anyone. There's someone down the street from me that was actively leading people away from the gospel and was excommunicated for those actions.

We know where the Lord stands on this matter. "The worth of souls is great," and if we choose to fight against God and his Church, it won't be pretty for us.

Questions to Ponder: What do you do to stay "on the straight and narrow"? How do you deal with someone attacking or questioning your faith? What would you do if a friend or family member left the Church and started speaking out against it?

Daily Challenge: Spend some time thinking about these questions, because it will be better to have thought about it before it happens than in the moment.

The Devil Will Not Support His Children

> *Alma 30:60 - ...the devil will not support his children at the last day, but doth speedily drag them down to hell.*

The Book of Mormon gives us more scriptures about Christ than about any other subject, but it also gives us some keen insight into Satan, his motivations, and warnings that we can heed to avoid being tempted by him. It is important to know the nature of the devil, just as it is important to know the nature and characteristics of our Savior.

Satan isn't interested in your salvation. He's not empathetic, or caring, or loving. He's self-interested through and through. Whatever things he's able to persuade us with in this life, he'll abandon us at the judgement day, leaving us standing there in our sins.

We're taught that every good thing comes from God, and that every bad thing comes from the devil. It's as black and white as it gets. If we want to avoid the temptations of the devil, we need to constantly seek out the good, in every aspect of our lives. When we slip up, we must repent and turn back to the Savior and the gospel.

Satan is constantly trying to drag us down to hell and make us miserable just as he is miserable. Let us not give him the satisfaction.

Questions to Ponder: What else do we know about Satan? What do the scriptures teach? What about the temple?

Daily Challenge: Repent! And take time to audit the things you consume, the choices you make, etc. Find the bad stuff and ruthlessly eliminate it, leaving room for more good to come into your life.

The Same Shall Be Blessed

Alma 32:15-16 - 15 Yea, he that truly humbleth himself, and repenteth of his sins, and endureth to the end, the same shall be blessed—yea, much more blessed than they who are compelled to be humble because of their exceeding poverty.

16 Therefore, blessed are they who humble themselves without being compelled to be humble; or rather, in other words, blessed is he that believeth in the word of God, and is baptized without stubbornness of heart, yea, without being brought to know the word, or even compelled to know, before they will believe.

These verses are so straightforward.

We learn here that humility is a choice, and an important one. We need to choose to be humble, rather than be compelled into humility from circumstances or outside forces. It is a quality that everyone needs to have, regardless of our situation.

Questions to Ponder: What makes humility such an important quality? What other blessings come from choosing to be humble?

Daily Challenge: Take a quick assessment - are you choosing to be humble? Or being compelled into humility because of your circumstance? How can you make it more of a choice in your life?

If Ye Have Faith...

> *Alma 32:21 - —faith is not to have a perfect knowledge of things; therefore if ye have faith ye hope for things which are not seen, which are true.*

I'm sure Alma's discourse on faith in Alma 32 is one of the most read and studied chapters in The Book of Mormon for most of us. I still have this verse memorized from scripture mastery in seminary nearly 20 years ago.

Faith - like repentance, which we've spent so much time on - is one of the fundamental doctrines of the gospel of Jesus Christ. Without faith, nothing else matters, nothing else works, and no blessings can be received. Even repentance requires faith, which is why the principles and doctrines we believe in are compiled into a grouping we call the Articles of Faith.

We learn in this verse what faith is and isn't. It's not to have a perfect knowledge of something - that would be...knowledge.

This is such a great definition of faith given here - that it is a "hope for things which are not seen, which are true." The truthfulness of the gospel is not dependent on our belief in it. It is eternally and unchangeably true regardless of our faith, which is a big part of why faith is so important. It allows us to tap into the saving power of the atonement and the gospel of Jesus Christ.

A recent example of faith in my own life:

I try to attend the temple as often as possible, sometimes as much as once a week. The Provo temple does an early 5:40am session every Tuesday morning and it fits perfect with my schedule so that I'm still home in time to take my oldest son to school.

The act of attending the temple is in itself an act of faith. We take 2+ hours out of our day, turn off the world, and focus on providing vicarious saving ordinances for people we have not met, cannot see, and cannot know if it is received on the other side.

We also attend in hopes that if we have something on our mind, or need special blessings, or would benefit from how thin the veil can be inside the temple, those things can happen there.

I went yesterday with the hopes of getting some guidance from my Heavenly Father as I recently left my position at my company where I had been the CEO for nearly 10 years. I've spent the last month or so pretty lost and frustrated with how slow the process of finding a new job has been.

In the celestial room, I waited and waited for something, anything. As is often the case, the thing that I received was much different than what I had anticipated going in.

I watched as those from my session left the room, to the point where I was the only one left. Then, after a few more minutes, I watched as the next session started coming into the room. I had this incredible feeling of anticipation wash over me. I sat there waiting to see someone I knew. I had this strong desire to see my mom who passed away nearly 6 years ago. I wanted to see my siblings who live a few states away, and my kids, who are currently 6, 4, and 3 years old. I felt a love and a desire that I can only imagine pales in comparison to the desire and love that our Heavenly Father has for us, and it was an incredible feeling. I realized in that moment that while things might be hard at the moment, both emotionally and financially, my problems are small in comparison to the purpose for which we're here on earth - to bring to pass the immortality and eternal life of man.

I realized while I was walking out that I was focusing too much on my own problems, and not thinking about how my next phase in life could be used to help others, to be more spiritual, to do more. I'm so grateful for the lesson, and for the renewed energy to pursue this book and whatever else is to come.

Questions to Ponder: Do you have a favorite faith-related memory? What happens when you replay it in your mind, or tell it to others? How do you grow your faith, or maintain it? What is faith to you? How did you gain your faith in Christ and the gospel?

Daily Challenge: Share a faith-related story from your life with a friend or loved one. Let the spirit into the conversation and see what it testifies and teaches you in the moment.

In The First Place

> *Alma 32:22 - ...God is merciful unto all who believe on his name; therefore he desireth, in the first place, that ye should believe, yea, even on his word.*

I'm a creative professional - I work as a film producer and screenwriter. One of the HARDEST things about being a self employed creative is that you have to be self-motivated, and the HARDEST part about being self-motivated is knowing what to do next.

This verse solves that problem, at least for those of us trying to live the gospel. Where do we start? With belief. With faith.

If you've ever thought about a situation where you've struggled with the Church, or have lost your faith or your testimony and you're working on it, this verse hopefully feels like a huge answer. "God is merciful unto all who believe on his name." He wants you to believe so that He can be merciful.

There are SO many blessings promised to the faithful in the Book of Mormon - I know, I've counted them - and all that's required of us is to believe. To humble ourselves, to have a desire to know, and to believe that if we put in the time to believe and have faith those blessings will come.

I can promise you that they will come. They've come in my life and countless others, and I know that the blessings you're seeking by living with faith will come to you too.

Questions to Ponder: How do you believe? What does that look like? How does it manifest itself in your actions and your thoughts?

Daily Challenge: Find one thing you can do to SHOW your belief in God. Tell a friend. Read the scriptures. Say a prayer. Serve someone in need. Then see how it feels, if it helps your faith grow, if you feel the Spirit.

Desire To Believe

> *Alma 32:27 - But behold, if ye will awake and arouse your faculties, even to an experiment upon my words, and exercise a particle of faith, yea, even if ye can no more than desire to believe, let this desire work in you, even until ye believe in a manner that ye can give place for a portion of my words.*

I like to think that this desire to believe is the humility that the Lord needs us to have in order to be disciples. The blessings of faith only come to those that exercise that faith, the belief that they have, and it requires humility.

I think the two are very intertwined. In my life it seems that my faith doesn't work at all unless I'm humble. I may be going through the motions of praying and studying and seeking answers, but if my other actions show the Lord that I'm only interested in my way of doing things, He can't help me. I've hardened my heart in a way that prevents the blessings of faith to happen.

The desire to believe is the act of humility. We have to show God that we are willing to listen, to act, to submit. That we don't know the answers, we don't know the outcomes, and we don't know the path to get there, but we know that His way is going to be better than the path we choose alone.

Questions to Ponder: What are our faculties in this verse? Why would Alma phrase it as an experiment? What does that mean to you? When in your life have you had a desire to believe? How can you have those experiences more often?

Daily Challenge: Spend some time thinking about something you desire to believe. Where is your testimony lacking, even a little? What principles do you wish you had a stronger testimony or understanding of? Ask the Lord for help as you work with faith to strengthen that testimony and understanding and see what comes of it.

It Shall Take Root

> *Alma 32:41-43 - 41 But if ye will nourish the word, yea, nourish the tree as it beginneth to grow, by your faith with great diligence, and with patience, looking forward to the fruit thereof, it shall take root; and behold it shall be a tree springing up unto everlasting life.*

> *42 And because of your diligence and your faith and your patience with the word in nourishing it, that it may take root in you, behold, by and by ye shall pluck the fruit thereof, which is most precious, which is sweet above all that is sweet, and which is white above all that is white, yea, and pure above all that is pure; and ye shall feast upon this fruit even until ye are filled, that ye hunger not, neither shall ye thirst.*

> *43 Then, my brethren, ye shall reap the rewards of your faith, and your diligence, and patience, and long-suffering, waiting for the tree to bring forth fruit unto you.*

To paraphrase: If you nourish the word, it will take root. Because of your diligence and faith, you can pluck the fruit, and feast until you are filled. You will reap the rewards of your faith.

So many promises in these short verses. It's the coolest thing to have these sort of principles laid out in the scriptures for us. Do this, get this. It's the perfect pitch - you want salvation? Have faith, be diligent and patient, keep working on it, and you'll get there.

There aren't any contingencies in this. If you are faithful - and everything that entails (obedience and repentance, for example) then you're promised these blessings.

Questions to Ponder: What "rewards of your faith" are the most exciting to you? What would your life be like with more of them? What changes do you need to make to have more of these rewards in your life.

Daily Challenge: It's worth taking some time to go back over these verses and "translate" them to modern language. What does nourishing mean for you and your faith? What about feasting on the fruit?

Ye Must Pour Out Your Souls

Alma 34:16-28 - 16 And thus mercy can satisfy the demands of justice, and encircles them in the arms of safety, while he that exercises no faith unto repentance is exposed to the whole law of the demands of justice; therefore only unto him that has faith unto repentance is brought about the great and eternal plan of redemption.

17 Therefore may God grant unto you, my brethren, that ye may begin to exercise your faith unto repentance, that ye begin to call upon his holy name, that he would have mercy upon you;

18 Yea, cry unto him for mercy; for he is mighty to save.

19 Yea, humble yourselves, and continue in prayer unto him.

20 Cry unto him when ye are in your fields, yea, over all your flocks.

21 Cry unto him in your houses, yea, over all your household, both morning, mid-day, and evening.

22 Yea, cry unto him against the power of your enemies.

23 Yea, cry unto him against the devil, who is an enemy to all righteousness.

24 Cry unto him over the crops of your fields, that ye may prosper in them.

25 Cry over the flocks of your fields, that they may increase.

26 But this is not all; ye must pour out your souls in your closets, and your secret places, and in your wilderness.

27 Yea, and when you do not cry unto the Lord, let your hearts be full, drawn out in prayer unto him continually for your welfare, and also for the welfare of those who are around you.

> *28 And now behold, my beloved brethren, I say unto you, do not suppose that this is all; for after ye have done all these things, if ye turn away the needy, and the naked, and visit not the sick and afflicted, and impart of your substance, if ye have, to those who stand in need—I say unto you, if ye do not any of these things, behold, your prayer is vain, and availeth you nothing, and ye are as hypocrites who do deny the faith.*

These verses sound and feel like a prayer on our behalf. There is a ton of pleading and emotion, he really wants us to do the things he's asking. I feel there's so much more weight in these verses than I ever give to faith, repentance, and prayer, which motivates me to work harder at putting more value and focus on these principles in my own life.

Questions to Ponder: Why is it important to exercise faith? To repent? To pray? How important is humility, and what role does it play in your practice of your faith?

Daily Challenge: Take some extra time today, have a heartfelt prayer and converse with your Heavenly Father. Thank Him for all of the things you are grateful for, and not just the broad stuff like the gospel and the atonement of Christ. Take some extra time afterward to sit and think and listen and feel the Spirit and what it has to say to you.

He Dwelleth Not In Unholy Temples

> *Alma 34:36 - ...the Lord hath said he dwelleth not in unholy temples, but in the hearts of the righteous doth he dwell; yea, and he has also said that the righteous shall sit down in his kingdom, to go no more out; but their garments should be made white through the blood of the lamb.*

I'd venture to say that most, if not all of us, have gone through a time in our lives where we struggled with our faith. In those moments it can be hard to find clarity because we've distanced ourselves from God and the Holy Ghost, making it hard to feel the promptings, and hear what they're saying.

Only when we repent and return are we able to fully understand what God has in store for us and receive the comfort the Holy Ghost provides. Through repentance we are made whole again ("their garments should be made white") thanks to the atonement of our Savior. And as we choose obedience over whatever it is we've chosen instead, we're able to feel the Lord's presence in our lives ("he dwelleth not in unholy temples").

It's imperative that if we make a mistake we repent as soon as possible, before it becomes a habit, before it distances us from the testimonies we hold and the faith we have. The Lord needs righteous disciples in order to carry out the work of salvation, and that's us. It's us! It may feel like a huge responsibility at times, but we can take comfort in the facts that a) we signed up for it, b) we'll be blessed for it, and c) the Lord won't give us anything we're not able to handle.

Questions to Ponder: What does the Lord need YOU for? What special talents do you have? What characteristics have you been blessed with? What can you do with the Lord's help if you just ask? What, if anything, do you need to repent of in order to feel those promptings more often?

Daily Challenge: Find something to repent for, and recommit to avoiding that sin or habit or mistake in the future.

Small And Simple Things

> *Alma 36:6-7 - 6 ...behold I say unto you, that by small and simple things are great things brought to pass; and small means in many instances doth confound the wise.*

> *7 And the Lord God doth work by means to bring about his great and eternal purposes; and by very small means the Lord doth confound the wise and bringeth about the salvation of many souls.*

I'm at least 40% creative. I work in film, am a screenwriter, am writing a book, studied music for most of my life, etc. But I also have a weird affinity for spreadsheets...

It can often be super hard to make progress on creative projects, but this principle is how to do it. By small and simple means - do a little bit every single day. 1000 words on your book. A sketch a day to improve your art. One hour of piano practice. Etc. etc. If you spend an hour a day writing 1000 words, in less than 3 months you'll have written an average length non-fiction book. You could write 2 to 3 screenplays a year. Write a song every week. The list goes on.

But the spiritual version of this is even more impactful. Often we study the outliers - the huge actions taken by incredible men and women in church history or in the scriptures - and we can feel...small. How can we ever live up to Alma, or Nephi, or Moroni, or the two young boys that carried people across a freezing river and then died while crossing the plains?

The Lord does not require us to be an outlier. All He asks is that we humble ourselves enough to become a vessel that He can use to further His purposes, and by these small means is how it's done. Saying hi to a neighbor. Choosing to be an example to others at the office. Keeping the commandments and living the principles of the gospel. Sharing your testimony with others.

None of these seem "scripture worthy" - they probably wouldn't make the cut. That's not what's important. There were a number of talks in the October 2017 General Conference where our leaders told us to not be so hard on ourselves or to hold ourselves to too high a standard. It's in part because of this principle - it's not how the Lord works. He works by small means, and He needs each of us in order to do it.

Questions to Ponder: How can you become a vessel for the Lord to use in His work? What small things can you do on a daily basis to live the gospel better? To reach your creative, or financial, or family goals? How can you humble yourself and adopt this perspective of progress?

Daily Challenge: Do something small today - whether for yourself or someone else. Test out this principle, and see how good it feels and how easy it is to do something small. Then do something tomorrow and the next day and the next and see how quickly you see progress.

A Wise Purpose

> *Alma 37:12 - 12 ...they are preserved for a wise purpose, which purpose is known unto God; for he doth counsel in wisdom over all his works, and his paths are straight, and his course is one eternal round.*

There is so much power in the chapters in Alma where he speaks directly to his sons. There's something different about how the gospel comes across when it's from a father to a son, and under these kind of circumstances. This verse comes after a verse about the records, verse 9:

> *Yea, I say unto you, were it not for these things that these records do contain, which are on these plates, Ammon and his brethren could not have convinced so many thousands of the Lamanites of the incorrect tradition of their fathers; yea, these records and their words brought them unto repentance; that is, they brought them to the knowledge of the Lord their God, and to rejoice in Jesus Christ their Redeemer.*

Alma holds the scriptures in such high regard. He has such incredible faith as to why they exist, and such reverence for the fact that they had them in their possession. In the middle of all of this he teaches Helaman, and us, about God - that He counsels in wisdom over all His works, His paths are straight, and His course is one eternal round.

How comforting are those qualities? I know I'd like to have a little more of each in my own character makeup, but to me it's extremely comforting that our Heavenly Father has these attributes. When we go through tough times especially, how great to know that He is eternally the same and that there is a purpose and a plan? While it doesn't mean there's a reason for everything that happens to us, it does mean that we can find meaning in the big moments in our lives, and look back on the experiences we go through and learn and grow from them.

Questions to Ponder: How do you treat the scriptures? With reverence? As if they were preserved for a wise purpose? What could that purpose be in your life? How does it feel to have a Heavenly Father with these eternal attributes?

Daily Challenge: Flip to your favorite chapter or verse in the scriptures and reread it today. Think about why it's important to you, what circumstances you were in when it became an important scripture to you, and what you should do about it today.

How Strict Are The Commandments

> *Alma 37:13 - O remember, remember, my son Helaman, how strict are the commandments of God. And he said, If ye will keep my commandments ye shall prosper in the land—but if ye keep not his commandments ye shall be cut off from his presence.*

I first read this scripture and thought the strictness was referring to God. However, that's not what it's saying. It's not saying that God is strict and gives us commandments to be hard on us. No, rather, the commandments are strict. Commandments are binary - either you keep them or you don't. Did you steal from that person? Did you covet? Did you break the law of chastity?

I think the commandments must be binary and strict this way so that we have the clarity we need, both now and at the judgement day. There can't be any grey area or else we'd be tempted to say, "Well, I was following the letter of the law..." That would cause a ton of problems.

With them being strict, we know with certainty when we messed up and when we need to repent. We know where we can do better, and where we've qualified for the blessings promised for keeping certain commandments.

The commandments, strict as they may be, bring blessings and prosperity. They are the way we work toward eternal salvation.

Questions to Ponder: Which commandments are hard for you to keep or to remember? Why do you think that is? What blessings are promised from keeping those commandments? What can you do about it?

Daily Challenge: Commit to keeping a commandment you struggle with, or repent for something you slipped up on recently. Study the blessings that come from obedience and repentance for inspiration.

God Is Powerful To The Fulfilling Of All His Words

> *Alma 37:15-17 - 15 And now behold, I tell you by the spirit of prophecy, that if ye transgress the commandments of God, behold, these things which are sacred shall be taken away from you by the power of God, and ye shall be delivered up unto Satan, that he may sift you as chaff before the wind.*

> *16 But if ye keep the commandments of God, and do with these things which are sacred according to that which the Lord doth command you, (for you must appeal unto the Lord for all things whatsoever ye must do with them) behold, no power of earth or hell can take them from you, for God is powerful to the fulfilling of all his words.*

> *17 For he will fulfil all his promises which he shall make unto you, for he has fulfilled his promises which he has made unto our fathers.*

There's this contract that we made with God when we chose sides and came down here to earth. We committed to keep the commandments. All blessings are predicated on obedience to a law or commandment, whether we know it or not.

It's comforting to me to know that God is so powerful. There is a plan, there is a reason for everything here on earth, and we have a purpose. All He asks us is that we try to keep the commandments, to be good people, to treat others kindly, and to live by a few rules. If we do that, we get blessed for it. Seems like a pretty great deal, and that's not to mention the fact that we are going to mess up, but that's ok because of the Atonement. Seriously - our Heavenly Father loves us SO MUCH. More than we know.

Questions to Ponder: How/when do you feel God's love the most? What blessings have come into your life from keeping the commandments? What happens if you disregard the scriptures and the teachings of the prophets? What's Satan's promise if you transgress?

Daily Challenge: Ponder the plan of salvation - how perfect it is, how much our Heavenly Father loves us, and the ways He shows us that love through the plan of happiness.

❖ ❖ ❖

When They Are Fully Ripe

> *Alma 37:28 - For behold, there is a curse upon all this land, that destruction shall come upon all those workers of darkness, according to the power of God, when they are fully ripe; therefore I desire that this people might not be destroyed.*

We learn about this in the temple. The land was cursed when Adam and Eve left the garden. The way the plan of salvation is set up is that those that choose wickedness will be destroyed. Destruction is such a harsh, descriptive way to teach us about the perils of wickedness.

The phrase "when they are fully ripe" gives insights as to why the prophets spend so much time teaching us to repent - if we repent then we prevent becoming fully ripe. Repenting when we sin, on a daily basis if necessary, helps keep us righteous and focused on progress in the right direction. When we abandon the atonement, stop repenting, and continue living in sin, we are "ripening" and heading towards the promised consequences.

All the more reason for us to repent, to rededicate ourselves to the service of God. To help our brothers and sisters to repent and remain faithful. To study the word of God so that we know the gospel and the principles we need to live our lives by.

Questions to Ponder: What is a worker of darkness? What does the imagery of "ripening" signify to you? What else can you do besides repenting to prevent being destroyed?

Daily Challenge: Think of a friend, a neighbor, or a family member that's not a member or no longer active. Pray for them. Pray for ways to serve them that helps them feel the love of God in their lives, then commit to helping the Lord in "bringing to pass the immortality and eternal life of man."

All Thy Doings

> *Alma 37:33-37 - 33 Preach unto them repentance, and faith on the Lord Jesus Christ; teach them to humble themselves and to be meek and lowly in heart; teach them to withstand every temptation of the devil, with their faith on the Lord Jesus Christ.*

> *34 Teach them to never be weary of good works, but to be meek and lowly in heart; for such shall find rest to their souls. 3*

> *5 O, remember, my son, and learn wisdom in thy youth; yea, learn in thy youth to keep the commandments of God.*

> *36 Yea, and cry unto God for all thy support; yea, let all thy doings be unto the Lord, and whithersoever thou goest let it be in the Lord; yea, let all thy thoughts be directed unto the Lord; yea, let the affections of thy heart be placed upon the Lord forever.*

> *37 Counsel with the Lord in all thy doings, and he will direct thee for good; yea, when thou liest down at night lie down unto the Lord, that he may watch over you in your sleep; and when thou risest in the morning let thy heart be full of thanks unto God; and if ye do these things, ye shall be lifted up at the last day.*

It's been nearly a year since I had the "moment" that made me reread the Book of Mormon, and later became the inspiration for this book. One thing that I've taken from this year of study and writing is the idea of practical Mormonism - taking the big principles, the eternal perspective of the gospel, and then breaking it down into smaller, daily actions. This chapter, where Alma is speaking to his son Helaman, provides a great place to start. Alma is just laying out the gospel and how to live it on a daily basis.

If all we ever do is read the scriptures and increase our knowledge of the gospel, but it never turns into daily action - repentance, faith, obedience, charity - then we haven't actually learned anything at all.

Questions to Ponder: Why does Alma keep using the phrase "all thy doings"? What is the significance of it? What are the blessings for doing these things? The consequences?

Daily Challenge: Think about the way your faith in God translates to your daily actions. Is there anything you could do differently, or more or less of? Commit to doing that and ask the Lord for guidance.

The Easiness Of The Way

> *Alma 37:46 - O my son, do not let us be slothful because of the easiness of the way; for so was it with our fathers; for so was it prepared for them, that if they would look they might live; even so it is with us. The way is prepared, and if we will look we may live forever.*

I still think of something our new bishop said during his first week conducting the sacrament meeting. He spoke of how the Lord comes to those who are actively working, while Satan seeks out those that are lazy and slothful. It was one of those "aha" moments for me. I need to be active in whatever it is I need help with, rather than waiting around for the Lord to do it for me. It doesn't work that way.

The footnote for "easiness" takes us to Matthew 11:30 - "For my yoke is easy, and my burden is light." When you put it in that context, yeah, the way is pretty easy, because the Lord made it so. He's taught us the gospel, and provided an atonement for us so that we can return to live with Him and God again. That doesn't mean it's a free ride. If we'll just "look" that's a start, and with the right perspective, that humility to look will lead us to faith which leads us to action. Let's choose that path so that we can live forever.

Questions to Ponder: Does the path feel easy right now? Why? Why not? Is there something you can be doing to actively show the Lord that you're working as hard as you can? How does the atonement provide a way for us to live forever?

Daily Challenge: See if there's an area in life where you're looking for help or praying, and if there's a way to be active and faithful. Are there areas in life where you're slothful? An audit every now and then can be helpful. Use it as a way to prune out the stuff that isn't helpful and find more time for the stuff that is.

Inasmuch...

> *Alma 38:1 - ...inasmuch as ye shall keep the commandments of God ye shall prosper in the land; and inasmuch as ye will not keep the commandments of God ye shall be cut off from his presence.*

Simple and straightforward. Sometimes we get lost in the weeds worried about a new policy that's hard to understand, or the spirit of the law vs. the letter of the law, that we forget the simpleness of the gospel. Keep the commandments and prosper, or don't and be cut off. Couldn't be more clear.

When we're in those times where we're struggling with the gospel, it helps to take a step back, get some perspective, and get right with God.

Questions to Ponder: Is there anything you're struggling with right now? Why do you think that is? Is there a way to step back and get some perspective? How about making it simpler, like "keep the commandments"?

Daily Challenge: Spend some time pondering the questions today, and be really honest. If you can't think of anything, think of someone you might be able to help who's currently struggling, and what you can do to serve them or help them.

As Much As Ye Shall Put Your Trust In God

> *Alma 38:5 - ...as much as ye shall put your trust in God even so much ye shall be delivered out of your trials, and your troubles, and your afflictions, and ye shall be lifted up at the last day.*

Anyone else going through a trial right now? No? Just me?

As I write this at the end of 2017, I have recently left my position as CEO of a video production company, and have "struck out on my own"...except that there isn't any work. I've applied for probably 30 jobs in the last month, and every single company is in a hiring freeze until January. Just a week ago I got an email from LinkedIn about a blog post on why December is the worst time to be looking for jobs...

Go figure.

To say it's been tough would be an understatement, but you know what? I have faith that it's all going to work out. I have a lot going on, found some work to tide me over until the new year, and I can feel that lifting and supporting and comforting companionship of the Holy Ghost getting me through all of it.

I don't think this verse applies only to the end of our lives and the "last day." I think it can be applied to every single trial, trouble, and affliction we go through here on earth. However much we put our trust in God is how much we reap the blessings of that faith.

Questions to Ponder: How do you show your trust in God? What actions does that translate to? What trials have you gone through in the past where God helped you through them?

Daily Challenge: Pray for help, or pray with gratitude. We're all on different parts of the path - some of us need help, some of us are in a position to do the helping. Ask God what you can do next.

There Is No Other Way Nor Means

> *Alma 38:9 - ...there is no other way nor means whereby man can be saved, only in and through Christ. Behold, he is the life and the light of the world. Behold, he is the word of truth and righteousness.*

This is a great reminder, no matter where we are on the path. It helps to reframe our desires and the direction we're headed, because there is only one way we can be saved, which is through Christ. If we're too focused on worldly things or worldly pursuits, we may be losing focus of what really matters and which way we should go.

If things feel dark and confusing, Christ is the light of the world. If we're unsure of the direction we should go, or what's true in our lives, we can look to Him as the word of truth. It's worth constantly checking in with God to make sure we're on the path and heading in the right direction, and to make sure we're focusing on Christ for our salvation.

Questions to Ponder: Where is your focus? How much time do you spend studying, reading, praying, pondering, serving, etc., compared to other activities? What, if anything, feels like it's lacking in your life? Where should you turn?

Daily Challenge: Spend some time pondering or meditating and checking in. Where is your focus? What do you need? What can you do and where can you turn?

This Is A Sin Which Is Unpardonable

> Alma 39:6 - For behold, if ye deny the Holy Ghost when it once has had place in you, and ye know that ye deny it, behold, this is a sin which is unpardonable; yea, and whosoever murdereth against the light and knowledge of God, it is not easy for him to obtain forgiveness; yea I say unto you, my son, that it is not easy for him to obtain a forgiveness.

Yikes.

I remember this verse, but never really paid attention to (or don't remember) the "murdereth" part. That's intense.

As important as it is for us to become friends with the Holy Ghost, to recognize his voice, understand how he speaks to us, and heed those promptings, it's equally important that we don't deny that knowledge if ever put in that situation. There aren't many unpardonable sins, so we know how serious it is from this phrase alone. But describing it as "murder[ing] against the light and knowledge of God" should really put it into perspective for us. Don't do it. Ever.

Questions to Ponder: Why would Alma be telling this to his son Corianton? Why use such vivid language? How should this effect our perspective of the importance of the Holy Ghost in our lives?

Daily Challenge: Spend some time getting to know the Holy Ghost better. Talk to God, listen for the Holy Ghost. Understand how he speaks to you and what he's trying to say now.

Ye Cannot Hide Your Crimes

> *Alma 39:8 - But behold, ye cannot hide your crimes from God; and except ye repent they will stand as a testimony against you at the last day.*

I just, tonight, watched the movie *The Circle* that came out in 2017, and they posed the question: are we better people when we know people are watching? The main character stood before a crowd of people and declared that when she thought no one was watching, she was a worse version of herself, at which point she committed to live stream every waking minute of her life for the foreseeable future.

Now, despite the movie being not great, the theory, I think, is sound. When we know that God is watching us at all times, it can be a check against some of our more "natural man" desires and actions. I don't think that being motivated by fear of being caught is the best way to go throughout life, but it may help us in a moment of weakness.

We also have the ability to repent, to change, and to grow and become better. The principles that are taught in The Book of Mormon are so essential to being happy and progressing in this life, and I'm extremely grateful for the truths contained in this book of scripture.

Questions to Ponder: What motivates you to keep the commandments and live the gospel? What prevents you from choosing otherwise? How has this knowledge that God knows all of our actions (and our crimes) helped you in your life?

Daily Challenge: Repent!

You Cannot Carry Them With You

> *Alma 39:14 - Seek not after riches nor the vain things of this world; for behold, you cannot carry them with you.*

This is a nice reminder. In the most recent Gospel Doctrine class that I taught, the conversation led to a comment about perspective, and how with so many things, if we just back up from whatever it is, and try to have a more eternal perspective, it makes that thing easier to deal with or to comprehend.

The riches and vain things of the world may seem like worthwhile pursuits in the moment. We can justify just about anything if we try hard enough. But the harder route is to take a step back and, like Alma teaches here, have a different perspective. The vain things of this world - financial pursuits for the sake of getting richer, chasing after status or fame - you cannot carry them with you. So why do they matter? Because the "natural man" part of our brain thinks they do. Because Satan uses those persuasions to tempt us and lead us astray, to shift our focus from the eternal to the mundane.

You cannot carry them with you. A great reminder that perspective matters. Perspective can save us.

Questions to Ponder: Where else in your life can you apply an eternal perspective? Does it mean that rich people are vain? Or worldly? How can you practice having an eternal perspective in all things?

Daily Challenge: Take something in your life, try to take a step back, and have a different perspective. See how it changes the situation.

They Are Consigned To Partake Of The Fruits Of Their Labors

> Alma 40:26 - But behold, an awful death cometh upon the wicked; for they die as to things pertaining to things of righteousness; for they are unclean, and no unclean thing can inherit the kingdom of God; but they are cast out, and consigned to partake of the fruits of their labors or their works, which have been evil; and they drink the dregs of a bitter cup.

Do the things we do here on earth matter? Are there eternal consequences, good or bad?

In Elder's Quorum recently we went deep on the topic of faith. Someone said that faith was like reading a 1000 page book, one page a day. You know at some point you'll finish the book, but in the first few days and weeks it may seem like an eternity away. (2.8 years, to be specific.)

Once you reach the end though, you'll have read a book. Not only that, you'll be able to partake of the fruits of your labors and take the lessons you learned and the insights you gained and apply it to every aspect of your life! That's the blessing of faith and obedience to the gospel.

The opposite, however, is also true. If we are wicked, we're consigned just the same - permanently committed to that outcome. Choosing wickedness for our whole lives would mean that the consequences would be eternal.

So, let's choose righteousness, yeah? With me? Good.

Questions to Ponder: How does this verse make you feel when you read it? How do you think Alma felt when he was speaking these things? How can we use it to motivate us to be righteous?

Daily Challenge: Repent! Why risk letting anything get in the way of progress and the blessings that come from faith?

The Desires Of Their Hearts Were Good

> *Alma 41:3-6 - 3 And it is requisite with the justice of God that men should be judged according to their works; and if their works were good in this life, and the desires of their hearts were good, that they should also, at the last day, be restored unto that which is good.*

> *4 And if their works are evil they shall be restored unto them for evil. Therefore, all things shall be restored to their proper order, every thing to its natural frame—mortality raised to immortality, corruption to incorruption—raised to endless happiness to inherit the kingdom of God, or to endless misery to inherit the kingdom of the devil, the one on one hand, the other on the other—*

> *5 The one raised to happiness according to his desires of happiness, or good according to his desires of good; and the other to evil according to his desires of evil; for as he has desired to do evil all the day long even so shall he have his reward of evil when the night cometh.*

> *6 And so it is on the other hand. If he hath repented of his sins, and desired righteousness until the end of his days, even so he shall be rewarded unto righteousness.*

"If the desires of your hearts are good." As much as we try, we sometimes fail, and it's easy to get discouraged. But here we're taught that if we just desire, if we try, if our heart is in the right place, we'll be okay.

Questions to Ponder: Do you find yourself being too hard on yourself when it comes to the gospel? Why is that? What can you do to change the perspective and realize the truth in these verses?

Daily Challenge: Find something in your life where you've set too-high expectations for yourself, and add some perspective. Realize you're doing a great job, that your heart is in the right place, and that it's ok to not be perfect.

The Decrees Of God Are Unalterable

> *Alma 41:8 - Now, the decrees of God are unalterable; therefore, the way is prepared that whosoever will may walk therein and be saved.*

There's a video circulating my facebook feed lately that feels timely with this chapter. It condemns the Church for a policy change, and, in essence, blames the Church's policies for the increased rate of teen suicide in Utah, specifically among LGBTQIA+ teens.

Now, there's probably some correlation, but I don't think that correlation always means causation.

Here's the thing. We need to separate Church doctrine from Church culture, sure, but we also need to remember this truth from this verse in Alma. The decrees of God are unalterable. It can't be any more clear than that. The gospel is the gospel. The doctrine is the doctrine. No video, no blog post, no protest is going to change that fact.

Rather, the way is prepared for those that will follow that doctrine, keep the commandments, and humble themselves before God, especially when it comes to the things that are hard. This is a hard topic. We've had other hard topics in the past. We must follow the decrees of God. It's the only way we can be saved.

Questions to Ponder: What should you do in situations like this? How can you focus on showing love to those that have chosen to not follow the decrees of God? How can you focus on serving and being charitable rather than judgmental?

Daily Challenge: Reach out to someone who is a non-member, less active, or no longer associated with the Church, and find a way to serve and show your love for them. When some have felt left out or unwelcome in the Church, it's the perfect time to reach out and make sure they know they're not alone.

Wickedness Never Was Happiness

> *Alma 41:10 - Do not suppose, because it has been spoken concerning restoration, that ye shall be restored from sin to happiness. Behold, I say unto you, wickedness never was happiness.*

There's a big principle that Alma is trying to get at in this chapter as he speaks to his son Corianton. As it says in chapter 39, it was Corianton's sin and wickedness that prevented an entire group of people, the Zoramites, from receiving the gospel.

I'd like to say that there's a difference between small sins that are quickly repented for and "living in sin," but I think the effects can be similar enough that we should worry about the little sins just as much. If we wait until we're "wicked," we're probably not going to be as quick to heed the call of repentance. That's why we have to be so vigilant with repentance for every little thing, so we never head too far down that track.

I don't think we're wicked people. The Book of Mormon teaches us that we are good because we come from God and are made in his image, and only good things can come from God. Yet, we also have the tendencies of the "natural man," and the temptations of the devil coming at us each and every day, and we are susceptible to those temptations, like it or not. So, we have to keep the commandments and try our hardest, because we don't know the effects of the sins we commit. Sometimes a lie doesn't just affect us, but those we're lying to, and the consequences could be incredibly far reaching. I'm sure Corianton didn't expect to prevent an entire people from hearing the gospel, but that's one of the results of sin. It blinds us to the truth.

What's more is that wickedness is not happiness, never was, and never can be. If we're here to have joy - another principle The Book of Mormon teaches - then we need to do our best to remain clean of sin, faithful to the teachings of the gospel, and steadfast in our commitments and covenants to the Lord.

Questions to Ponder: If there is no happiness in sin, why do you make those (sinful) choices? Why is it so hard to withstand the temptations of the world? How do you overcome it? Why should you want to?

Daily Challenge: Ponder these questions today. See if there's some perspective you can add to them that will help you in your desire to be righteous and keep the commandments.

That Which Ye Do Send Out Shall Return Unto You Again

> Alma 41:14-15 - 14 Therefore, my son, see that you are merciful unto your brethren; deal justly, judge righteously, and do good continually; and if ye do all these things then shall ye receive your reward; yea, ye shall have mercy restored unto you again; ye shall have justice restored unto you again; ye shall have a righteous judgment restored unto you again; and ye shall have good rewarded unto you again.

> 15 For that which ye do send out shall return unto you again, and be restored; therefore, the word restoration more fully condemneth the sinner, and justifieth him not at all.

These are Alma's words to his son who had sinned beyond what we would ever want for a child or friend. As stern as Alma was to Corianton, he also has such wise advice. I love to think of it in the context of the rebuke though. Just as we're taught in D&C 121, Alma is sharply reproving his son in this chapter, but then showing forth an increase of love and teaching him the gospel in the process. There is a way back if we have sinned, and we can have all of these incredible blessings back in our life through living the gospel.

Whether we use the principle in this verse for a loved one or for ourselves, it's such a valuable lesson. Deal justly. Judge righteously. Do good continually. What you send out shall return unto you again.

Questions to Ponder: How can you do better at heeding these words of Alma? Do you believe the principles taught, especially in verse 15? Do you live according to that belief?

Daily Challenge: Go do something great to day. Be kind to someone. Go out of your way to help someone. Put the principle to the test and see if it "returns unto you again."

God Himself Atoneth

> *Alma 42:15-16 - 15 ...God himself atoneth for the sins of the world, to bring about the plan of mercy, to appease the demands of justice, that God might be a perfect, just God, and a merciful God also.*

> *16 Now, repentance could not come unto men except there were a punishment, which also was eternal as the life of the soul should be, affixed opposite to the plan of happiness, which was as eternal also as the life of the soul.*

The gospel is centered on Jesus Christ and His atonement. None of the other stuff - repentance, obedience, faith, baptism, ordinances, temples, etc. - matters at all without an atonement for us by a Savior. It's also important that these principles, as well as the atonement, are eternal, unchanging, true forever and ever. Without them, we cannot be saved.

Alma is talking to Corianton about how to resolve in his mind the reason a sinner should be judged and sent to live in his misery for eternity. Alma is helping him through that, but gets back to the atonement. It's the focal point, the big picture, the most important aspect of the entire plan of salvation and happiness.

Because there was an atonement, we can repent and prevent that awful consequence of living in our sin for eternity. I hate feeling guilty for a day if I messed up. I would HATE that feeling for eternity. Thanks to our Savior and the atonement, we don't have to worry. We can repent, we can rely on Him for our salvation, and live with Him and God and our families for eternity.

Questions to Ponder: What feelings do you have about our Savior's atonement? About repentance and forgiveness? How has it affected your life?

Daily Challenge: Ponder these questions, think about the big picture, how perfect the plan of happiness is, and how it has brought happiness into your life.

If There Was No Law Given...

> *Alma 42:20 - And also, if there was no law given against sin men would not be afraid to sin.*

It's important to read this in the same context as the last few chapters, as Alma is still talking to his wayward son Corianton and giving him a bit of a rebuke. But the principle is still there for all of us reading these words hundreds (thousands) of years later. There's a purpose for laws and commandments. There is a reason for everything. It's all part of our Heavenly Father's plan of salvation for us.

Just as we're taught that there had to be opposition in all things, there is a law and there is breaking a law. It's also an interesting insight into our nature. Would it even be considered a sin if there was no law?

Questions to Ponder: What do you think about this verse? What does it teach about human nature? About sin? About the laws and commandments we've been given?

Daily Challenge: Commit to being better - more diligent in keeping the commandments, more obedient to the laws of God.

But There Is A Law Given

> *Alma 42:22-24 - 22 But there is a law given, and a punishment affixed, and a repentance granted; which repentance, mercy claimeth; otherwise, justice claimeth the creature and executeth the law, and the law inflicteth the punishment; if not so, the works of justice would be destroyed, and God would cease to be God.*

> *23 But God ceaseth not to be God, and mercy claimeth the penitent, and mercy cometh because of the atonement; and the atonement bringeth to pass the resurrection of the dead; and the resurrection of the dead bringeth back men into the presence of God; and thus they are restored into his presence, to be judged according to their works, according to the law and justice.*

> *24 For behold, justice exerciseth all his demands, and also mercy claimeth all which is her own; and thus, none but the truly penitent are saved.*

This is a great follow up to the last chapter's verse: 'if there were no law given against sin men would not be afraid to sin." This whole chapter is so great at laying out the foundations of the gospel and the plan of happiness. Alma really got it.

I feel like each of us needs to go through our own version of what Alma went through in order to really understand the need for, and gain gratitude for, the atonement of our Savior. The entire plan truly rests upon that act. Without it there would be no mercy, and we would all find ourselves subject to the demands of justice. None of us would be able to escape it because none of us are perfect. Yet it's easy to downplay a little sin here and there, which is why I wonder if God gives us certain trials and hardships to try and humble us to the point where we have an Alma-like reverence and gratitude for the atonement.

That perspective certainly makes some of our trials easier to get through. It doesn't make it any easier in the moment, but any time we can look at our lives the way Alma is trying to help his son look at his, we'll be strengthened and comforted as we go through life.

Questions to Ponder: What comes to mind when you think of the topics of justice, executing the law, inflicting of punishment, and exercising of demands? What about the atonement being claimed by mercy, and being restored to the presence of God?

Daily Challenge: Take some time to imagine this conversation between Alma and Corianton. Try to put yourself in the same emotional place as Alma trying to teach and convince his wayward son of the truthfulness of the gospel and the perfection of the plan, and the enormity of the Atonement.

Ye Shall Not Suffer Yourselves

> *Alma 43:46 - ...Inasmuch as ye are not guilty of the first offense, neither the second, ye shall not suffer yourselves to be slain by the hands of your enemies.*

This statement applies to us as much as our enemies. We can be so hard on ourselves sometimes for not living up to these insane expectations we have of ourselves - being great parents, providing for our families, fulfilling our calling, studying the scriptures every day, etc. etc. etc. The list is endless sometimes.

But what is the principle? We don't have to be perfect. We're allowed to make mistakes.

Also, we don't have to live up to the crazy standards of others. "Keeping Up With The Joneses" is a real phenomenon, and it's brutal! I've experienced it first hand with members of my family where they constantly talk about their neighbors and what they might think about this or that. It's completely unfair to them that they hold themselves to a standard no one else is even holding them to.

You shall not suffer yourselves. That's the principle. If you're living right, doing what the Lord asks, and trying your best, then realize that you're doing enough, and stop the suffering.

Questions to Ponder: Do you have stress from "suffering from the hands of" yourself/your friends/your enemies? Where is it coming from? Why? What can you do about it?

Daily Challenge: Let it go! Find some stress in your life and just let it go. You'll quickly realize it was unnecessary and you'll feel so much better for it!

This Is The True Faith Of God

> Alma 44:4 - Now ye see that this is the true faith of God; yea, ye see that God will support, and keep, and preserve us, so long as we are faithful unto him, and our faith, and our religion; and never will the Lord suffer that we should be destroyed except we should fall into transgression and deny our faith.

As with every principle in this book, it doesn't matter if it's true, if it's written in scripture or spoken by prophets, IF we don't do anything about it. It's like it never existed in the first place if we don't apply the teachings and the principles that the scriptures and the prophets teach.

Faith is an action word. More than simply believing, faith is the step that we take between hoping something is true and knowing something is true - the reward for our faith. It's like taking a step into a dark room, reaching around for the light switch, and hoping - having faith - that the actions will lead to the room being filled with light.

God has promised to support and keep and preserve us so long as we are faithful. His end of the promise will be kept. The question is, will we do the same?

Questions to Ponder: Where else in the scriptures does it mention the "true faith"? How is it different from faith? What are the consequences for denying or abandoning your faith? What are your reasons for being faithful?

Daily Challenge: Take some time to do a scripture chase on "True Faith" and see where it leads.

Like Unto Moroni

> *Alma 48:17 - Yea, verily, verily I say unto you, if all men had been, and were, and ever would be, like unto Moroni, behold, the very powers of hell would have been shaken forever; yea, the devil would never have power over the hearts of the children of men.*

This may be the first verse I've included that points to a specific person besides the Savior. They easily could have written "be strong and humble and awesome" and not included Moroni, but I don't think it would have had the same effect.

I think it is important for us to have role models. Obviously the Savior provides us the perfect example, but by giving us other people to look to and follow, it gives us a better chance. It makes the gospel twice as accessible. We can take the things we love about each of them and focus on those qualities in our own lives.

One way we could motivate ourselves to be righteous and awesome is to think of someone one day writing or saying this about us: if all men had been, and were and ever would be, like unto [your name], the very powers of hell would have been shaken forever...

Questions to Ponder: What are the qualities of Moroni that you love the most? What attributes are worth emulating? What can you do to be more like him? More like our Savior?

Daily Challenge: Read the chapters about Moroni in Alma to remember who he is, the choices he made, and why we would want to emulate them.

Inasmuch...

> Alma 50:19-20 - 19 And thus we see how merciful and just are all the dealings of the Lord, to the fulfilling of all his words unto the children of men; yea, we can behold that his words are verified, even at this time, which he spake unto Lehi, saying:

> 20 Blessed art thou and thy children; and they shall be blessed, inasmuch as they shall keep my commandments they shall prosper in the land. But remember, inasmuch as they will not keep my commandments they shall be cut off from the presence of the Lord.

Two things. First, I'm grateful that we have a merciful and just God, rather than just one or the other. The balance makes sense, and it feels just perfect. It's an essential part of the plan, to have both justice and mercy.

Second: inasmuch. It's conditional, as with almost all blessings from God. He wants to bless us as much as possible, but there are conditions. Inasmuch as they (we) keep the commandments. Over and over again in the scriptures we read these essential words. This isn't a gospel of being "saved" once and then being good from then on out regardless of our choices and actions. No. We believe in agency, in choice and accountability, in there being consequences and blessings that stem from the decisions we make. The decision to turn our lives over to God in faith, repentance, and baptism is just the start. "Inasmuch" is closely related to "endure to the end." Each and every day our choices matter, and the blessings that come from our obedience and righteousness are proof that they do.

Questions to Ponder: What other attributes of God do you love? How does it make you feel to know that He is a just and merciful God? How would things be different if He were just one or the other? How important are agency and consequences in the plan of salvation?

Daily Challenge: Pray. Talk with your Heavenly Father on a deep level. Try to express gratitude for the plan, for the Savior, for agency, for anything else that comes to mind. See how it affects your day to have that time with Him.

Whosoever Did Not Doubt

> *Alma 57:26 - ...And we do justly ascribe it to the miraculous power of God, because of their exceeding faith in that which they had been taught to believe—that there was a just God, and whosoever did not doubt, that they should be preserved by his marvelous power.*

My guess is that each and every one of us has had moments of doubt in our lives, whether in ourselves, or in what we believe, or even in God. I went through a divorce in my mid-twenties that rocked me pretty hard. I didn't know what to do or what I believed because everything I knew up to that point had basically failed me.

Moments of doubt are just that. Moments. They're opportunities to make decisions and choices, and it's how we come out of those moments that ends up defining us and our faith. Those that come out of those moments are the ones that are "preserved by his marvelous power," and I can absolutely say that that is what happened to me. I feel it to this day, that I'm being "preserved," or looked after, or taken care of. It motivates me every day to continue in my faith and to strengthen my relationship with my Heavenly Father. His power is miraculous, and we can feel that in our own lives as long as we take those moments of doubt and turn them into moments of faith.

Questions to Ponder: Have you had similar moments of doubt? What did they feel like? How did you react? What did you do? What resulted from those actions? How can that strengthen your faith for those potential future moments of doubt?

Daily Challenge: Find a way today to strengthen your relationship with Heavenly Father.

Resist With Our Words

> *Alma 61:14 - Therefore, my beloved brother, Moroni, let us resist evil, and whatsoever evil we cannot resist with our words, yea, such as rebellions and dissensions, let us resist them with our swords, that we may retain our freedom, that we may rejoice in the great privilege of our church, and in the cause of our Redeemer and our God.*

This one might be pushing the boundaries of a "statement" verse, but there certainly is a principle in there: that as we resist evil - whether it be with our words or other actions - we'll receive the blessings promised by the gospel.

Who knows what the future will bring and what "evils" will come at us, as a church, in our homes, or in our personal lives. Just this last year alone some things have occurred that shocked me in disbelief. The promise is that as we resist those evils that we'll be blessed, and we'll know we'll be on the right side when it comes to God's judgement.

Questions to Ponder: What evils are you confronted with on a daily basis? How do you resist them? How do you fight them? What is your responsibility in those moments?

Daily Challenge: Resolve to resist the evils that will come into your life, and stay true to the gospel of Jesus Christ.

HELAMAN

The Lord Is Merciful

> Helaman 3:27-30 - 27 Thus we may see that the Lord is merciful unto all who will, in the sincerity of their hearts, call upon his holy name.

> 28 Yea, thus we see that the gate of heaven is open unto all, even to those who will believe on the name of Jesus Christ, who is the Son of God.

> 29 Yea, we see that whosoever will may lay hold upon the word of God, which is quick and powerful, which shall divide asunder all the cunning and the snares and the wiles of the devil, and lead the man of Christ in a strait and narrow course across that everlasting gulf of misery which is prepared to engulf the wicked—

> 30 And land their souls, yea, their immortal souls, at the right hand of God in the kingdom of heaven, to sit down with Abraham, and Isaac, and with Jacob, and with all our holy fathers, to go no more out.

The book of Helaman is a fairly dramatic change in tone and pace from the war chapters in Alma, and there is such great doctrine in these pages. Since these verses were written/presented as a single thought, it felt right to keep them together.

It's always emotional when I think about how easy the gospel is, how much our Heavenly Father loves us and wants to bless us. And all He asks for is a little faith, talking with him in prayer, keeping the commandments, and living the gospel. None of it is physically hard. It may be emotionally hard at times, or our pride might get in the way, but the gospel isn't difficult to live. And the gate of heaven is open to us for doing so little when you put it in perspective. That's what a loving father would do, and that's what He's done for us.

Questions to Ponder: How often do you talk with your Heavenly Father in prayer? How are the conversations? How well do you know His voice?

Daily Challenge: Set aside time to have a nice long prayer, a conversation with God about everything in your life, and take time to listen for the Spirit.

They Were Lifted Up In Pride

> *Helaman 3:34-36 - 34 And they were lifted up in pride, even to the persecution of many of their brethren. Now this was a great evil, which did cause the more humble part of the people to suffer great persecutions, and to wade through much affliction.*

> *35 Nevertheless they did fast and pray oft, and did wax stronger and stronger in their humility, and firmer and firmer in the faith of Christ, unto the filling their souls with joy and consolation, yea, even to the purifying and the sanctification of their hearts, which sanctification cometh because of their yielding their hearts unto God.*

> *36 And it came to pass that the fifty and second year ended in peace also, save it were the exceedingly great pride which had gotten into the hearts of the people; and it was because of their exceedingly great riches and their prosperity in the land; and it did grow upon them from day to day.*

I remember teaching the lesson about the pride cycle in Gospel Doctrine back in 2016. It was one of my favorite lessons to prepare and study for. As I've been writing about pride over the last few days, it's been enlightening to revisit.

I was really intrigued by two things in particular, both mentioned in these verses. First, that pride often comes after prosperity which comes from our living the gospel and receiving blessings from God. I think it's because as we get richer and more prosperous we start to think that we were somehow responsible, when in reality we know that all good things come from God. That slight distortion of our perspective leads to pride, which is why it's so important to stay vigilant in repenting often and remaining obedient to God's commandments.

Second, why is it that pride leads people to persecution of others? Is it to justify what we have? Is it a defense mechanism? A lashing out that stems from some weird form of guilt? I'm genuinely curious, because it is unclear to me how people go from pride to persecution. Other verses in The Book of Mormon talk about pride leading to all sorts of wickedness, from lying to priestcrafts and secret combinations to murder. Murder! All in order to protect their riches and their status, to maintain their prideful state. It's so weird to me that it happens that way.

Obviously it doesn't happen overnight, but it is surprising how quickly a group of prosperous people can turn to pride and then wickedness and then get destroyed or go through some form of suffering, which then leads them to humility and repentance and back to the start of the cycle again.

We'll talk a lot about pride over the next few chapters of Helaman verses.

Questions to Ponder: What is pride? How does it manifest itself? How does it show up in your own life? What can you do to prevent entering the pride cycle?

Daily Challenge: Repent! And ponder on how important it is to be humble, and what you're grateful for.

It Was Because...

> *Helaman 4:11-13 - 11 Now this great loss of the Nephites, and the great slaughter which was among them, would not have happened had it not been for their wickedness and their abomination which was among them; yea, and it was among those also who professed to belong to the church of God.*

> *12 And it was because of the pride of their hearts, because of their exceeding riches, yea, it was because of their oppression to the poor, withholding their food from the hungry, withholding their clothing from the naked, and smiting their humble brethren upon the cheek, making a mock of that which was sacred, denying the spirit of prophecy and of revelation, murdering, plundering, lying, stealing, committing adultery, rising up in great contentions, and deserting away into the land of Nephi, among the Lamanites—*

> *13 And because of this their great wickedness, and their boastings in their own strength, they were left in their own strength; therefore they did not prosper, but were afflicted and smitten, and driven before the Lamanites, until they had lost possession of almost all their lands.*

It's almost a self-fulfilling prophecy. Because of the pride of their hearts, and their boasting in their own strength, they were left in their own strength.

What strikes me about this section is that it was among those who professed to belong to the church. Going to church and calling ourselves members isn't enough. Going through the motions, being "seen as" a good, faithful, obedient disciple isn't enough. We actually have to do the things that bring the spirit into our lives and the things that bring the promised blessings of the gospel.

It's not something we can fake. God knows us. He knows our hearts and He sees the actions we take - how we treat others, how we see things, how we feel - and He responds accordingly. If we're taking all of the credit for the good things in our lives (pride) then He leaves us to our own strength, essentially to show us how wrong we are, in the hope that we have to - sometimes painfully - confront the reality that we truly do need him.

We also get the word *because* repeated in these verses. It's rare that the scriptures give such a specific reason for the consequences that came to a person or group of people. Yet here it's laid out very clearly, and I think it's for us, the readers who are coming to these pages thousands of years later. We need to know that the members of the church grew prideful and wicked, and it was because of their pride, their riches, the way they treated the poor, the hungry, the naked.

See any of that in the world today?

Questions to Ponder: How could the destruction among the Nephites have been avoided? What can you do in your own lives to prevent pride from entering your heart?

Daily Challenge: Serve someone. Find someone in a humble circumstance and do something to lift their spirit, to bring some light into their lives.

Inasmuch As They Did Repent

> *Helaman 4:15 - ...inasmuch as they did repent they did begin to prosper.*

I always feel like these verses pop up on days that I need them most. This is as simple and clear a reason for repentance as I've ever read.

As they repented, they began to prosper.

Repentance is the way out of the pride cycle. Once we're caught up in our own strength, forgetting God and abandoning our commitments to live the gospel, the way back is through repentance. The great part is we can do it at the slightest mistake or misstep. We can use repentance as a preventative measure to keep us from ever entering the pride cycle in the first place.

If things aren't going the way you think they "should," maybe repentance is the next thing to try. Sincere, honest repentance. A long conversation with God about what to do next. The principle is right there in front of you.

Questions to Ponder: Why does repentance lead to prosperity? How have you experienced that in your life in the past? Do you believe this principle is true?

Daily Challenge: Repent!

Who Shall Come

> *Helaman 5:9 - ...there is no other way nor means whereby a man can be saved, only through the atoning blood of Jesus Christ, who shall come; yea, remember that he cometh to redeem the world.*

I'm so grateful for the knowledge I have of the atonement, for these scriptures that preach to us about the importance of that act, and what it means in our lives. I'm grateful for my Savior and what He did for me and for all of us.

Then the part of this verse "who shall come." It's such a definitive statement. This isn't faith, this is knowledge. This is someone preaching truth. The atonement provides such incredible, eternal gifts to us. I cannot wait until that time when I get to see my Savior again and hug Him and thank Him for what He did for us. For providing a way for us to live with our families again.

Questions to Ponder: How do you feel when you read this verse? How does it affect your faith? How important is the atonement to you?

Daily Challenge: Experience gratitude today. It may be in serving others, or writing in a journal about what you're thankful for, or through prayer. Find a way to show God that you're grateful for the plan of salvation and for our Savior, Jesus Christ.

Remember, Remember

> *Helaman 5:12 - And now, my sons, remember, remember that it is upon the rock of our Redeemer, who is Christ, the Son of God, that ye must build your foundation; that when the devil shall send forth his mighty winds, yea, his shafts in the whirlwind, yea, when all his hail and his mighty storm shall beat upon you, it shall have no power over you to drag you down to the gulf of misery and endless wo, because of the rock upon which ye are build, which is a sure foundation, a foundation whereon if men build they cannot fail.*

This verse encapsulates the Book of Mormon scripture so perfectly. If there were only one scripture to take from this entire book, it's likely this one.

Many of us have felt the "hail and mighty storm" of the devil. I was there after my first marriage ended in divorce. I felt like a failure, like I had let God down and that he was displeased with me - a belief I managed to fabricate myself, unfortunately.

I stopped attending church - it was too hard to go. When we were married, church meetings were the only real time we were happy, but even then there were a few sacrament meetings that ended with her storming into the halls. I could have done more. I should have done more, I thought. Then came the shame, which led to me checking out. I stopped going to church.

Then came the shafts in the whirlwind. The mighty winds. The temptations, the shame and guilt, the loneliness, the anger, the doubt, the frustration. The devil isn't messing around. If he can get ahold of you in the slightest, he takes everything he can get.

The ONLY way back, the only way to fight that onslaught, is side-by-side with our Savior. The ONLY way back is to remember His sacrifice, to humble ourselves to the point where we remember that we cannot do it alone - nor do we have to - and then to exercise our faith. To repent. To go back to church. To study the scriptures. To pray for the Spirit. To ask for help. To believe that we'll receive answers.

I consider myself lucky. It only took me about 7 or 8 months to snap out of it and get back to church. I had great home teachers and an incredible bishop that helped me through it even though I didn't want the help. Because I turned back to the Savior, I wasn't "dragged down to the gulf of misery and endless wo" where the devil resides. His power was limited because of the Savior. I don't know how to express how eternally grateful I am that this verse is true, that this principle is true, and that we have a Savior willing to die for us, to guide us, to fight with us, to rescue us.

Questions to Ponder: What does the Savior want for you? What does the devil want for you? What signs are

there that you're forgetting, or building on a sandy foundation?

Daily Challenge: Write or journal your thoughts about the atonement and our Savior. Write what you're grateful for. Write about a time where you dealt with some of the things in this verse and how you got through it.

Seek No More To Destroy My Servants

> *Helaman 5:29 - ...Repent ye, repent ye, and seek no more to destroy my servants whom I have sent unto you to declare good tidings.*

At first I assumed this verse was for those attacking the Church from the outside, and was struggling to figure out how to apply it to us that are active and faithful. But then I thought back to a recent event, where there was a policy change, and many of my member friends left the Church and added their voices to those outside that were criticizing the Church and its leaders.

The counsel - the principle - is to not "destroy" the Lord's servants who have been sent to guide us and lead us. Now, I don't think that means "follow everything they say blindly" either, because that principle isn't supported in the scriptures. We will sometimes be challenged by changes that occur in the Church, whether it be policy or leadership or a number of other things. In those moments we need to take the problem we're having to the Lord, and ask for help, for comfort. At the very least, "seek no more to destroy my servants."

Questions to Ponder: What other ways do people seek to destroy the Lord's servants? How do you do it? Why? What should you do when you're tempted to do so?

Daily Challenge: Take something you're struggling with to the Lord, and ask for help with it, for comfort, for guidance, for testimony.

That Same Being

> *Helaman 6:23-31 - 26 Now behold, those secret oaths and covenants did not come forth unto Gadianton from the records which were delivered unto Helaman; but behold, they were put into the heart of Gadianton by that same being who did entice our first parents to partake of the forbidden fruit—*

> *27 Yea, that same being who did plot with Cain, that if he would murder his brother Abel it should not be known unto the world. And he did plot with Cain and his followers from that time forth.*

> *28 And also it is that same being who put it into the hearts of the people to build a tower sufficiently high that they might get to heaven. And it was that same being who led on the people who came from that tower into this land; who spread the works of darkness and abominations over all the face of the land, until he dragged the people down to an entire destruction, and to an everlasting hell.*

> *29 Yea, it is that same being who put it into the heart of Gadianton to still carry on the work of darkness, and of secret murder; and he has brought it forth from the beginning of man even down to this time.*

> *30 And behold, it is he who is the author of all sin. And behold, he doth carry on his works of darkness and secret murder, and doth hand down their plots, and their oaths, and their covenants, and their plans of awful wickedness, from generation to generation according as he can get hold upon the hearts of the children of men.*

> *31 And now behold, he had got great hold upon the hearts of the Nephites; yea, insomuch that they had become exceedingly wicked; yea, the more part of them had turned out of the way of righteousness, and did trample under their feet the commandments of God, and did turn unto their own ways, and did build up unto themselves idols of their gold and their silver.*

One thing stands out among all of these examples provided in these verses - Satan uses pride to take people down. All of these examples are basically the different symptoms of pride entering into the hearts of an individual or group of people. Pride starts small, but look where it can lead! It's crazy - the amount of destruction, death, and suffering the devil has evoked through people's pride.

The scriptures teach us an incredible amount about our Savior, His ministry, and His atoning sacrifice. But they also teach us about the devil and his methods and his motivations. What does he get when he brings people down into misery? Company. He's a miserable being, and desires that others join him. That's all. And by any means necessary.

The scriptures give us these examples so we know what to look for and how to prevent it. These verses reinforce the need for humility, for repentance, for faith and obedience. It's imperative that when we sin, we repent. We need to constantly refocus on the Savior and His atonement, rather than our own strength.

Questions to Ponder: How has Satan tried to affect you or tempt you? What methods does he use? What does it look/feel like? How do you combat it? How has your faith in Christ helped you?

Daily Challenge: One place to learn of Satan's methods and motivations is in the scriptures, but another is in the temple. If you can, find a time to visit the temple soon, and pay attention to what the temple teaches us about the devil and how we can avoid his temptations.

Because

> *Helaman 6:35-36 - 35 And thus we see that the Spirit of the Lord began to withdraw from the Nephites, because of the wickedness and the hardness of their hearts.*

> *36 And thus we see that the Lord began to pour out his Spirit upon the Lamanites, because of their easiness and willingness to believe on his words.*

X happened because of Y.

I read a book recently called *Principles* by Ray Dalio, and in it he talks about how everything that is happening today - whether in the financial markets, politics, your personal lives - is just "another one of something." The market crash of 2008 was just another crash, with similar qualities to previous crashes. The housing bubble was another bubble, like those that had come before it.

The point he was making is to learn from history. To be aware of patterns that have occurred in the past and learn how to apply those patterns to what is happening now.

It's easy to read about the pride cycle in The Book of Mormon and apply it to what is happening today in our political climate. It's easy to see dissension in the church as "another one of these," as it's happened before and will happen again.

When we get verses like this, they are trying to teach us something: these consequences came because of wickedness and the hardening of their hearts (pride), or on the flip side, these blessings are because of their humility and teachability.

So, Questions to Ponder: What's going on in your life? What is it "another one" of? What patterns are reoccurring, and how have you dealt with them in the past? What do the scriptures teach you to do?

Daily Challenge: Spend some time writing out some patterns that you're seeing. See if you can connect them to other experiences, and start looking for solutions from those past examples.

Wo Be Unto You

Helaman 7:17-28 - 17 O repent ye, repent ye! Why will ye die? Turn ye, turn ye unto the Lord your God. Why has he forsaken you?

18 It is because you have hardened your hearts; yea, ye will not hearken unto the voice of the good shepherd; yea, ye have provoked him to anger against you.

19 And behold, instead of gathering you, except ye will repent, behold, he shall scatter you forth that ye shall become meat for dogs and wild beasts.

20 O, how could you have forgotten your God in the very day that he has delivered you?

21 But behold, it is to get gain, to be praised of men, yea, and that ye might get gold and silver. And ye have set your hearts upon the riches and the vain things of this world, for the which ye do murder, and plunder, and steal, and bear false witness against your neighbor, and do all manner of iniquity.

22 And for this cause wo shall come unto you except ye shall repent. For if ye will not repent, behold, this great city, and also all those great cities which are round about, which are in the land of our possession, shall be taken away that ye shall have no place in them; for behold, the Lord will not grant unto you strength, as he has hitherto done, to withstand against your enemies.

23 For behold, thus saith the Lord: I will not show unto the wicked of my strength, to one more than the other, save it be unto those who repent of their sins, and hearken unto my words. Now therefore, I would that ye should behold, my brethren, that it shall be better for the Lamanites than for you except ye shall repent.

24 For behold, they are more righteous than you, for they have not sinned against that great knowledge which ye have received; therefore the Lord will be merciful unto them; yea, he will lengthen out their days and increase their seed, even when thou shalt be utterly destroyed except thou shalt repent.

> *25 Yea, wo be unto you because of that great abomination which has come among you; and ye have united yourselves unto it, yea, to that secret band which was established by Gadianton!*

> *26 Yea, wo shall come unto you because of that pride which ye have suffered to enter your hearts, which has lifted you up beyond that which is good because of your exceedingly great riches!*

> *27 Yea, wo be unto you because of your wickedness and abominations!*

> *28 And except ye repent ye shall perish; yea, even your lands shall be taken from you, and ye shall be destroyed from off the face of the earth.*

This passage contains multiple verses with the "qualifying" statements in them - because of the added context. The book of Helaman has many of these passages:

Because you have hardened your hearts...he shall scatter you forth.

Ye have set your hearts upon the riches and vain things of the world...and for this cause wo shall come unto you except ye shall repent.

If ye will not repent, ...this great city...shall be taken away.

I will not show unto the wicked my strength.

Except ye repent ye shall perish.

In case you were wondering if pride was a serious sin, this passage provides a pretty serious answer.

Questions to Ponder: What verses or principles stand out to you? What causes pride? What are the consequences? How have you seen pride show up in your life?

Daily Challenge: Repent! It's the best way to avoid entering the pride cycle, to stave off wickedness, and to remain close to our Father in Heaven.

Look Upon The Son Of God With Faith

> *Helaman 8:15 - ...as many as should look upon the Son of God with faith, having a contrite spirit, might live, even unto that life which is eternal.*

Lest we forget, it always comes back to a focus on our Savior and His atonement for us. The only way to attain eternal life is through Christ. This verse includes a nod to humility as well - having a contrite spirit. So much of the book of Helaman focuses on pride and how it incorporates a turning away from Christ, thinking we can go it alone. I always feel so bad for people who leave the Church because there is usually (if not always) an element at pride at play. No matter the reason for leaving, they ultimately are saying that they're better off without God, His church, the gospel, and everything that entails. We are constantly told throughout the scriptures that the only way is through Christ, and this verse teaches us the importance of humility in that process as well.

Questions to Ponder: Are there any exceptions to those who can attain eternal life? What else is asked of you? How do you reach eternal life with God?

Daily Challenge: Find a way to add some humility into your life today. Admit fault, say sorry, listen more, ask more questions. See if you can cultivate it on demand.

The Unsteadiness Of Our Hearts

> *Helaman 12:1 - And thus we can behold how false, and also the unsteadiness of the hearts of the children of men; yea, we can see that the Lord in his great infinite goodness doth bless and prosper those who put their trust in him.*

In my paperback copy of The Book of Mormon I used to mark all of the scriptures for this book, I ended up highlighting the entirety of Helaman Chapter 12. The chapter starts out with this verse about our nature and our hearts. The heart is linked to trust; if we put our trust in the Lord, we're allowing our hearts - our desires, passions, etc - to turn to the Lord and follow Him. To trust Him with our lives and our salvation.

The opposite of this is what we've talked in recent chapters: pride. As we harden our hearts, we're both literally and figuratively turning away from the Lord, and trusting rather in ourselves. Yet, it teaches us here that our hearts are false. Why is that?

Our hearts can be tempted and can be persuaded. They can be misled and driven by the wrong things. Our hearts are unsteady, and given the choice we should always trust in the Lord rather than in ourselves. Only when we know our hearts are in the right place should we set to work with our hearts and bodies and minds, putting our talents to work. Only then will we receive the blessings that come from obedience and faith in God.

Questions to Ponder: How else are our hearts false and unsteady? What blessings have come into your life because of your trust in God? What does that trust look like? How does it manifest in your life on a daily basis?

Daily Challenge: Think about other ways you can put your trust in the Lord, and what you can do to show that trust.

At The Very Time...

> Helaman 12:2 - Yea, and we may see at the very time when he doth prosper his people, yea, in the increase of their fields, their flocks and their herds, and in gold, and in silver, and in all manner of precious things of every kind and art; sparing their lives, and delivering them out of the hands of their enemies; softening the hearts of their enemies that they should not declare wars against them; yea, and in fine, doing all things for the welfare and happiness of his people; yea, then is the time that they do harden their hearts, and do forget the Lord their God, and do trample under their feet the Holy One—yea, and this because of their ease, and their exceedingly great prosperity.

Such an incredible lesson here. Mormon pinpoints the process with which the pride cycle takes hold of us. It's incredible that this is how it works, but it's also an incredible statement as to all of the things that God can do in our lives.

The thing we need to not forget, this verse teaches, is that when we're experiencing prosperity, where that prosperity came from. It's not because we're hustling, working 80+ hour weeks. It's not because we're good salespeople, or because we're great at social media, or because we're great at anything. Are you able to deliver people out of the hands of their enemies? Or soften the hearts of people to prevent a way? NO? Didn't think so.

All good things come from God, especially the things we want to try and take credit for. By maintaining humility in times of prosperity we can avoid the pride cycle and the perils that come from entering into it.

Questions to Ponder: What thoughts come to you in times of prosperity? How do you avoid letting it get to your head? How do you stay humble?

Daily Challenge: Thank God for something good in your life, any type of prosperity. Thank him for His hand in helping that come into your life.

Except The Lord Doth Chasten His People...

> *Helaman 12:3 - And thus we see that except the Lord doth chasten his people with many afflictions, yea, except he doth visit them with death and with terror, and with famine and with all manner of pestilence, they will not remember him.*

Chastening is used to humble individuals or a group of people. The hope is that they come around, see the error of their ways, remember the Lord, repent, and start to live righteously (again). It's unfortunate that it has to get to that point, because when you think about it, God has made it so easy for us in the church to stay faithful and righteous. We have the plan of salvation laid out for us. Scriptures. Modern prophets and revelation. The Holy Ghost. Prayer. The temple. All there to help us along the path through this mortal existence so that we can progress and ultimately become like Him. Not only that, He rewards us for doing the things He's helping us do by giving us blessings as often as he can without disrupting the way the plan is set up.

Yet, Satan can gain a foothold at a moment's notice. He sneaks in, tells us we're responsible for all the good stuff in our lives. Pride enters our lives and it's all downhill from there, and if we don't catch it in time, the only thing the Lord can do at that point is chasten us, humble us, try and help us remember.

This verse reveals the nature of man, the realities of the earth we live in, and the way the plan of salvation works. Hopefully we choose the path that avoids the chastening altogether as often as possible.

Questions to Ponder: When have you been chastened by the Lord? What happened? How did it feel? Why do you think you were chastened? Why else does the Lord chasten you at times?

Daily Challenge: Think of someone who is struggling right now. Is there something you can do to help them? To reach out so they know they're not alone? How can you help them? Try and find a way and do that today.

O How Foolish

> Helaman 12:4-6 - 4 O how foolish, and how vain, and how evil, and devilish, and how quick to do iniquity, and how slow to do good, are the children of men; yea, how quick to hearken unto the words of the evil one, and to set their hearts upon the vain things of the world!

> 5 Yea, how quick to be lifted up in pride; yea, how quick to boast, and do all manner of that which is iniquity; and how slow are they to remember the Lord their God, and to give ear unto his counsels, yea, how slow to walk in wisdom's paths!

> 6 Behold, they do not desire that the Lord their God, who hath created them, should rule and reign over them; notwithstanding his great goodness and his mercy towards them, they do set at naught his counsels, and they will not that he should be their guide.

Anyone else feel a little guilty? This is some heavy stuff to learn about ourselves here. It feels like the deck is stacked against us, that we've got a lot of obstacles to overcome in order to be successful here.

Guess what though - read these verses again, but as if it were the opposite. It's a pretty great guide for the path ahead. Be humble, righteous, do good, and remember you're a child of God. Hearken to the words of Christ and set your hearts on things with eternal value. Remember the Lord in all times and all places. Listen to His counsels. Look to the Lord for guidance, remember His atonement for you, and strive to follow Him.

The other thing is: we signed up for this! We knew what we were getting into when we raised our hands and chose to follow Christ in the pre-mortal existence. We knew that we needed to come here in order to progress and become like God, even if it was going to be hard at times. And we had to have these obstacles because there must be opposition in all things. That's what helps us grow and progress.

While one could read these verses and give up hope, I hope that we can read them and feel energized and purpose-driven in our desire to choose the right and follow God.

Questions to Ponder: How do you feel when you read these verses? What do they mean to you? What should we do about it? What do you do to overcome the natural man?

Daily Challenge: Do something awesome today, because you can. You're capable - you're a son or daughter of God, who has infinite power. Go do something awesome!

How Great Is The Nothingness Of The Children Of Men

Helaman 12:7-21 - 7 O how great is the nothingness of the children of men; yea, even they are less than the dust of the earth.

8 For behold, the dust of the earth moveth hither and thither, to the dividing asunder, at the command of our great and everlasting God.

9 Yea, behold at his voice do the hills and the mountains tremble and quake.

10 And by the power of his voice they are broken up, and become smooth, yea, even like unto a valley.

11 Yea, by the power of his voice doth the whole earth shake;

12 Yea, by the power of his voice, do the foundations rock, even to the very center.

13 Yea, and if he say unto the earth—Move—it is moved.

14 Yea, if he say unto the earth—Thou shalt go back, that it lengthen out the day for many hours—it is done;

15 And thus, according to his word the earth goeth back, and it appeareth unto man that the sun standeth still; yea, and behold, this is so; for surely it is the earth that moveth and not the sun.

16 And behold, also, if he say unto the waters of the great deep—Be thou dried up—it is done.

17 Behold, if he say unto this mountain—Be thou raised up, and come over and fall upon that city, that it be buried up—behold it is done.

18 And behold, if a man hide up a treasure in the earth, and the Lord shall say—Let it be accursed, because of the iniquity of him who hath hid it up—behold, it shall be accursed.

> *19 And if the Lord shall say—Be thou accursed, that no man shall find thee from this time henceforth and forever—behold, no man getteth it henceforth and forever.*

> *20 And behold, if the Lord shall say unto a man—Because of thine iniquities, thou shalt be accursed forever—it shall be done.*

> *21 And if the Lord shall say—Because of thine iniquities thou shalt be cut off from my presence—he will cause that it shall be so.*

I realized something while driving to work, thinking about these verses. I think when the Lord is talking about the natural man, or the children of men, he's talking about our physical bodies. Our spirits are amazing - think about what they did! We all, through our faith, decided to follow Christ in the council in heaven, to come down to earth to gain a body with the hope that we would be able to progress and become like God. We had no guarantee that this would work, as it required faith in God and Christ to be our Savior. Our spirits are intelligences, eternal, without beginning or end. They're pretty incredible.

We chose to come down here and take on these imperfect bodies, to submit ourselves to temptation, to sloth and laziness, to carnal desires. Our bodies don't always listen, as they are just a vehicle for our spirits' progression. So, if we want to be more like God, we need to focus on finding ways for our spirits to take control of these bodies, something they're perfectly capable of. All of these verses are talking about things we're easily capable of overcoming. Our spirits are obviously greater than the dust and the earth and the mountains, as long as we listen and obey.

Questions to Ponder: What else are our spirits capable of? What is it that makes it so hard to overcome our natural tendencies?

Daily Challenge: Do something today to overcome a temptation. Skip the morning soda run. Do 20 pushups. Get up early. Leave the binging for another night and use that extra time to write or read or create. Allow yourself to see what your spirit is capable of.

For This Cause, That Men Might Be Saved

> *Helaman 12:22 - And wo unto him to whom he shall say this, for it shall be unto him that will do iniquity, and he cannot be saved; therefore, for this cause, that men might be saved, hath repentance been declared.*

We've heard it many times: we cannot be saved in our sins. I love this verse because of how straightforward it is. Repentance is part of the plan because of our iniquity, which we all knew was going to be a part of the plan. We knew we would need a Savior because we knew we were going to sin. I wonder how many of us cried at that moment when we learned what we'd be capable of - some of us denying that there is a God or a Savior, or breaking sacred covenants that we knew we would make here on earth. Yet, even knowing that, we still agreed and probably wept more tears of joy for the opportunity to come to earth, obtain a body, and be able to finally progress from our state in the pre-mortal existence.

God knew we could not be saved in iniquity, so He proposed a plan that required a Savior. Our brother Jesus Christ stepped forward and volunteered. Think of the immense amount of love and charity they had and have for us in order to make these choices. And it's all for us.

Questions to Ponder: What do you love most about the plan of salvation? How does it make you feel to know that Jesus Christ gave His life for yours? What role does repentance play in your life?

Daily Challenge: Repent! We're so lucky to have such an incredible gift. Let's not take it for granted.

That Men Might Be Brought Unto Repentance

> Helaman 12:23-24 - 23 Therefore, blessed are they who will repent and hearken unto the voice of the Lord their God; for these are they that shall be saved.

> 24 And may God grant, in his great fulness, that men might be brought unto repentance and good works, that they might be restored unto grace for grace, according to their works.

We learned that repentance was declared by God as a part of the plan so that we could be saved. These verses expound on that thought. "Therefore..." this is what the author wants us to focus on - "blessed are they who will repent and hearken unto the voice of the Lord."

How many times has this thought been reiterated so far? In nearly 200 chapters it feels like close to half of them touch on either repentance or humility. Yes, it's THAT important. It's a fundamental, foundational aspect of the gospel, to have humility and let that humility drive us to repent of our sins.

While the prophets were witnessing incredible downfalls of entire groups of people, of cities and groups of often great men and women, they were also thinking of us and the challenges we would be facing in our lives when we'd turn to these accounts looking for help and guidance. And what do they choose to talk about? Humility and repentance. Listen to the plea in verse 24! Read it out loud if you need to:

"And may God grant, in his great fulness, that men may be brought unto repentance..."

This is a prayer to God. It's a plea by a prophet over the people he has been called to lead and guide, who have fallen away. What does he want for them more than anything? For them to repent. Notice that he can't force them to. "That they may be brought unto repentance." It's such an important thing that he's praying that they be *brought* to repentance, because he knows they're beyond the point of listening to him or those calling them to repentance.

There's such emotion and fervor in his words, it's impossible to mistake how important repentance was for him and his people.

DAILY MORMON

Questions to Ponder: Why else do you think repentance was so important? What do you think they knew that maybe we don't? How do you feel about repentance? How is that reflected in your daily life?

Daily Challenge: Repent! Yes, again! But guess what? We still need to repent. We can still become better.

And Thus It Is

> *Helaman 12:25-26 - 25 And I would that all men might be saved. But we read that in the great and last day there are some who shall be cast out, yea, who shall be cast off from the presence of the Lord;*

> *26 Yea, who shall be consigned to a state of endless misery, fulfilling the words which say: They that have done good shall have everlasting life; and they that have done evil shall have everlasting damnation. And thus it is. Amen.*

Which life will we choose? We made the choice once already, or else we wouldn't be here. Our spirits desire nothing more than to be righteous, to follow God, to progress and become like him someday. Yet, our bodies often want something more...mortal. More immediate. Less important.

The choice is right in front of us, each and every day, yet so are the consequences. Which will we choose?

Questions to Ponder: How does it feel knowing that some of your brothers and sisters will choose evil, wickedness, and to be cast off from the presence of the Lord? What, if anything, should you do about it? How does it feel to know that your spirit wants eternal life with our Father in Heaven?

Daily Challenge: Do something good today. Make the choice, and do something good. Let it compound each and every day until, with the Lord's help, you attain eternal life through His atonement.

Nothing Can Save This People

> *Helaman 13:6 - ...and nothing can save this people save it be repentance and faith on the Lord Jesus Christ, who surely shall come into the world, and shall suffer many things and be slain for his people.*

After really diving into Helaman 12 the last few chapters, we get this great verse that kind of sums everything up for us. It all comes back to the atonement and to our Savior, Jesus Christ. Without Him, salvation is not possible.

I constantly have this thought - I wonder if my actions line up with the statement "I believe in Christ." I wonder if I truly have a testimony. If you were to look at my life would it seem at a glance, "yeah, that guy believes in Christ"? I pray daily, I study my scriptures, I'm an active member of the Church and fulfill my calling to the best I know how. Yet, I still feel like I should be doing more. Like there are too many distractions, too many pointless thoughts and action that don't help me progress.

If I "truly" believed in Christ, I think to myself, how would my life be different? Now, I don't know how "truly" is different than how I believe in Christ now, but it's an interesting thought nonetheless. I wonder why it keeps coming up.

What I really think at the end of the day though is that if we "truly" believe in Christ, we will take all of these teachings at face value and turn them into actions and choices in our daily lives. If you didn't believe in Christ, why would you ever repent, or act according to your faith? Yet that's something I, and I imagine most of us, do every day. We repent. We pray. We go to church. We attend the temple. We live the word of wisdom. So, while we may not say it specifically every day, our actions show that we truly believe in Christ.

And for that I'm grateful.

Questions to Ponder: How does your faith influence your daily life? What actions bring you the most joy, the most comfort, make you feel the closest to your Savior?

Daily Challenge: Find some time to ponder about the life of our Savior; His incredible sacrifice on our behalf and what the atonement provides for us.

If Ye Will Repent

> Helaman 13:11 - But if ye will repent and return unto the Lord your God I will turn away mine anger, saith the Lord; yea, thus saith the Lord, blessed are they who will repent and turn unto me, but wo unto him that repenteth not.

I love, LOVE, these simple statements. If ye will repent, [then] I will turn away mine anger. Sweet! Done deal! Let's do this!

There's something about how straightforward it is. I think my logical brain needs that kind of structure. There's a book I read by Gretchen Rubin called Better Than Before, and she outlines this framework she came up with based on how we respond to internal and external expectations. If we're really good at doing things when the pressure is external, like from a parent, or a boss, or a gospel doctrine, and if we're not good at self motivating or following our own internal pressure, then she'd call us an Obliger. I fall under the semi-rare category of being good at both internal desire and external accountability, dubbed an Upholder. (You can find your tendency by taking her free quiz. Just Google "four tendencies quiz Gretchen Rubin". Why bring this up? Because the scriptures do an incredible job of addressing each of us with our specific tendencies. Some of us question everything that comes our way and we don't act until it makes sense. Some of us rebel no matter what. Others can be told to do something and it's fixed for life.

The scriptures have verses like today's that are super straight forward - good for my "Upholder" brain - but also include stories, anecdotes, testimony, and truth, all meant to help each one of us gain both external and internal reasons for living the gospel each day.

Questions to Ponder: Do you tend to believe everything you read, or question it? How did you come to gain your testimony of the gospel? How are you strengthening it now?

Daily Challenge: Do something today to act with faith and strengthen your testimony. Pray, repent, serve, read the scriptures, fast, attend the temple - whatever it is, we need to put in the time to live the gospel each day so that it's a part of our lives, not just a part of our beliefs.

For Them Will I Spare

> *Helaman 13:13 - But blessed are they who will repent, for them will I spare...*

Every book. Every prophet. Nearly every chapter of The Book of Mormon speaks of repentance. And I get it, it's hard to remember sometimes. I mean, I'm the one sitting here writing about it every night and even I forget at times. It's pathetic really.

I find it interesting how many ways they can say the same thing. "For them will I spare" is a new one. What does it mean? That we qualify for the Lord's saving grace. We have to do our part to be able to receive the full blessings of the atonement.

The principle is the same no matter how it's worded or who says it - we must repent in order to be saved.

Questions to Ponder: How do you feel about repentance? How often do you repent? Why? (Why not?)

Daily Challenge: Have a conversation with the Lord. Repent. Ask for forgiveness. Ask him to teach you and help you grow and progress through the process.

Treasures In The Earth

> *Helaman 13:18-20 - 18 And it shall come to pass, saith the Lord of Hosts, yea, our great and true God, that whoso shall hide up treasures in the earth shall find them again no more, because of the great curse of the land, save he be a righteous man and shall hide it up unto the Lord.*

> *19 For I will, saith the Lord, that they shall hide up their treasures unto me; and cursed be they who hide not up their treasures unto me; for none hideth up their treasures unto me save it be the righteous; and he that hideth not up his treasures unto me, cursed is he, and also the treasure, and none shall redeem it because of the curse of the land.*

> *20 And the day shall come that they shall hide up their treasures, because they have set their hearts upon riches; and because they have set their hearts upon their riches, and will hide up their treasures when they shall flee before their enemies; because they will not hide them up unto me, cursed be they and also their treasures; and in that day shall they be smitten, saith the Lord.*

Our focus and our intent matters. If we spend our lives pursuing worldly treasures, it's a fool's errand. We can't keep it, it doesn't help us, and it actually hurts our salvation. If our motivation is to help others progress, to come unto Christ, to be a disciple of Jesus Christ and obediently keep our covenants, worldly treasure may follow, but we'll have the proper intentions, and the proper perspective on what that worldly treasure is. Really, it's an opportunity to do more of what you've been doing! You like serving people? You can serve more. Like donating to charity? You can donate more.

Like the parable of the talents, we've all been given ways to succeed here on earth. If we use those talents and put them to work to better the world and the kingdom of God, they will grow and double. If, however, we bury our talents out of fear or out of our own desires for something else, we'll lose even that which we have.

The Lord needs disciples that are willing to put worldly things aside and help build the kingdom. I wonder, often - probably too often - whether my personal pursuits are interfering with the things the Lord needs me for. Is trying to be a film producer a worldly pursuit of worldly treasures? Or is it just trying to use my talents the best way I know how?

Again, it comes down to the intent. What are we after? The fame? The money? The accolades? Or trying to reach as many people as possible, sharing the light of Christ, helping provide jobs and stability and enjoyment... believe me, I've overthought this one way too much. All I know is that it comes down to intent, and that God knows what's in our hearts. As long as we're trying to make the world a better place, we're good.

Questions to Ponder: What treasures are a part of your life? How do they get in the way? What can you focus on instead? How do you change your intentions?

Daily Challenge: Find one worldly pursuit that could be curtailed or lessened, or one "heavenly treasure" to pursue instead.

Whosoever Shall Believe

> *Helaman 14:8 - And it shall come to pass that whosoever shall believe on the Son of God, the same shall have everlasting life.*

I was lucky enough to have a conversation over dinner tonight with two of my favorite people, and, as it often does, the conversation turned to religion. The state of the Church, The Book of Mormon, friends who have left, etc etc. It's always a rousing conversation that leaves me with lots to think about for the days that follow.

One thing that always comes up is no matter what is going on, whether or not things are difficult, or confusing, or flat out maddening, the gospel will always be true.

One friend mentioned that when Mormons leave the Church they typically leave everything, including their faith in God and Jesus Christ, where her friends in other faiths just leave one church or congregation and go down the road to the next best church.

I'm not sure why that is. That's probably what I'll spend the next few days thinking about, but for now, it's interesting that this verse came up next to write about. Whatever happens, Jesus Christ is the way, the truth, and the life. Whosoever shall believe on the Son of God, the same shall have everlasting life.

Questions to Ponder: Why is it that people abandon their faith when they leave the Church? What can you do to help those that are struggling? What course of action should you take if you are struggling yourself?

Daily Challenge: If you're like me, you thought about someone as you were reading today's chapter. Send them a text, an email, call them on the phone - reach out to them in some way today. They probably are struggling and they need you, and the Lord needs you as well.

If Ye Believe On His Name

> *Helaman 14:13 - And if ye believe on his name ye will repent of all your sins, that thereby ye may have a remission of them through his merits.*

Belief leads to repentance, which leads to a remission of sins through Christ. How wonderful is that statement? How incredible is that concept?

All it takes on our part is a desire to believe. "If ye will believe..." there aren't any other conditions. If we'll humble ourselves enough to believe, then to repent, asking God in prayer, we can receive a remission of our sins through Christ.

Questions to Ponder: What are Christ's "merits"? How can you strengthen your belief in God and Christ and the gospel? What other blessings come from your desire to believe and then acting in faith?

Daily Challenge: Make an act of faith today. Pray, repent, study, serve, ponder. Find ways to strengthen your belief and your testimony of the gospel.

The Resurrection of Christ

> *Helaman 14:17 - But behold, the resurrection of Christ redeemeth mankind, yea, even all mankind, and bringeth them back into the presence of the Lord.*

Just think about those words for a minute.

The resurrection of Christ redeems mankind. Nothing else. Not our effort. Not how much money we make or how many instagram followers we have. Not how much power or influence we have. It's the most egalitarian principle I can think of, the most level playing field in the whole world. Everyone will be resurrected because of Christ. There are no conditions, no quotas, no expectations. It just happens.

It brings us back into the presence of the Lord. It is the entire purpose for which we are here on earth - to receive a body, use our agency to the best of our ability, and try to become like God. Yet, no matter how well we do, how hard we try, we will always fall short if it isn't for the atonement of Christ. HE makes it possible for us to accomplish our great purpose here - the immortality and eternal life of man. There is no other way that is possible.

Questions to Ponder: If you actually believe those words, how would you act? Would it be different from how you act now? How?

Daily Challenge: Take some time today to ponder the incredible scope and effect of these statements in this verse. How does it make you feel? What thoughts come to your mind? What actions are you inspired to take?

Lest By Knowing These Things

> Helaman 14:19 - Therefore repent ye, repent ye, lest by knowing these things and not doing them ye shall suffer yourselves to come under condemnation, and ye are brought down unto this second death.

Samuel the Lamanite was the man. His prophecy to the Nephites encompasses Helaman chapters 13-15, so he is the prophet speaking in these verses.

He obviously had a clear testimony of Christ and the gospel. It is evident in the simplicity of his words, how he is able to distill these massive concepts into a single verse or a single thought.

The other reason is the concern he has for others. "Lest..." that word almost has a pleading to it. He's seemingly begging the Nephites to understand the gravity of the words he's saying, and the consequences to the actions they're taking in their lives. How many of us have been in a similar situation, pleading with a loved one who knows these things and yet doesn't do them?

These great prophets have that same love and desire for not just their family and their close friends, but entire groups of people. Samuel is preaching to a large group of Nephites! Who does that? Someone with a deep understanding of the reality of the gospel and immense love for his spiritual brothers and sisters.

Questions to Ponder: Who in your life "knows these things and [is] not doing them"? What can you do to help them? What do they need from you? Why is repentance often a part of the plea from the prophets in these moments?

Daily Challenge: Reach out to a loved one, not to call them to repentance or talk to them of the error of their ways, but just so that they know you're there, and that you're thinking of them.

Behold, Ye Are Free

> Helaman 14:30 - And now remember, remember, my brethren, that whosoever perisheth, perisheth unto himself; and whosoever doeth iniquity, doeth it unto himself; for behold, ye are free; ye are permitted to act for yourselves; for behold, God hath given unto you a knowledge and he hath made you free.

Tonight I was having a conversation with my brother about how I could stand to lose about 10 pounds in order to get back to a physique I'm happy with. I had been doing a strength building workout the last few months, and while I put on a solid 8+ pounds of muscle over that time, I also managed to gain a few pounds of the undesirable squishy stuff.

He echoed similar sentiments, but added how hard it is to control the cravings for sugar and carbs. I too struggle. You see, as kids we used to eat cereal at all times of the day... bowls and bowls of cereal. Breakfast, afternoon snack, and late night nibble. And we'd often have a heaping spoonful (or two) of sugar to top it off and sweeten the deal.

Ugh. Just thinking about it now gives me the shivers.

Point is, we ate a lot of carbs, and a lot of sugar. There were always sugary treats to be found all over the house. I don't know how the four of us kids managed to maintain fairly healthy physiques through our lives. Gotta be that English blood or something.

I told my brother that, believe it or not, he is actually stronger than a bowl of cereal. Well, maybe not Lucky Charms, but they are magically delicious.

We are in truth not our bodies. We are eternal, intelligent spirits without beginning or end, created in the image of Almighty God who created the Heaven and Earth. Doubtful that He ever succumbed to a second helping of Cap'n Crunch.

Our spirits reside in these bodies and have full control over them. Want proof? Stand up. Reach for something in front of you. Smile. Close your eyes and think of a beach.

See?

Your spirit can tell your body to do anything it wants. EVEN (gasp!) avoid carbs.

Now this is a silly, extreme example of the principle described in this verse, but it is, I believe, the exact same principle. "Ye are free; ye are permitted to act for yourselves."

Questions to Ponder: How does this principle apply to your salvation? To your physical health? To your mindset? To your outlook on life? What is possible if you let your spirit take full control of your body and use it to further progress and become like God?

Daily Challenge: Do something today to overcome the natural man that we all have. Resist a temptation. Get up early. Call a friend. Share your testimony or a copy of The Book of Mormon. Prove to yourself that you are capable of literally anything with enough faith and belief.

3 NEPHI

He Hath Blessed Them And Prospered Them

> 3 Nephi 5:22 - And insomuch as the children of Lehi have kept his commandments he hath blessed them and prospered them according to his word.

This is a nice reminder of how simple the gospel is. Keep the commandments, be blessed and prosper. Simple. Clean. Elegant. No fuss.

Whenever we're struggling, we can turn to this principle to reset and fix the issue. Keep the commandments. See what principle is at play in your life and start there. The Lord needs people who are obedient at keeping the commandments, as they are the ones He uses to build the kingdom here on earth. He can't use us the same way if we're not being obedient or focused.

When we see others struggling, we should find ways to help them remember the gospel. Help them live the gospel. Bring the light of Christ into their lives. These blessings are all predicated on obedience to the principle they are based on. We have to be obedient in order to gain the blessings.

Questions to Ponder: What blessings are you seeking in your life? What principles are those blessings based on or connected to? Have you tested it to see if obedience to that principle brings blessings?

Daily Challenge: Test a principle today. Find one that you've struggled with in the past, are currently struggling with, or that could use some reinforcing. Live the principle. See if the Lord blesses you for your obedience, and once he does, keep living it!

Wo Unto The Inhabitants Of The Whole Earth

> *3 Nephi 9:2 - Wo, wo, wo unto this people; wo unto the inhabitants of the whole earth except they shall repent; for the devil laugheth, and his angels rejoice, because of the slain of the fair sons and daughters of my people; and it is because of their iniquity and abominations that they are fallen.*

Some context is in order. The chapter heading for 3 Nephi 9 reads: In the darkness, the voice of Christ proclaims the destruction of many people and cities for their wickedness."

Christ has been crucified, and the sign of that event has occurred, just as Samuel the Lamanite prophesied. The people are experiencing three days of darkness when the voice of the Lord speaks to them from above. And what does He say? "Hey guys! How's it going? I'm so happy to see you soon!"

No...

Wo, wo, wo... THREE Wo's! Wo unto this people, to the whole earth except they shall repent. The FIRST thing He talks about is the importance of repentance. Why? Because when we don't repent, the devil wins. He wins because pride leads to a fall, spiritual and then physical, which is what the devil wants more than anything else, for us to be miserable just as he is.

This is serious. These are not just words on a page. Not some annual gospel doctrine lesson. This is a foundational doctrinal principle, one which if we neglect or fail to practice in our lives, we will fall. We will fail. We will be cut off, forever.

Questions to Ponder: Why would the Lord start His proclamation this way, with such a strong warning? What does it say about Him? What does it say about the devil?

Daily Challenge: I'm gonna side with the Lord on this one. Repent!

Because...

> 3 Nephi 9:12 - And many great destructions have I caused to come upon this land, and upon this people, because of their wickedness and their abominations.

The word *because* is often the difference between a verse that ends up in this book and one that doesn't. The cause and effect is important for us to learn from because there's an action, a choice involved. If we want the outcome from that choice, we make the choice! If we don't want the outcome, say, many great destructions, we can choose that as well.

These verses teach us that this life is in our control. We are able to make choices based on the agency we've been blessed with, and much of the difficulty and frustration we deal with can be avoided if we just remember that fact.

We're in charge of our bodies, our actions, our thoughts. This verse is an extreme example of what happens when we let our "natural man" take over and lead us to wickedness and abominations. That doesn't ever have to happen, if we just remember who's in charge.

Questions to Ponder: What, if anything, is not in your control? What do you do about it? How should you let it affect you?

Daily Challenge: Try a daily affirmation. Currently in my bathroom I have two quotes: "For God hath not given us the spirit of fear, but of power and of love and of a sound mind." and "I can be whatever I will to be." Try either one out. Say it out loud 10+ times, visualize what it means, what changes if you really believe what you're saying, and feel more powerful. It's a great way to start the day.

If Ye Will Come Unto Me

> 3 Nephi 9:14-15 - 14 Yea, verily I say unto you, if ye will come unto me ye shall have eternal life. Behold, mine arm of mercy is extended towards you, and whosoever will come, him will I receive; and blessed are those who come unto me.

> 15 Behold, I am Jesus Christ the Son of God. I created the heavens and the earth, and all things that in them are. I was with the Father from the beginning. I am in the Father, and the Father in me; and in me hath the Father glorified his name.

This reminds me of humility. "If ye will come unto me." It's really on us, as the Lord has already done His part. As long as we will have enough humility, we will have eternal life, as humility leads to every other aspect of the gospel - faith, repentance, obedience, prayer, sacrifice, service, attending the temple... it all comes back to humility and remembering the perspective of how great God is.

"Whosoever will come." It's up to us.

Questions to Ponder: What keeps you from being humble? How does it manifest in your life? What can you do to become more humble?

Daily Challenge: Offer a prayer of pure gratitude. Thank your Heavenly Father for every blessing in your life individually, and remember how lucky we are for everything we have.

To Them Have I Given To Become The Sons of God

> *3 Nephi 9:17 - And as many as have received me, to them have I given to become the sons of God; and even so will I to as many as shall believe on my name, for behold, by me redemption cometh, and in me is the law of Moses fulfilled.*

We're now to the section of The Book of Mormon where Christ visits the people in America after His death. All of the prophecies, the visions and dreams, everything has been pointing to Him and His life and His atoning sacrifice.

After all of that, all that He asks of us is to receive Him humbly, to believe in Him, and we can be redeemed by Him. To believe and to have faith requires action on our part, and obedience and discipleship, but the path is still a simple and straightforward one.

I was thinking about how my three boys learn new things, and how hard it is to be patient as they figure things out. My instinct is to reach in and help them as much as I can because I don't want them to fail. I can only imagine that our Heavenly Father has that same instinct, multiplied billions of times for the number of His children here on the earth. That, and the stakes are so much greater than learning to ride a bike or draw the number 7 in the right direction. "To them have I given to become the sons of God." No wonder they want to help us so much!

They could have made it so hard, but they didn't. They really have given us every advantage imaginable. That is how much they love us. They want us to succeed. They want us to learn and figure it out. They want us to return home to live with them again. We just have to choose it for ourselves.

Questions to Ponder: If you have children, what about that relationship reminds you of your relationship with your Heavenly Father? How do you think He and Christ feel about you?

Daily Challenge: Spend some extra time with a loved one today. Sit down, talk about the gospel, share how much you love them.

A Broken Heart And A Contrite Spirit

> 3 Nephi 9:20-22 - 20 And ye shall offer for a sacrifice unto me a broken heart and a contrite spirit. And whoso cometh unto me with a broken heart and a contrite spirit, him will I baptize with fire and with the Holy Ghost, even as the Lamanites, because of their faith in me at the time of their conversion, were baptized with fire and with the Holy Ghost, and they knew it not.

> 21 Behold, I have come unto the world to bring redemption unto the world, to save the world from sin.

> 22 Therefore, whoso repenteth and cometh unto me as a little child, him will I receive, for of such is the kingdom of God. Behold, for such I have laid down my life, and have taken it up again; therefore repent, and come unto me ye ends of the earth, and be saved.

THERE IT IS! The scripture that supports my theory that humility is a foundational gospel principle. Look at verse 20: Humility - a broken heart and a contrite spirit - comes before faith and baptism!

Again, in verse 22: "whoso repenteth and cometh unto me as a little child." "For such is the kingdom of God." He's teaching us right here the importance of humility.

It is a topic that often gets glossed over or looped in with other principles like faith and repentance and we don't give it enough time and weight. Humility is SO important. Christ is giving a sermon to the entire people there, and what does He speak about? HUMILITY! It's the HUMBLE that He has laid his life down for. They are those who will be saved.

I hope this is exciting some of you the same way it's exciting me. I know that often it's easy to have a spiritual breakthrough and everyone else around you is like, "yeah, dude, we know. We've known that, like, forever and stuff." (Apparently the people around me speak like a bunch of millennials...)

I hope that you'll take time to ponder these scriptures today, and really think about and pray about the importance of humility.

Questions to Ponder: Why do you think that Christ took the time to talk about humility - having a broken heart and contrite spirit? Why do these qualities help us gain eternal life? How did Christ exemplify humility in His life?

Daily Challenge: Ponder these verses throughout the day. Find ways to apply humility to every part of your life, every relationship, every interaction.

If Ye Will Repent...

> *3 Nephi 10:6-7 - 6 O ye house of Israel whom I have spared, how oft will I gather you as a hen gathereth her chickens under her wings, if ye will repent and return unto me with full purpose of heart.*

> *7 But if not, O house of Israel, the places of your dwellings shall become desolate until the time of the fulfilling of the covenant to your fathers.*

Such an interesting image, the hen gathering her chickens. I don't know much about farming or the gathering habits of certain birds, but I do know how it feels. The hen is the mother. The idea of "under her wings" feels like a protection, a safeguard, being not only huddled close, but protected from anything on the other side of that motherly wing.

There's so much love in that statement. And, again, all we are asked to do is repent and follow Christ - "return unto me with full purpose of heart."

There are often scriptures that state the opposite, as this one does. "But if not..." says Christ. The gospel is very, very clear. Think about the commandment God gave Adam and his posterity after the fall. The firstling of the flock. Simple. Clear. Yet, what did Cain do? Offered something completely different, almost as if he were mocking God. His sacrifice wasn't rejected because he got 90% on the "test," but because his effort was in vain. He loved Satan more than God, and his actions revealed that relationship.

We need to be like the good examples in the scriptures, following the teachings and the examples of the prophets who teach us to obey, to be humble, to repent, and to have faith. If we do that, we will be able to return to live with God again.

Questions to Ponder: Why is it hard at times to repent and be vulnerable? What prevents you from doing it? How do you overcome that fear or that hesitation?

Daily Challenge: Think about ways you can overcome any obstacles between you and repentance. If there are none, a) I'm jealous, and b) then keep repenting!

Whoso Readeth, Let Him Understand

> 3 Nephi 10:14 - And now, whoso readeth, let him understand; he that hath the scriptures, let him search them, and see and behold if all these deaths and destructions by fire, and by smoke, and by tempests, and by whirlwinds, and by the opening of the earth to receive them, and all these things are not unto the fulfilling of the prophecies of many of the holy prophets.

This one seems different from the rest of the scriptures I've written about over the last 7 months. I think it's because the Lord is speaking in His way, where He is almost tempting you to try or test Him. "See if all these things are not unto the fulfilling of the prophecies of many of the holy prophets." It's like He's saying, "sure, just go back and check. I'll wait..."

Yet there still is a promise and a statement in this verse. The scriptures contain some incredible truths, some perfect examples of gospel principles, and the words of the Lord and His prophets here on the earth. This is, in a way, the Lord's testimony of that fact. It's all here.

If that is true, what about the words of the prophets in our day? What about the things they teach and prophesy of over the pulpit during General Conference? What about their messages each month in the Ensign magazine? Are they any less true because they aren't contained in the pages of the scriptures?

"Whoso readeth, let him understand" could also read "whoso listens, let him understand. whoso reads/prays/ponders/asks/studies - let him understand." The scriptures, I believe, contain every truth that we need in order to live a happy life, to progress, to become more Christlike, to help our fellow man, and to ultimately return to live with Him again.

Questions to Ponder: What answers have you found in the scriptures in the past? How did you find them? What was the process like? Can you replicate it?

Daily Challenge: Take a question to the Lord. Pray, ponder, then search the scriptures and diligently seek for the answer. It's there. There is a principle for you and your question right now, if you'll take the Lord up on His offer to read and search.

I Am The Light And Life Of The World

> 3 Nephi 11:11 - And behold, I am the light and the life of the world; and I have drunk out of that bitter cup which the Father hath given me, and have glorified the Father in taking upon me the sins of the world, in the which I have suffered the will of the father in all things from the beginning.

Every time I read the phrase "I am the light/life of the world" I feel like I could probably spend an entire year studying just that one topic and still end up with much more to learn. There is so much meaning to the word light, and how it's used in different ways by our Savior in the scriptures.

Christ is speaking. It's not someone else talking about the atonement at some future date and an unfamiliar location. It's the Savior speaking of actions He had just barely taken on our behalf. This is the very first thing He says to the people gathered around Him right after He states his name. He wants us to know and understand His life and what it means for us and our loved ones. He wants us to believe in Him, and trust Him, and love Him.

The Book of Mormon truly is another testament of Jesus Christ, and these next dozen or so chapters are some of my favorite, because they contain the words of the Savior. I know with all of my heart that this book of scripture is true, that it was translated by the prophet Joseph Smith by the power of God, and that if we will study it earnestly and strive to live by its principles, we will be happy, blessed, and ultimately saved by the grace of our Savior, Jesus Christ.

I know He lives, I know He loves us, and I know that this gospel is true.

Questions to Ponder: How/when did you gain your testimony of Jesus Christ? Of The Book of Mormon? How do you maintain your testimony today? How do you help others that are struggling or have struggled with theirs?

Daily Challenge: Share your testimony with a friend or family member. Let the spirit come through you to touch their hearts and reinforce that testimony.

The God Of The Whole Earth

> *3 Nephi 11:14 - ...I am the God of Israel, and the God of the whole earth, and have been slain for the sins of the world.*

I wonder if at times I forget this truth, or at least "forget" about it long enough that it stops influencing my thoughts and actions. I often ask my gospel doctrine class, "what would it look like if you fully and completely believed this principle? How would it show up in your daily lives?"

I think this verse helps me with my perspective. Just today, for example, I was so focused on a single problem at work that was frustrating me because I had no control over it. I was stuck, waiting on people to answer or return my phone calls and emails. The frustration permeated my entire day, and I couldn't focus on anything else.

Then, I sit down, read this verse as I write this chapter, and WHAM! There it is. The exact verse I need.

There are SO MANY things that are more important and bigger than our problems, but in that moment when we're staring them in the face, our problems can seem insurmountable. But guess what? There is a God. We have a Heavenly Father looking out for us. A Savior who atoned for our sins. Our daily struggles pale in comparison to what they have had to go through for this plan of salvation to work.

These larger, eternal thoughts instantly pull me out of my funk, and I feel better. That's how the gospel works. It's the good news, the map and the blueprint, all created to teach and lead and guide us to live a life full of happiness, one centered on our Savior Jesus Christ. And the best part? It works. Because it's true.

Questions to Ponder: When did you last sit and ponder the grandeur of the plan of salvation? The gospel? How The Book of Mormon came to be? The Atonement of our Savior? How can you spend time with those thoughts on a more frequent basis?

DAILY MORMON

Daily Challenge: Take some time to ponder this verse today. Play out in your mind the entirety of the plan of salvation, from inception in the pre-earth life, through the creation, the fall, the life of our Savior and His atonement and resurrection, to you, to your children and your family, all the way to when you leave this earth to join your other loved ones who have passed on. Then think of His return, the millennium, and the incredible, eternal future we can have with them someday.

Whoso...Desireth To Be Baptized In My Name

> 3 Nephi 11:23-28 - 23 Verily I say unto you, that whoso repenteth of his sins through your words, and desireth to be baptized in my name, on this wise shall ye baptize them—Behold, ye shall go down and stand in the water, and in my name shall ye baptize them.

> 24 And now behold, these are the words which ye shall say, calling them by name, saying:

> 25 Having authority given me of Jesus Christ, I baptize you in the name of the Father, and of the Son, and of the Holy Ghost. Amen.

> 26 And then shall ye immerse them in the water, and come forth again out of the water.

> 27 And after this manner shall ye baptize in my name; for behold, verily I say unto you, that the Father, and the Son, and the Holy Ghost are one; and I am in the Father, and the Father in me, and the Father and I are one.

> 28 And according as I have commanded you thus shall ye baptize. And there shall be no disputations among you, as there have hitherto been; neither shall there be disputations among you concerning the points of my doctrine, as there have hitherto been.

Just this last week my oldest son Eli turned 7. For the first time since he was born I started really thinking about how to teach him about, and prepare him for, baptism. I don't see it as purely a ritual, something like a rite of passage. To hear the Lord speak about baptism in these verses reinforces that for me. Sure, there are the practical steps for how to baptize, but even in these short verses there are phrases that teach us that this is more than just going into the water and coming out.

I imagine I'll be referring to these verses often over the next year as I help my son make a decision about being baptized. Perhaps he'll want to wait? Perhaps he won't want to at all. I've thought about these possibilities and what I would do, but then quickly realized, thanks to the Holy Ghosts gentle influence, that I cannot nor should I try to coerce him or manipulate him. I can only testify and teach and pray with him, helping him understand and come to a decision one way or another. On his own.

In order for him to value something like baptism and confirmation, receiving the gift of the Holy Ghost, and taking upon the name of Christ, I first have to value those things, both internally - which is how most of us value those things - but now also externally. I have to talk about them, and through that example and how I value them myself I can help him understand their importance in my life.

Questions to Ponder: When did you get baptized? Do you remember making that choice? How did you come to make that decision? How can you teach and show your children that you value spiritual things?

Daily Challenge: Talk with someone - a friend or family member - about your faith, about the gospel, the Holy Ghost, or a recent spiritual experience. Practice having these discussions so that if someone struggling with their faith, or who is not a member of our faith, comes to you with questions, you'll feel more comfortable chatting with them about it.

He Stirreth Up The Hearts Of Men

> 3 Nephi 11:29-30 - 29 For verily, verily I say unto you, he that hath the spirit of contention is not of me, but is of the devil, who is the father of contention, and he stirreth up the hearts of men to contend with anger, one with another.

> 30 Behold, this is not my doctrine, to stir up the hearts of men with anger, one against another; but this is my doctrine, that such things should be done away.

Only recently did I receive the insight that the principle that "all good things come from God, and all bad things come from the devil" (I'm paraphrasing) also includes the good and evil thoughts that we have. Our desires, our motives, our internal things, not just the external things in this world. It changed something for me. I realized that any time I spent focused on negative thoughts - stress, anxiety, frustration, bitterness, anger - was time that I was not able to feel the Holy Ghost. It's like I was throwing a negative thought rave in my head and the music and the darkness was too much for the still, quiet voice of the Spirit to cut through.

In order for us to progress, we need to not only make great choices when it comes to our actions, the "fruits" by which we will be judged, but also when it comes to our thoughts and what we choose to focus on. If we have negative thoughts or are letting them dominate our minds, that's Satan stirring up our hearts. This is not the Lord's doctrine, but "that such things should be done away."

Questions to Ponder: How much of your day is consumed with negative thoughts or emotions? How often do you focus on the problems rather than listening for the solution? How can you nurture the Lord's doctrine, rather than allowing yourself to be stirred up with anger or other negative persuasions?

Daily Challenge: Commit to a day of positivity. Focus only on the good, the solutions, the blessings, the friendships and relationships, the good news of the gospel. See how your day changes when you leave no room in your day for any negativity whatsoever.

This Is My Doctrine

3 Nephi 11:31-41 - 31 Behold, verily, verily, I say unto you, I will declare unto you my doctrine.

32 And this is my doctrine, and it is the doctrine which the Father hath given unto me; and I bear record of the Father, and the Father beareth record of me, and the Holy Ghost beareth record of the Father and me; and I bear record that the Father commandeth all men, everywhere, to repent and believe in me.

33 And whoso believeth in me, and is baptized, the same shall be saved; and they are they who shall inherit the kingdom of God.

34 And whoso believeth not in me, and is not baptized, shall be damned.

35 Verily, verily, I say unto you, that this is my doctrine, and I bear record of it from the Father; and whoso believeth in me believeth in the Father also; and unto him will the Father bear record of me, for he will visit him with fire and with the Holy Ghost.

36 And thus will the Father bear record of me, and the Holy Ghost will bear record unto him of the Father and me; for the Father, and I, and the Holy Ghost are one.

37 And again I say unto you, ye must repent, and become as a little child, and be baptized in my name, or ye can in nowise receive these things.

38 And again I say unto you, ye must repent, and be baptized in my name, and become as a little child, or ye can in nowise inherit the kingdom of God.

39 Verily, verily, I say unto you, that this is my doctrine, and whoso buildeth upon this buildeth upon my rock, and the gates of hell shall not prevail against them.

> *40 And whoso shall declare more or less than this, and establish it for my doctrine, the same cometh of evil, and is not built upon my rock; but he buildeth upon a sandy foundation, and the gates of hell stand open to receive such when the floods come and the winds beat upon them.*

> *41 Therefore, go forth unto this people, and declare the words which I have spoken, unto the ends of the earth.*

The thought that comes to mind when I read these verses is from my work as a film producer and screenwriter. One thing that happens in many movies is that the opening scene provides a microcosm, or a foreshadowing of the movie you're about to see. Take the movie Moana:

In the opening sequence you have most of the main characters introduced - Moana, her people, her grandmother - and an explanation of the challenges that lie ahead for them to get what they want. If you try hard enough you can work out most of the story you're about to watch. The fun, then, isn't in watching the story you know is going to take place, but seeing how these characters deal with the situations they get themselves into, and the unexpected ways the storytellers deliver on the promise they set up in the opening scenes.

Back to these verses. Christ is starting at the beginning. "This is my gospel..." and lays out the story. Belief. Humility. Repentance. Baptism. The Godhead. Prophets. Truth. Revelation...

The specifics aren't laid out for us, because that would be so boring, like a movie where you can anticipate what a character is going to say before they even say it. I remember watching one of *The Fast And The Furious* movies (don't ask why I was doing this...) and Dwayne "The Rock" Johnson is in some hospital room when things are really hitting the fan. His arm is in a cast. He gets up, heroically, and I knew, I just knew he was about to flex-bust out of his cast and run to save the day with the rest of the team. Mere seconds later, it transpired exactly how I expected. Now, I wanted that to happen, but that's not the point. It was fairly lazy writing.

I digress.

The Lord through His prophets and through the scriptures gives us the beginning of the story, the foundation, the "cinematic world" we're going to be living in here on earth. It's up to us to write the story, the scenes, the dialog. We make the choices, the decisions, on who to follow, what to believe, how to act, whether to be obedient and faith-

DAILY MORMON

ful. It's those decisions that not only reveal who we are, but also the path that we walk here on earth.

Part of me often wishes that there were more specifics. I'd love to know what I'm going to be doing 5 years from now, if I'll ever actually make a movie, if my kids are going to grow up and be healthy, faithful, serve missions, what they'll do with their lives. But that would be just as big a let down as lazy movie writing. Which I despise.

As hard as life is, we can always go back to the foundations of the gospel, and do a "page-one rewrite" any time we want. That's repentance. We can reset, change, and start over.

When we get off track, we can go back to the things that we know - God lives, His son came to earth to suffer and die on our behalf, and that the Holy Ghost provides guidance and comfort and helps us as we strive to be obedient and faithful.

When we don't know what to do, we can rely on our faith and our belief. We can humbly pray and listen and be led to righteous choices and decisions that help us get to the desired ending we are all hoping for.

The same way we want The Rock to heroically save the rest of the Fast and Furious family from whatever crazy individual is trying to mess up the world, or from some imaginary volcano monster trying to destroy all the islands of the sea. You know, because The Rock was the voice of Maui in the movie Moana. That dude can do pretty much anything. #fullcircle

Questions to Ponder: What parts of the doctrine give you the most comfort? What do you rely on when times get hard, when things aren't going your way, when external pressures are increasingly too hard to bear?

Daily Challenge: Reread these verses. What principles of the gospel can you spend more time studying to get a deeper understanding? Turn to that principle in the Bible Dictionary or Topical Guide, and start there. See what you can learn.

Give Heed Unto The Words Of These Twelve Whom I Have Chosen

> *3 Nephi 12:1 - ...Blessed are ye if ye shall give heed unto the words of these twelve whom I have chosen from among you to minister unto you, and to be your servants; and unto them I have given power that they may baptize you with water; and after that ye are baptized with water, behold, I will baptize you with fire and with the Holy Ghost; therefore blessed are ye if ye shall believe in me and be baptized, after that ye have seen me and know that I am.*

This verse feels especially poignant as I write it in early 2018. We're coming out of a few years of statements and policy changes made by the twelve that have rocked the world and a decent percentage of the Church membership, from what I've heard and seen. I have friends who used these moments to leave the Church, some to even abandon their faith in Christ and the gospel altogether.

So, the question is, at what point do we stop giving heed to the words of the twelve, at what point do we stop believing in Christ, if what they say is different than what we believe or feel is right? Are the twelve capable of making mistakes? Is God? How long are we expected to continue on if we feel this way? What should we do in these situations instead?

I pose all of these questions because they are questions I've asked myself over the last two years. Does that make me unfaithful? I hope not. I hope it makes me humble.

I think that confronting hard questions is an essential part of our faith, and required for growth. Blind obedience only takes us so far because we're not actually making choices, but rather continually making a single choice, to follow God. Now, I just don't think it's that realistic for most people. At least not for me.

We all have doubts at different times. We all have different things that will set off the alarm, so to speak, and cause us to question things that we thought we knew. It's better to know that this type of scenario is a possibility in all of our lives, so better to prepare for it now, and anticipate how we are going to deal with it, rather than wait until it happens and try and overcome these hard questions in the moment of doubt.

I can safely say that I still have a testimony, in both the leadership of the Church and in God and Christ. Why? Because God does not make mistakes. Sure, we do. Even the prophets and the apostles. They are human, after all, prone to the same biases, temptations, and paradigms that we all are prone to. What I hope makes them different is their willingness to humbly go to the Lord in prayer and ask for guidance on our behalf, and then to act on those answers, whether they align with their personal inclinations or not. That's the lesson and the takeaway for us. "Blessed are ye if ye believe in me...after that ye have seen me and know that I am." Important words whether we're a witness, or a special witness, of our Savior, Jesus Christ.

Questions to Ponder: What do YOU do when you have doubts? Where do you turn? What is your process? How have you dealt with doubts successfully in the past?

Daily Challenge: Ponder these questions and this scripture today. Ask the Lord for help, and strengthen your relationship with the Spirit in some way today, so that when the next doubt arises, you'll be more prepared to listen and have your heart softened by the comforter, and to be able to hear and heed the counsel you receive.

More Blessed Are They

> 3 Nephi 12:2 - And again, more blessed are they who shall believe in your words because that ye shall testify that ye have seen me, and that ye know that I am. Yea, blessed are they who shall believe in your words, and come down into the depths of humility and be baptized, for they shall be visited with fire and with the Holy Ghost, and shall receive a remission of their sins.

As we were studying Adam and Eve and Cain and Abel earlier in the year as part of the Old Testament curriculum, I was thinking how awesome it would be to be just barely removed from the Garden of Eden. I mean, obviously not as awesome as the garden, but still, it was, like, right over there. AND they got to hear the voice of the Lord all the time, AND they lived to like 800 or 900 years old!

Yet, the Lord teaches here, more blessed are they who shall believe in your words. He's talking to the twelve at this point, and says that the more removed we are from the Lord, the more blessed we are for our belief. The further away we get from the time that Christ walked the earth, the more faith it takes to believe in these stories that we read in the scriptures. The more we have to rely on the Holy Ghost for our testimony, rather than seeing the Lord heal someone with our own eyes, the more blessed we are because of that faith.

Faith is often hard, especially now that opposing voices are so prevalent and pervasive, sitting just in our pockets or our purses just a few taps away on our phones. It's a much harder time to be faithful.

I ran into a friend today at lunch (Hey Paul!) and we were talking about this very thing, how it seems like one of the most important times for faith is between 30 and 45, because for whatever reason there are many who fall away into inactivity, doubt, disbelief, and more during this time. It's a hard time, but we need to double down and recommit to the things we covenanted to at baptism and throughout our lives. As we do so, we're promised to have the Holy Ghost support and guide us.

DAILY MORMON 285

Questions to Ponder: Where is your faith weak? What daily actions can you take in order to strengthen it? Who can you rely on if things get hard? What scriptures can help you through those tough times?

Daily Challenge: Do one faith building thing today. Read this scripture today. Say a prayer. Study a favorite scripture. Pay your tithing. Go to church. Visit a family in the ward. Call a friend or family member. Do something today to strengthen your faith.

Great Shall Be Your Reward In Heaven

> *3 Nephi 12:3-12 - 3 Yea, blessed are the poor in spirit who come unto me, for theirs is the kingdom of heaven.*

> *4 And again, blessed are all they that mourn, for they shall be comforted.*

> *5 And blessed are the meek, for they shall inherit the earth.*

> *6 And blessed are all they who do hunger and thirst after righteousness, for they shall be filled with the Holy Ghost.*

> *7 And blessed are the merciful, for they shall obtain mercy.*

> *8 And blessed are all the pure in heart, for they shall see God.*

> *9 And blessed are all the peacemakers, for they shall be called the children of God.*

> *10 And blessed are all they who are persecuted for my name's sake, for theirs is the kingdom of heaven.*

> *11 And blessed are ye when men shall revile you and persecute, and shall say all manner of evil against you falsely, for my sake;*

> *12 For ye shall have great joy and be exceedingly glad, for great shall be your reward in heaven; for so persecuted they the prophets who were before you.*

Wherever your testimony is at, however deep or however new, I feel like these verses are just plain universal truths. I have atheist friends who still believe these words - maybe not in the person who said them, but still, these truths are just universal, eternal truths that resonate with everyone.

I think these verses work even without the "for they..." parts. We can all agree, I hope, that being humble, meek, merciful, and pure in heart are all admirable, desirable qualities to have. Yet, beyond that are these incredible blessings of, among other things, the kingdom of heaven! How incredibly awesome is that?!

My guess is that there are a number of us tonight that are mourning. It seems like there is a school shooting every month. There are friends of mine whose loved ones are sick and who are holding on to life. Family members going through divorce. Dear friends struggling with their testimonies and their faith. We are all struggling in some way, great or small. But, reading these verses, we're taught that we can have comfort. We can have peace. We can receive blessings, even in trying times.

For that to happen, we must put our faith in Christ, we must strive to humbly live the gospel to the fullest extent we can. The joy and comfort that come from the Spirit when we're striving this way is immense, and real, and tangible. These words from the Lord are so simple and straightforward, yet often so hard to live. I just hope we'll all work toward becoming more like Him, and that we'll all receive the blessings that we need tonight, tomorrow, and whenever we need them.

Questions to Ponder: Do you feel the comforting companionship of the Holy Ghost? What things cause that to happen? How can you do more to have his presence be more constant, to be felt more easily?

Daily Challenge: Pray today - for yourselves, for your friends, for those suffering and in mourning. I feel like the world could use a few extra prayers tonight...

Let Your Light So Shine

> 3 Nephi 12:14-16 - 14 Verily, verily, I say unto you, I give unto you to be the light of this people. A city that is set on a hill cannot be hid.

> 15 Behold, do men light a candle and put it under a bushel? Nay, but on a candlestick, and it giveth light to all that are in the house;

> 16 Therefore let your light so shine before this people, that they may see your good works and glorify your Father who is in heaven.

The topic of "light" is one I could spend years studying and still only scratch the surface. I love these verses because the blessing is for others this time, not just for us. If we let our light shine, it's to bless others, not ourselves. To be a light unto the people, so they can see our good works and glorify God.

There's a lot of focus in The Book of Mormon on how to become better, but this verse is strictly about enriching the lives of others. It's an important part of the gospel - to get our own lives right, and then to go out and bring that same joy and faith out into the world.

Questions to Ponder: What does being a light look like? What actions does it involve? How can you strive to be a light to those around you?

Daily Challenge: Smile extra today. Let your face light up when you see people. Let them see the light that's in you through the joy and happiness you bring into the world.

I Have Given You The Law

> *3 Nephi 12:17-20 - 17 Think not that I am come to destroy the law or the prophets. I am not come to destroy but to fulfil;*

> *18 For verily I say unto you, one jot nor one tittle hath not passed away from the law, but in me it hath all been fulfilled.*

> *19 And behold, I have given you the law and the commandments of my Father, that ye shall believe in me, and that ye shall repent of your sins, and come unto me with a broken heart and a contrite spirit. Behold, ye have the commandments before you, and the law is fulfilled.*

> *20 Therefore come unto me and be ye saved; for verily I say unto you, that except ye shall keep my commandments, which I have commanded you at this time, ye shall in no case enter into the kingdom of heaven.*

These laws that Christ is speaking about are eternal laws. One jot nor one tittle hath not passed away from the law. He's basically saying it's unchanged, same as it's always been.

So what happens when we are living our lives out of harmony with these laws? I think you can guess.

Because these laws are eternal, they are true. If we're living according to the laws, we are in alignment, we're good. When we don't, or when we break the laws, that's when things start getting out of whack.

The only way we'll ever progress is when we are living in harmony with these eternal laws set forth by God and reiterated by His prophets.

Questions to Ponder: What other spiritual laws can you think of? What other laws are mentioned in the scriptures?

Daily Challenge: Start in the Topical Guide or the Bible Dictionary, and head off on a scripture chase about laws. See where you end up and what you discover.

First Be Reconciled To Thy Brother

> *3 Nephi 12:21-26 - 21 Ye have heard that it hath been said by them of old time, and it is also written before you, that thou shalt not kill, and whosoever shall kill shall be in danger of the judgment of God;*

> *22 But I say unto you, that whosoever is angry with his brother shall be in danger of his judgment. And whosoever shall say to his brother, Raca, shall be in danger of the council; and whosoever shall say, Thou fool, shall be in danger of hell fire.*

> *23 Therefore, if ye shall come unto me, or shall desire to come unto me, and rememberest that thy brother hath aught against thee—*

> *24 Go thy way unto thy brother, and first be reconciled to thy brother, and then come unto me with full purpose of heart, and I will receive you.*

> *25 Agree with thine adversary quickly while thou art in the way with him, lest at any time he shall get thee, and thou shalt be cast into prison.*

> *26 Verily, verily, I say unto thee, thou shalt by no means come out thence until thou hast paid the uttermost senine. And while ye are in prison can ye pay even one senine? Verily, verily, I say unto you, Nay.*

Some strong words from the Savior about anger and how we deal with others. I hadn't really given this topic a ton of thought, until we moved into our current ward, and in the first year we had two or three separate lessons about anger. Two on our relationships with our spouses, and one specifically geared toward the men in the ward about dealing with anger before it turns into something worse like physical action or emotional abuse.

I came to find out that anger is often linked to shame, and that men especially deal with shame in one of two ways - checking out or lashing out. I've seen it in my own life, though on a smaller scale. If I had an unproductive day at work, I'd come home and be short or impatient with my kids, who were only guilty of being excited that I was finally home. Other times I'd check out completely and turn on a podcast, go mow the lawn, or do something else that would separate me from them. It wasn't out of anger, it was out of shame, feeling that I wasn't a better provider or wasn't doing more for them. It has been a hard issue to deal with and overcome.

Self awareness is a place to start. Being able to admit that we have some shame takes a ton of vulnerability, and many of us have been raised in a way that looks down on men (and women) being vulnerable.

The Lord says that it's important for us to deal with our anger and our other issues. "First be reconciled unto thy brother" is the principle. We have to repent and make amends and take care of our mistakes and our shortcomings before going to the Lord. He then likens it to being in prison, which is absolutely what it feels like. Being trapped, having limited options available to you... it's a terrible place to be stuck.

Live a life of kindness, honesty, and forgiveness. Look to the Lord as an example and strive to treat others as He did, and find the blessings and the rewards that follow.

Questions to Ponder: Where in your life is there anger, or vengefulness, or any other negative emotion? How can it be dealt with? What would the Savior have you do if He were counseling you? What steps can you take today to make it right, as vulnerable and ashamed as it might make you feel?

Daily Challenge: Do one thing today to either work on a weakness, or make amends for weakness in the past.

I Give Unto You A Commandment

> 3 Nephi 12:27-30 - 27 Behold, it is written by them of old time, that thou shalt not commit adultery;

> 28 But I say unto you, that whosoever looketh on a woman, to lust after her, hath committed adultery already in his heart.

> 29 Behold, I give unto you a commandment, that ye suffer none of these things to enter into your heart;

> 30 For it is better that ye should deny yourselves of these things, wherein ye will take up your cross, than that ye should be cast into hell.

I read verses like this and it makes me wonder what life was like back around the time of Christ. For this, specifically, like, how big a problem was this that He brought it up so often? I don't hear modern prophets talking about adultery over the pulpit every General Conference...

Point being, we should look at these verses from the Lord and not only learn the law that He's teaching, but also try to infer the underlying principles and figure out how to apply them to our lives.

Questions to Ponder: Why is lust something the Lord would warn against? What do we lust after besides the opposite sex? How does lust impede our progress in becoming more like Christ?

Daily Challenge: Think of ways to avoid lustful thoughts, and commit to a day of pure thoughts for any of the things you lust after, promising to not entertain those thoughts.

Old Things Are Done Away

3 Nephi 12:31-48 - 31 It hath been written, that whosoever shall put away his wife, let him give her a writing of divorcement.

32 Verily, verily, I say unto you, that whosoever shall put away his wife, saving for the cause of fornication, causeth her to commit adultery; and whoso shall marry her who is divorced committeth adultery.

33 And again it is written, thou shalt not forswear thyself, but shalt perform unto the Lord thine oaths;

34 But verily, verily, I say unto you, swear not at all; neither by heaven, for it is God's throne;

35 Nor by the earth, for it is his footstool;

36 Neither shalt thou swear by thy head, because thou canst not make one hair black or white;

37 But let your communication be Yea, yea; Nay, nay; for whatsoever cometh of more than these is evil.

38 And behold, it is written, an eye for an eye, and a tooth for a tooth;

39 But I say unto you, that ye shall not resist evil, but whosoever shall smite thee on thy right cheek, turn to him the other also;

40 And if any man will sue thee at the law and take away thy coat, let him have thy cloak also;

41 And whosoever shall compel thee to go a mile, go with him twain.

42 Give to him that asketh thee, and from him that would borrow of thee turn thou not away.

43 And behold it is written also, that thou shalt love thy neighbor and hate thine enemy;

44 But behold I say unto you, love your enemies, bless them that curse you, do good to them that hate you, and pray for them who despitefully use you and persecute you;

> 45 That ye may be the children of your Father who is in heaven; for he maketh his sun to rise on the evil and on the good.

> 46 Therefore those things which were of old time, which were under the law, in me are all fulfilled.

> 47 Old things are done away, and all things have become new.

> 48 Therefore I would that ye should be perfect even as I, or your Father who is in heaven is perfect.

It's a pretty amazing sermon He lays out here. Divorce, oaths, retribution, humility, charity and love. What do they all have in common? That in the Lord all of these old things are done away. He came and fulfilled the law of Moses, and gave people the gospel of Christ.

What is the principle we need to take away from this? For me it's that we believe in modern revelation through prophets. There are things that will change. There will be new procedures and policies. We will be called to repentance, given commandments, and expectations to act upon. What are we going to do when that happens?

Questions to Ponder: When was the last trial of your faith? What was it? How did you handle it? What was the result? What did you learn from it?

Daily Challenge: Take some time to think about this scenario. How will you act if something hard happened that shook your faith and made you doubt? What would you do? Play it out and think about how the Lord would hope you would respond in that situation.

Thou Shalt Not Do As The Hypocrites

> 3 Nephi 13:1-8 - 1 Verily, verily, I say that I would that ye should do alms unto the poor; but take heed that ye do not your alms before men to be seen of them; otherwise ye have no reward of your Father who is in heaven.

> 2 Therefore, when ye shall do your alms do not sound a trumpet before you, as will hypocrites do in the synagogues and in the streets, that they may have glory of men. Verily I say unto you, they have their reward.

> 3 But when thou doest alms let not thy left hand know what thy right hand doeth;

> 4 That thine alms may be in secret; and thy Father who seeth in secret, himself shall reward thee openly.

> 5 And when thou prayest thou shalt not do as the hypocrites, for they love to pray, standing in the synagogues and in the corners of the streets, that they may be seen of men. Verily I say unto you, they have their reward.

> 6 But thou, when thou prayest, enter into thy closet, and when thou hast shut thy door, pray to thy Father who is in secret; and thy Father, who seeth in secret, shall reward thee openly.

> 7 But when ye pray, use not vain repetitions, as the heathen, for they think that they shall be heard for their much speaking.

> 8 Be not ye therefore like unto them, for your Father knoweth what things ye have need of before ye ask him.

The principle in these verses can be applied to so many things, not just to alms - money or food given to the poor - or prayer. The principle speaks to our intention, our desires. Are we making the choices we make to be seen of men?

Why do we go to church? Why do we study the scriptures? Why do we pay our tithing, do our ministering, accept callings, and live the Word of Wisdom?

The principle teaches that we need to have personal reasons for practicing the gospel that go deeper than the surface level of being seen of men. It's hard, certainly, but through the process of discovering our "why" for these different things, we are blessed with the things that our "Father knoweth...we have need of before [we] ask him. "

Questions to Ponder: If you were to go over the different practices you have in the gospel, how many would have an external motivation (to be seen of men, for example) and how many have an internal motivation? What can you do to internalize those that you're doing for other reasons?

Daily Challenge: Pray for help with anything that you don't have a strong internal testimony of or a strong internal motivation for. Ask the Lord for help that as you practice with faith that He'll bless you with the testimony you're seeking.

Forgive Men Their Trespasses

> *3 Nephi 13:14-15 - 14 For, if ye forgive men their trespasses your heavenly Father will also forgive you;*

> *15 But if ye forgive not men their trespasses neither will your Father forgive your trespasses.*

Do you think this applies to driving on the freeway? Even when some huge, lifted truck cuts us off when our young kids are in the back seat?

Yeah?

Dang. Well, I've failed at this one then. Like, today...

We don't often talk about this principle, this concept of having to live both sides of the law. You have to forgive in order to be forgiven. It makes sense - we wouldn't want to be hypocritical about it. But how often do we think about this?

Recently I've heard a number of stories from friends, from members in the ward, and from people who are no longer active - stories about how hard it is to be a member of the Church sometimes. The main reason? Other members of the Church.

Honestly, at first, I had a hard time believing them, because I just hadn't experienced it myself. But like anything, that shouldn't negate or lessen their experience. So, I inquired. I asked them to share their stories and their feelings.

The main thing I heard was how women especially - but men also - held some standard in their minds about what a "good mormon" looks like, dresses like, talks like, and acts like, and then felt that it was perfectly okay to judge and speak badly about those that didn't live up to that standard.

I call B.S.

Where in the scriptures is that principle taught? Yeah, didn't think so. Quite the opposite actually, but we'll get to that in 3 Nephi 14. But isn't that the same principle? If you don't want people to judge you, then don't judge them! If you don't want people to talk behind your back, don't do it about them! None of us are perfect, and there is NO such thing as a singular description of what a Mormon looks, dresses, talks, OR acts like.

I realize now I'm up on a soap box, and that wasn't my intention. But wow, the stories I heard made me incredibly sad. Our calling as members and disciples of Christ is to help bring people closer to Him, not to turn them away with our judgements and our unwillingness to forgive. That's what I believe the principle teaches. So, I'd ask that if you see it happen around you, call it out, explain that it's not Christlike to talk about others that way or to exclude others, and strive to act with charity and love for everyone you come in contact with, especially other members of the Church.

Questions to Ponder: What other ways does hypocrisy creep into the culture of the church or in your own life? What is your responsibility when you see it? How do you help change it?

Daily Challenge: Think about someone that may have been or felt excluded or ostracized, and reach out to them. Welcome them in, show them a better example than what they've seen in the past, and help bring the light of Christ to them.

But Unto Thy Father

> *3 Nephi 13:16-18 - 16 Moreover, when ye fast be not as the hypocrites, of a sad countenance, for they disfigure their faces that they may appear unto men to fast. Verily I say unto you, they have their reward.*

> *17 But thou, when thou fastest, anoint thy head, and wash thy face;*

> *18 That thou appear not unto men to fast, but unto thy Father, who is in secret; and thy Father, who seeth in secret, shall reward thee openly.*

The topic comes up again and again. So today, just a bunch of questions:

Questions to Ponder: We covered a similar topic just a few days ago. Why do you think Christ would bring up the concept of hypocrisy twice in one sermon? What types of hypocrisy plague the Church and the world today? What does hypocrisy look like in your life? And what is the solution that Christ dictates in the scriptures?

Daily Challenge: Do something "in secret" today. Pay tithing or send in a fast offering, serve someone without recognition, pray for someone, anything you can. See how it feels to serve, and think back to why our Heavenly Father wants us to do things that way, rather than to be seen of men.

Treasures In Heaven

> *3 Nephi 13:19-21 - 19 Lay not up for yourselves treasures upon earth, where moth and rust doth corrupt, and thieves break through and steal;*

> *20 But lay up for yourselves treasures in heaven, where neither moth nor rust doth corrupt, and where thieves do not break through nor steal.*

> *21 For where your treasure is, there will your heart be also.*

I was just reading through my lesson for this Sunday before turning to this chapter, and the topics are very similar. The lesson is on being in the world and not of the world, about choosing God and heavenly things over worldly things.

It comes down to a matter of priorities. What do we value? If we don't know, we can look at our actions. How we spend our time, the things we choose to do, the people we interact with and the content we consume all point to what we value.

I've always struggled a bit with the idea of being 100% righteous 100% of the time. Partly because it seems impossible, but also because I think part of my brain saw it as boring. Yet, the older I get, and the more I study, and the more spiritual experiences I have, the more I realize that the heavenly treasures are much greater than the worldly ones, no matter how appealing they are in the moment.

It reminds me of the Pepsi Challenge. (Go with me here...)

Back in 1975 Pepsi created a blind taste test where a representative from PepsiCo would set up a table and invite a passerby to take a sip of Pepsi and their big competitor Coca-Cola to see which they preferred. The customer didn't know which was which, but overwhelmingly people chose Pepsi over Coke.

Decades later, however, the author Malcolm Gladwell in his book Blink presented evidence that suggests Pepsi's success over Coca-Cola in the challenge was a result of the flawed nature of the "sip test" method. His research showed that tasters will generally prefer the sweeter of two beverages based on a single sip, even if they prefer a less sweet beverage over the course of an entire can.

That's right. People preferred a sip of the sweeter Pepsi, but found it too sweet when consuming an entire can. Now, I'm by no means saying that the Gospel is like a can of Coke, but what I am saying is that our human nature is perfectly encapsulated by this flawed test. Satan would have us believe that we will like the worldly things, the treasures of earth, but if we go too far down that path we'll ultimately find it to be an unsatisfying way to live our lives.

The real reward comes as we seek after and lay up for ourselves treasures in heaven.

Questions to Ponder: What are some modern day worldly or earthly treasures? Which ones are you most tempted by? How do you reframe those things to be undesirable and learn to seek after heavenly treasures?

Daily Challenge: Talk with a spouse or friend or loved one about this topic. See how they deal with life's temptations. Share with them how you deal, and try and strengthen one another.

Thy Whole Body Shall Be Full Of Light

> *3 Nephi 13:22-24 - 22 The light of the body is the eye; if, therefore, thine eye be single, thy whole body shall be full of light.*

> *23 But if thine eye be evil, thy whole body shall be full of darkness. If, therefore, the light that is in thee be darkness, how great is that darkness!*

> *24 No man can serve two masters; for either he will hate the one and love the other, or else he will hold to the one and despise the other. Ye cannot serve God and Mammon.*

We talked about laying up treasures in heaven, and the next verses from our Savior go deeper on that thought. By having a singular focus, an eye single to the glory of God, we're promised the blessing of having our whole body full of light.

What does that look like? What does it feel like? Is it something we want?

These are the kinds of questions I was asking myself before I started working on this book. Do we really believe the things The Book of Mormon says? The things that Christ told His disciples, and us? Having our whole body be full of light sounds pretty incredible. I know what a singular, intense spiritual experience feels like, as I've had a few, but what about this? Is it different? Does it last longer?

If we believe it's possible, if we believe that it's worth pursuing, why is it so hard to align our actions with those desires and beliefs? Is that what sets us apart? Our actions? What else do we have to go on?

When I read these verses again tonight, all of the questions came rushing back. How do YOU feel about these verses? Have you ever felt like your whole body was filled with light?

Questions to Ponder: This whole chapter was a series of questions!

Daily Challenge: Take one of the questions from this chapter, any that stood out to you, and ponder it today. Seek answers through study and prayer, and see what comes to you through the power of the Holy Ghost.

❖ ❖ ❖

Therefore Take No Thought

> 3 Nephi 13:25-34 - 25 And now it came to pass that when Jesus had spoken these words he looked upon the twelve whom he had chosen, and said unto them: Remember the words which I have spoken. For behold, ye are they whom I have chosen to minister unto this people. Therefore I say unto you, take no thought for your life, what ye shall eat, or what ye shall drink; nor yet for your body, what ye shall put on. Is not the life more than meat, and the body than raiment?

> 26 Behold the fowls of the air, for they sow not, neither do they reap nor gather into barns; yet your heavenly Father feedeth them. Are ye not much better than they?

> 27 Which of you by taking thought can add one cubit unto his stature?

> 28 And why take ye thought for raiment? Consider the lilies of the field how they grow; they toil not, neither do they spin;

> 29 And yet I say unto you, that even Solomon, in all his glory, was not arrayed like one of these.

> 30 Wherefore, if God so clothe the grass of the field, which today is, and tomorrow is cast into the oven, even so will he clothe you, if ye are not of little faith.

> 31 Therefore take no thought, saying, What shall we eat? or, What shall we drink? or, Wherewithal shall we be clothed?

> 32 For your heavenly Father knoweth that ye have need of all these things.

> 33 But seek ye first the kingdom of God and his righteousness, and all these things shall be added unto you.

> 34 Take therefore no thought for the morrow, for the morrow shall take thought for the things of itself. Sufficient is the day unto the evil thereof.

Can we take these words of counsel from the Lord to his apostles and apply them to our lives? I think we can, as we have been called in a similar fashion. All of the blessings promised to his disciples are available for us as well, but requires the same responsibility - to act in faith before those blessings reveal themselves.

So often the blessings of the gospel are so distant and disconnected from our daily lives that it becomes hard to act in faith. But that's the whole point of faith. Faith is the gap between what we know and what we're trying to know. That's why Christ says to take no thought about what we shall eat or drink or how we will clothe ourselves. If we act in faith, the promise is that he'll take care of the things we need. That's a pretty incredible promise.

How many of us in the last year have wondered how we're going to pay our bills due to an unexpected expense or circumstance? How many have wondered how we will find time to spend with our kids, our calling, our spouses, and still have time for the Lord? We all ask these questions throughout our lives, and the only answer is to act in faith, focusing on the things that matter most, and trust that God will handle the rest.

Questions to Ponder: What were your favorite verses from 3 Nephi 13? What stood out as something you hadn't thought about before? How can you act with more faith in your daily life?

Daily Challenge: Reread 3 Nephi 13 and see what stands out to you. Focus on that verse and do some extra study - look at the footnotes or find a talk that references that verse.

Judge Not, That Ye Be Not Judged

> *3 Nephi 14:1-5 - 1 ...Verily, verily, I say unto you, Judge not, that ye be not judged.*

> *2 For with what judgment ye judge, ye shall be judged; and with what measure ye mete, it shall be measured to you again.*

> *3 And why beholdest thou the mote that is in thy brother's eye, but considerest not the beam that is in thine own eye?*

> *4 Or how wilt thou say to thy brother: Let me pull the mote out of thine eye—and behold, a beam is in thine own eye?*

> *5 Thou hypocrite, first cast the beam out of thine own eye; and then shalt thou see clearly to cast the mote out of thy brother's eye.*

We talked about this recently, about how devastating judging others can be, both to the "judger" and the "judgee." It's one of the worst aspects of our church culture, in my opinion, that there are those that judge rather than act with charity, especially when we're all just doing our best to live the gospel and strive to become more like our Savior.

It's a bit comforting to know that the problem isn't just limited to us today, but has been around since, well, forever I guess. Look back at Cain and Abel.

What would the Church be like if those that are inactive didn't have to fear any judgement upon coming back to church? If instead they were welcomed with loving arms by those who have missed their presence?

How many more people would see the light of Christ in us and our homes if we treated them with charity and love?

If we all made a concerted effort to stem the tide of judgement and gossip in our wards and our homes, the world would be better for it.

Questions to Ponder: Is judgement or gossip something you see in your ward or your social circles? What can you do to stop it? How can you show a better example? Why is judgement such a pernicious and terrible thing? What makes it so effective in hurting others?

Daily Challenge: Take a stand against judgement and gossip if you come across it. Call it out for what it is, and help those that are participating understand how hurtful it is and encourage them to change and be more careful in the future.

That Which Is Holy

> *3 Nephi 14:6 - Give not that which is holy unto the dogs, neither cast ye your pearls before swine, lest they trample them under their feet, and turn again and rend you.*

In these first verses of chapter 14 the Savior is teaching us about certain righteous behaviors. In verses 1 & 2: judging righteously. Verses 3-5: focusing on our own faults instead of the faults of others. Here in verse 6 He teaches about showing respect for things that are sacred.

"That which is holy" could be anything from answers to prayers, the ordinances of the temple, a priesthood blessing or sacred experience.

We can look to the Doctrine and Covenants for a little more context as well. D&C 63:64 says:

> *Remember that that which cometh from above is sacred, and must be spoken with care, and by constraint of the Spirit; and in this there is no condemnation, and ye receive the Spirit through prayer; wherefore, without this there remaineth condemnation.*

Sacred things are things that come from God and the Holy Ghost. We're counseled to treat them as sacred, which I believe comes down to trust. If the Lord is going to bless you with guidance or revelation and you go blab about it to someone, I wonder how it makes Him feel. Can you be trusted with sacred things? Will you do it again the next time?

It's important for us to keep these things in the proper perspective and treat them accordingly.

Questions to Ponder: What danger is there in talking about sacred experiences with people who cannot - or will not - understand them? Why is it important to keep things sacred? Why is it important that the Lord is able to trust you with sacred things?

Daily Challenge: The next time you're tempted to talk about a sacred thing with someone who may not be able to understand or be edified by it, maybe hold back. Consider the motivation for sharing, and if it's to show off or to be "seen of men," it may not be the best motivation to share such things.

Everyone That Asketh, Receiveth

> *3 Nephi 14:7-12 - 7 Ask, and it shall be given unto you; seek, and ye shall find; knock, and it shall be opened unto you.*

> *8 For every one that asketh, receiveth; and he that seeketh, findeth; and to him that knocketh, it shall be opened.*

> *9 Or what man is there of you, who, if his son ask bread, will give him a stone?*

> *10 Or if he ask a fish, will he give him a serpent?*

> *11 If ye then, being evil, know how to give good gifts unto your children, how much more shall your Father who is in heaven give good things to them that ask him?*

> *12 Therefore, all things whatsoever ye would that men should do to you, do ye even so to them, for this is the law and the prophets.*

This may be one of the most important principles in The Book of Mormon: Ask and it shall be given unto you.

In these few short verses, there are no qualifications, no caveats, not exceptions. *Every one that asketh, receiveth*. Now, we know that you need to have faith and that the things you're asking for need to be "good" things.

Give yourself a minute to think about what this means. What would you do if *anything* were possible? If you could be given anything you ask for, find anything you seek?

Yes, I'm taking these verses *extremely* literally. But what other way is there?

Just imagine, for one minute, that these verses were meant to be taken extremely literally. What would you ask for? What would you do? How would your life be different if you had this incredible power given to you?

I fully believe that this principle is meant to be taken literally. I believe that God wants to give us as much as He possibly can. You know how I know? Because when I go shopping with my kids I have zero ability to say no to them when they ask for a snack. It's just not possible. Ask my wife, she love-hates that about me.

Think of the things that we read about in The Book of Mormon. Visitation by angels. Seeing God. If these things are possible, surely the things that we seek are possible as well, right?

What about finding a job that pays our bills and helps us save for the future? What about the help that we need to raise our children to be good people? What about creating work that benefits others and makes the world a better place?

What is it that you hope for? When you're driving to work, or are up late at night stirring because this idea, this dream won't let you fall asleep? What is it?

Do you believe that you can ask God for help? Do you believe that He will hear you and answer your prayers? Do you believe that that thing is possible?

I also know that He doesn't just give us things because we want them. God blesses those that are acting in faith, working toward that thing that they want. It really is as simple as focusing on something you want, asking God for help achieving that thing, and then taking a step in that direction, acting in faith, working toward that goal?

What might happen if you do this?

Questions to Ponder: What do you want? What can you do today as an act of faith? Can God help you achieve it?

Daily Challenge: Spend some time thinking about these questions today, and test it out. Try it on one thing for the next few weeks and see what happens.

Strait Is The Gate, And Narrow Is The Way

> 3 Nephi 14:13-14 - 13 Enter ye in at the strait gate; for wide is the gate, and broad is the way, which leadeth to destruction, and many there be who go in thereat;

> 14 Because strait is the gate, and narrow is the way, which leadeth unto life, and few there be that find it.

After all of that talk last chapter about how God has made it as simple as possible for us to be saved and given eternal life, it's followed by this principle: that despite all of that, the way is still narrow, and the gate is still strait. Now, that doesn't mean it's not possible. In fact, it's much more specific than the alternative. It's easier to understand the path one must take to enter into that gate, *because* it is so strait and narrow.

The reason many will be led to destruction is because of lack of effort. It's hard, some will say. Or, I can just wander over here a bit and I'll catch up with you guys later.

That's not how it works.

Like the rod of iron in Lehi's dream, we must cling to it, hold fast. We have to live our most obedient and disciplined life. But that discipline and obedience ultimately leads to freedom and *eternal* life. That can't be said for the lazy approach "which leadeth to destruction."

Something I tell my creative friends all the time is that the thing that sets apart a professional creative from an amateur is that professionals do the work. They understand that it's the day in, day out process that ultimately gets them where they want to go. Not some viral fluke. It's writing 1,000 words a day, doing a sketch daily, taking and posting a picture online. It's mastering your craft, not hoping for a miracle.

The gospel is the same way. It's not some miraculous event that will save you in the end, it's your works, your fruits. It's your daily choices and actions that determine your outcome.

It's absolutely possible for us to conquer the natural man and become masters of our discipleship.

Questions to Ponder: What are the daily actions that you need to do in order to stay on the strait and narrow path? What habits or actions should you avoid?

Daily Challenge: Do something today that puts you or keeps you on the strait and narrow. Focus on making the right, sometimes hard choices, rather than taking an easy way out.

By Their Fruits Ye Shall Know Them

> 3 Nephi 14:15-20 - 15 Beware of false prophets, who come to you in sheep's clothing, but inwardly they are ravening wolves.

> 16 Ye shall know them by their fruits. Do men gather grapes of thorns, or figs of thistles?

> 17 Even so every good tree bringeth forth good fruit; but a corrupt tree bringeth forth evil fruit.

> 18 A good tree cannot bring forth evil fruit, neither a corrupt tree bring forth good fruit.

> 19 Every tree that bringeth not forth good fruit is hewn down, and cast into the fire.

> 20 Wherefore, by their fruits ye shall know them.

The obvious takeaway here is the literal one: to judge prophets by their fruits, by the good or bad things that they do. But I think the more important takeaway is a personal one. What do our "fruits" - our actions, our choices, our decisions - say about us? If someone were to judge us by our fruits, what would they see?

Would they see a disciple of Christ? A Latter-day Saint? An honest, honorable person?

What do we want people to see? Is that outward persona just a façade, or is it true to who we really are?

The verse that rings true - and to be honest, kind of stings a little - is verse 18. "A good tree cannot bring forth evil fruit, neither a corrupt tree bring forth good fruit." When that time for judgement comes, there's no hiding. We are who we are, not who we claimed or pretended to be. If we feel like we're just going through the motions, it may be time to have a personal "come to Jesus" moment, to get real, to assess our choices, our lives, the direction we're headed, what we want, why we want it, and what it's all for.

This isn't something that takes 15 minutes one day. This is a process of becoming better and understanding why we want to in the first place.

How well do we know ourselves? If we look at our "fruits", is that the person we want to be?

Questions to Ponder: Again, apologies, this whole email today was a series of questions. Which one stood out to you? Which do you need to spend some time pondering?

Daily Challenge: Take some time to ask yourselves the hard questions. Read through the email and find the question that gives you the most discomfort, and let that discomfort be your compass. Start there, take the time you need to get answers, and let that guide you.

I Never Knew You

> *3 Nephi 14:21-27 - 21 Not every one that saith unto me, Lord, Lord, shall enter into the kingdom of heaven; but he that doeth the will of my Father who is in heaven.*

> *22 Many will say to me in that day: Lord, Lord, have we not prophesied in thy name, and in thy name have cast out devils, and in thy name done many wonderful works?*

> *23 And then will I profess unto them: I never knew you; depart from me, ye that work iniquity.*

> *24 Therefore, whoso heareth these sayings of mine and doeth them, I will liken him unto a wise man, who built his house upon a rock—*

> *25 And the rain descended, and the floods came, and the winds blew, and beat upon that house; and it fell not, for it was founded upon a rock.*

> *26 And every one that heareth these sayings of mine and doeth them not shall be likened unto a foolish man, who built his house upon the sand—*

> *27 And the rain descended, and the floods came, and the winds blew, and beat upon that house; and it fell, and great was the fall of it.*

Following up on yesterday's chapter, these verses contain the consequences for having our fruits and our desires out of alignment. If we say we want eternal life but our actions say otherwise, the Lord will judge us on our actions. We not only have to understand the gospel, but *live* the gospel.

To attend church every week but not live the gospel the other six days (i.e. to live the gospel constantly), is foolish. Why? Because it doesn't work. You'll never get the desired effect from a 15% effort.

To quote Jacob 6:12, "O be wise; what can I say more?"

Questions to Ponder: What are some things you do that could be considered foolish? How can you actively be more wise in how you live the gospel? What are the consequences of having your actions out of alignment with your desire for salvation and eternal life?

Daily Challenge: These are a few hard days of personalizing the Lord's words and applying them to our life, but it's the only way to grow and get better, just as a muscle needs resistance and to be broken down in order to grow. Take some time today to ponder these verses, see if the Holy Ghost reveals any aspects of your life that could use some attention.

Ye Have Heard The Things Which I Taught

> *3 Nephi 15:1 - ...Behold, ye have heard the things which I taught before I ascended to my Father; therefore, whoso remembereth these sayings of mine and doeth them, him will I raise up at the last day.*

A gentle and simple reminder for us who are reading (and writing) this book, those who are studying the words of Christ in The Book of Mormon.

First, we must hear and read the words. Second, remember them. And most importantly, do them. If all we ever do is read and learn the teachings of the Savior, yet it never translates into action or how we live our lives, how we treat others, or our perspective, then we're lost. The promise here in this verse doesn't apply to those that ignore His teachings. Worse, those of us that know the gospel and still chose not to live it will suffer even worse consequences.

We must remember the things we're taught but also apply those teachings to our lives in order to reap the blessings. It's as true a principle as any other in these chapters, and I'm grateful for it. It helps me to remember the importance of living the gospel, not just studying the gospel.

Questions to Ponder: What teachings of the savior over the last few days have resonated the most? Why do you think those verses stood out? How are you going to change your life as a response?

Daily Challenge: Do something Christlike today. Go out of your way to serve, show or tell someone you love them, be slower to anger. Find a way to live the gospel to its fullest.

I Am The Law And The Light. Look Unto Me...

> 3 Nephi 15:3-9 - 3 And he said unto them: Marvel not that I said unto you that old things had passed away, and that all things had become new.

> 4 Behold, I say unto you that the law is fulfilled that was given unto Moses.

> 5 Behold, I am he that gave the law, and I am he who covenanted with my people Israel; therefore, the law in me is fulfilled, for I have come to fulfil the law; therefore it hath an end.

> 6 Behold, I do not destroy the prophets, for as many as have not been fulfilled in me, verily I say unto you, shall all be fulfilled.

> 7 And because I said unto you that old things have passed away, I do not destroy that which hath been spoken concerning things which are to come.

> 8 For behold, the covenant which I have made with my people is not all fulfilled; but the law which was given unto Moses hath an end in me.

> 9 Behold, I am the law, and the light. Look unto me, and endure to the end, and ye shall live; for unto him that endureth to the end will I give eternal life.

As we're studying the Old Testament this year (2018) in Gospel Doctrine, this topic has a ton of meaning. The people that Moses led were wandering around in the desert for a long time in a fairly unstructured manner. No rules, no gospel, lots of sinning.

It makes sense that, coming out of that, they would need a lot of structure and many rules to help keep them in line. They needed much more direction. By the time Christ came to earth to teach the gospel it had then been long enough for Him to fulfill the law, to provide the ultimate sacrifice, and to do away with the old law and institute a new, higher law.

It was hard for those that clung more to the rules than the purpose for the rules, and I think the same thing can be said for us today. We can lose sight of the important parts of the gospel and get lost in the minutiae. Christ gave us the proper guidance: "Look unto me. I am the law and the light."

If we find ourselves getting frustrated over policy, or aggravated by others who aren't fully living up to our personal standard of the gospel, we're just as wrong as they are, just for different reasons. We never know the circumstances of others, but it is up to us to focus on Christ, which means to focus on charity and love and service, not on condemnation or judgement.

Questions to Ponder: Why is a focus on Christ important when trying to live the gospel? What should you do if you disagree with the way someone is acting, or certain policies in your wards, stakes, or the church at large?

Daily Challenge: If you or someone you know has struggled with this principle, find time to go to God in prayer and ask for guidance and comfort and for the Holy Ghost to soften hearts and minds. Lets all commit to focusing on Christ, not the trivialities that sometimes pop up in the culture of the church.

I Have Given Unto You The Commandments

> *3 Nephi 15:10-15 - 10 Behold, I have given unto you the commandments; therefore keep my commandments. And this is the law and the prophets, for they truly testified of me.*
>
> *11 And now it came to pass that when Jesus had spoken these words, he said unto those twelve whom he had chosen:*
>
> *12 Ye are my disciples; and ye are a light unto this people, who are a remnant of the house of Joseph.*
>
> *13 And behold, this is the land of your inheritance; and the Father hath given it unto you.*
>
> *14 And not at any time hath the Father given me commandment that I should tell it unto your brethren at Jerusalem.*
>
> *15 Neither at any time hath the Father given me commandment that I should tell unto them concerning the other tribes of the house of Israel, whom the Father hath led away out of the land.*

How often do we think about the commandments? Personally - not that much. I'm well past the age where I'm trying to figure out what commandments I want to keep and which ones I struggle with. (Anyone else have a rough time in their 20s?)

I feel like we all ultimately reach a point where we get what Christ is saying here: "I gave you commandments. So, keep them. It isn't that difficult."

Sure, we all slip and fall, and we each have our temptations and our vices. But when it comes down to it, it's not difficult. Either keep them or don't.

I like to read the rest of the verses as if He's speaking directly to me. "Ye are my disciple. [I need you to be] a light unto this people." Keeping the commandments is the foundation of being a disciple of Christ, and if we're truly striving to be one, we shouldn't have any problem with these simple rules.

If we're struggling with any of the commandments, it may help to reframe the commandments into something simple, like how we would teach our children. Don't touch the stove, it's hot. Don't break the commandments, it's bad for your eternal salvation...

I realize I come from a very privileged position as I write this. Yet, I still think that these principles are true because of how Christ Himself talked about them. I can see Him standing before us today saying, essentially, "Guys, it's not that hard. Come on."

Questions to Ponder: What makes certain commandments easier for you to keep than others? What do you do to avoid the temptations that lead you to those commandments?

Daily Challenge: Ponder the commandments. Imagine standing there as Christ gives this sermon to you, one of His disciples. How does it feel? What does the Spirit teach you as you ponder these things?

Other Sheep I Have

> *3 Nephi 15:16-17 - 16 This much did the Father command me, that I should tell unto them:*
>
> *17 That other sheep I have which are not of this fold; them also I must bring, and they shall hear my voice; and there shall be one fold, and one shepherd.*

I love the way verse 17 is phrased. They *shall* hear my voice. There *shall* be one shepherd. There is no chance here, no alternative outcomes. It's a singular plan with a singular purpose, reinforcing the eternal, unchanging nature of our Father in Heaven.

Every time I read verses like this it reminds me how perfect the plan of happiness is. It's not something that changes at the whims of a fickle God. It's something we were all present for when it was presented. We all understood the purpose. We understood our parts in the plan. We understood the need for a Savior and an atoning sacrifice. We understood how the gospel would be taught to us on earth.

It gives clarity. It helps me know that there's a purpose, a reason, that it had been thought out. When things get hard we can *always* think back to how well thought out the plan is. People have gone through this before, it's all going to work out okay.

The gathering of Israel and the preaching of the gospel is one small part of a grand, eternal plan. Just as our lives are a part of a grand, eternal plan. Our Heavenly Father knows us and has enacted a plan that takes care of each and every one of us.

Questions to Ponder: How does your knowledge of the Plan of Happiness help you in your life? How has it helped you in the past? How does it feel to know you have a Savior who atoned for you to be able to return to Heavenly Father's presence once again?

Daily Challenge: Ponder these verses. Read the chapter in context and see what stands out, how you feel, what the Spirit teaches you.

Because Of Stiffneckedness

> *3 Nephi 15:18 - And now, because of stiffneckedness and unbelief they understood not my word; therefore I was commanded to say no more of the Father concerning this thing unto them.*

"Because of stiffneckedness and unbelief." This was a massive breakthrough for me when I was going through and highlighting verses in The Book of Mormon last year, and it was one of the big reasons I felt like I wanted to write a book. Not because I know all the stuff about all the things, but because of this one thought.

Humility is a prerequisite for progress.

Progress in knowledge, in experience, in growth of any kind. In order for us to learn, we have to be humble.

What happened when Christ realized that the people were stiffnecked and unbelieving? He stopped talking. No more sermons, no more commandments, no more gospel, no more light. Done. All because the people felt like they had enough, that they knew better, and that they didn't need to progress any further.

What a terrifying thought. I hope I never get to a point in my life where I feel like I don't need any more.

It's a powerful lesson for all of us to "check our necks", so to speak. I may have just coined a phrase...

Let's make sure that we're being humble, teachable, thirsting for knowledge, and searching the scriptures. Always looking for ways to progress and become better.

Questions to Ponder: Are there parts of your life where you feel a little stiff-necked? How do you know? What are the signs? What can you do to change it?

Daily Challenge: Do some figurative neck-stretches to relieve the tension and relax a little. Find some part of your life where you feel like you've got it all figured out and see if there is a way to approach it that allows you to be more humble and teachable.

Because Of Their Belief In Me

> 3 Nephi 16:6-8 - 6 And blessed are the Gentiles, because of their belief in me, in and of the Holy Ghost, which witnesses unto them of me and of the Father.

> 7 Behold, because of their belief in me, saith the Father, and because of the unbelief of you, O house of Israel, in the latter day shall the truth come unto the Gentiles, that the fulness of these things shall be made known unto them.

> 8 But wo, saith the Father, unto the unbelieving of the Gentiles—for notwithstanding they have come forth upon the face of this land, and have scattered my people who are of the house of Israel; and my people who are of the house of Israel have been cast out from among them, and have been trodden under feet by them;

Blessed are the gentiles, because of their belief.

There it is again. *Because*. This time, *because* of their belief they were blessed with a witness of the father and of Christ.

It's as simple as the gospel gets. If you believe, blessings come.

That belief leads to faith, which incorporates action, and at that point or sometime after that come the blessings. I've seen it in my own life countless times, and it's a big part of why I have a testimony of a loving Father in Heaven who has a plan for us and a way for us to return to Him.

If you're looking at your life and it makes you happy or sad, excited or fearful, hopeful or discouraged, it's because of something. So, figure out what that is, and do more of the things that bring happiness into your life, and less of the stuff that brings negative things or feelings into your life.

Questions to Ponder: What is an experience you remember where your actions led to blessings? How did it make you feel? How does it make you feel now? How can you do more things like that that bring blessings into your life?

Daily Challenge: Do something today that makes you happy. Study the scriptures. Take a walk. Serve someone. Take some time to go up into the mountains or near some water like a lake or a river. Find time to be alone. Write in your journal about all of the things you're grateful for. Anything that makes you happy, do that today. Prove out this principle.

If They Shall Do All Those Things

> 3 Nephi 16:10 - And thus commandeth the Father that I should say unto you: At that day when the Gentiles shall sin against my gospel, and shall reject the fulness of my gospel, and shall be lifted up in the pride of their hearts above all nations, and above all the people of the whole earth, and shall be filled with all manner of lyings, and of deceits, and of mischiefs, and all manner of hypocrisy, and murders, and priestcrafts, and whoredoms, and of secret abominations; and if they shall do all those things, and shall reject the fulness of my gospel, behold, saith the Father, I will bring the fulness of my gospel from among them.

It's important to remember that this is Jesus Christ speaking at this point in The Book of Mormon. He's speaking to us through this book.

He gave us a number of verses of what to do, but now we get a verse that essentially tells us what not to do. Don't sin against the gospel, avoid pride, don't lie, deceive, be mischievous or hypocritical, and (obviously) avoid murdering people, priestcrafts, whoredoms and secret combinations.

There's a broad spectrum here, but I believe - since none of us are perfect - that we're all somewhere on that spectrum. What happens if we go all the way to the point where we reject the gospel and are committing grievous sins? The fulness of the gospel is taken away.

Why would that be the punishment? Because it's the greatest gift that God has ever given us.

As I've been spending more time thinking about why I'm writing this book and who it's for, and how I hope it changes those who read it, I keep thinking about the person I once was. I was inactive for a good 8 months or so after my first marriage ended in divorce, and while the sins I committed were on the smaller side - staying home from church, buying a stuffed crust Pizza Hut pizza (in and of itself a sin) on Sunday and having it delivered, and a few decisions that flirted with the middle range of the spectrum - all of them involved pride. All of them came from a misunderstanding of how important the gospel and living the gospel was and is.

It's prideful to think that we don't need to go to church, to think that we know enough, or can do a better job than those that God has chosen and who have been given keys to lead and guide us. It's prideful to think that our salvation will work itself out despite the sins we commit and don't repent of.

It's also prideful to think that we don't need to study the gospel or pray every day. That we can manage on our own strength without the constant companionship of the Holy Ghost. It's prideful to think that just a little sin isn't so bad.

If there's one thing I hope that these emails and ultimately the book will help people realize - and ultimately make accompanying changes to their lives - is that we need the gospel. We need the atonement made by our Savior Jesus Christ. We need humility, we need the Holy Ghost, we need prayer, and we need the blessings that the gospel promises. All it takes is living the principles of the gospel to the fullest extent we are capable of, which means that each of us can improve.

Each of us carries some amount of pride, and if we can learn how to pinpoint it, to remove it, and to become more humble, then we'll receive more and more incredible blessings that our Father in Heaven has in store for us. If we can't see that - and I'm very guilty of this - then we are being prideful. That's not the place we want to be. So I hope that we can all realize how important the gospel is, and act in a way that reveals those beliefs.

Questions to Ponder: Where is there pride in your life? What actions make it seem like you don't cherish and appreciate the gospel or the atonement? How do you actively work at becoming more humble?

Daily Challenge: Spend some extra time praying today, have a conversation with your Heavenly Father, and ask him for help pinpointing the pride and for the understanding of how to remove it and become more humble.

Ye Shall Come To A Knowledge

> *3 Nephi 16:12 - And I will show unto thee, O house of Israel, that the Gentiles shall not have power over you; but I will remember my covenant unto you, O house of Israel, and ye shall come unto the knowledge of the fulness of my gospel.*

We just studied the Abrahamic Covenant in Sunday school (early 2018) and this verse stands out even more now than it did a year ago when I first highlighted it. The blessings that come to us through that covenant are incredible, and we're all given that blessing. We have a reminder that part of that blessing is one of knowledge, to coming to a fulness of the gospel.

I'm not sure what that looks like or feels like, I just know I want it. I want it more than pretty much anything I can think of at this point. And we can all have it, if we work toward it.

Questions to Ponder: What can we do to show the Lord that we value this gift of knowledge? That we want to know Him and have a fulness of the gospel?

Daily Challenge: Do something today to show Him how much you value these gifts and these promises.

If The Gentiles Will Repent

> *3 Nephi 16:13-14 - 13 But if the Gentiles will repent and return unto me, saith the Father, behold they shall be numbered among my people, O house of Israel.*

> *14 And I will not suffer my people, who are of the house of Israel, to go through among them, and tread them down, saith the Father.*

There are numerous blessings that come from repentance. We're being obedient to the laws of this world. We're humbling ourselves. We're remembering the atonement and submitting to the need for a Savior.

Then there are the side effects, the blessings that come into our lives when we are repenting often. This is one example. "AND I will not suffer my people... to go through among them and tread them down."

The Lord looks out for His people. I've seen in my own life the unexpected ways I and my family are blessed when we're living the gospel to its fullest.

Questions to Ponder: Do you repent often? If not, why? How has repentance blessed your life in the past?

Daily Challenge: Repent! It will bring incredible and unexpected blessings into your life, sometimes immediately.

They Shall Be As Salt

> 3 Nephi 16:15 - 15 But if they will not turn unto me, and hearken unto my voice, I will suffer them, yea, I will suffer my people, O house of Israel, that they shall go through among them, and shall tread them down, and they shall be as salt that hath lost its savor, which is thenceforth good for nothing but to be cast out, and to be trodden under foot of my people, O house of Israel.

The flip side.

If we don't humble ourselves to the point where we listen to the voice of the Lord, or repent, or do any of the other things He asked us, there are consequences to that as well. When we're living in alignment with the commandments and the gospel, our actions are good. When we aren't they are bad. All good things come from God, and we know that all bad things stem from Satan.

Like a tree that brings forth bad fruit, if we aren't living the gospel, if we aren't humble and willing to help the Lord with His work, we're, essentially, good for nothing. Now, that's not referring to our character or our eternal worth, as we know that the worth of souls is great in the sight of God, but it means that we aren't helpful. We are like the wicked and slothful servant who buried his talent.

I don't like going through suffering. It sucks. I've been there. It's hard, it's humbling, it's terrible. Life is so much easier when we're living the gospel.

Questions to Ponder: How has the Lord "suffered" you in the past? How did it feel? How does it feel when you're living the gospel and are living humbly?

Daily Challenge: Offer a prayer of gratitude today. Humbly thank the Lord for all of the good things in your life, and for the strength to be shown your weaknesses and for help in turning them into strengths so that He can better use you in his work.

Ponder Upon The Things Which I Have Said

> *3 Nephi 17:3 - Therefore, go ye into your homes, and ponder upon the things which I have said, and ask of the Father, in my name, that ye may understand, and prepare your minds for the morrow, and I come unto you again.*

I'm not sure there's anything to add to this. After many chapters of sermon, the Lord leaves the people with this admonition: to go and pray, to ponder the things He taught, and to prepare for more. That should be our admonition as we go to sleep each night. To ponder, to pray, and to prepare. Why? Because the promise is that the Lord will come again. We don't know when or if we'll be there, but we still must listen to Him and prepare nonetheless.

Questions to Ponder: What have you pondered lately? How do you ponder? What does it look like, feel like? How do you know when you've succeeded at it?

Daily Challenge: Do these three Ps tonight, pondering on the Lord's sermon over the last few chapters in 3rd Nephi. Then pray and ask for guidance, and prepare for the day ahead tomorrow with the new understanding and knowledge you've gained.

He Knoweth Whither He Hath Taken Them

> 3 Nephi 17:4 - ...for they [the lost tribes] are not lost unto the Father, for he knoweth whither he hath taken them.

This comforting scripture came at a very cool time tonight. I started working on a TV show called Relative Race at the beginning of this year (2018), and tonight I had a conversation with my contestant's father. She was placed in foster care at a very young age and adopted by her foster mom, and hasn't had contact with her birth parents for well over 20 years.

I was speaking with her father tonight, who was talking about how he had been lost for so long. He had made some choices that led to his family being broken and split up, and he is really remorseful for those actions. He's made significant strides over the last two decades to improve his life and repent for the things he did, and he's been praying for a chance to be reconnected to his children.

It was very clear to me, speaking with him on the phone, that God was aware of him and his struggles this whole time. God knows each of us, individually, deeply, intimately. He helps us when we are choosing to work hard and live right. It was a perfect, modern example of this verse, for he knoweth wither he hath taken them.

Questions to Ponder: Have you ever felt lost? What did it feel like? What did your life look like at that time? How does it feel now to hear, or to know that God knows you, that He knows where you are, what you're dealing with in your life, and that He wants to help you?

Daily Challenge: If you're struggling, talk with your Heavenly Father about it. See how He can help you. If you're not, look for someone you can help or serve and help them feel the love that God has for them through you.

Ye Shall Have My Spirit To Be With You

> *3 Nephi 18:10-16 - 10 ...Blessed are ye for this thing which ye have done, for this is fulfilling my commandments, and this doth witness unto the Father that ye are willing to do that which I have commanded you.*

> *11 And this shall ye always do to those who repent and are baptized in my name; and ye shall do it in remembrance of my blood, which I have shed for you, that ye may witness unto the Father that ye do always remember me. And if ye do always remember me ye shall have my Spirit to be with you.*

> *12 And I give unto you a commandment that ye shall do these things. And if ye shall always do these things blessed are ye, for ye are built upon my rock.*

> *13 But whoso among you shall do more or less than these are not built upon my rock, but are built upon a sandy foundation; and when the rain descends, and the floods come, and the winds blow, and beat upon them, they shall fall, and the gates of hell are ready open to receive them.*

> *14 Therefore blessed are ye if ye shall keep my commandments, which the Father hath commanded me that I should give unto you.*

> *15 Verily, verily, I say unto you, ye must watch and pray always, lest ye be tempted by the devil, and ye be led away captive by him.*

> *16 And as I have prayed among you even so shall ye pray in my church, among my people who do repent and are baptized in my name. Behold I am the light; I have set an example for you.*

The scriptures are just so incredible. They provide the principles that we can follow to get pretty much anything we want in life. Sometimes it's completely laid out step by step for us, as faith and knowledge is laid out by Alma. Here, we can use the trick of reverse engineering from the desired outcome to figure out what we need to do.

Want to be blessed? Do these things (keep the commandments, be baptized, always remember Christ). Want to have the Spirit to be with you always? Remember Christ.

Sometimes I don't know why spiritual things work. All I know is that they do work. When I read the scriptures, I'm happier. When I spend my days thinking about Christ and good things (because good things come from Christ), I have a much stronger connection to the Spirit and feel led and influenced by Him. When I pray, I feel like I get answers and extra help. I don't know how it works. I just know it works.

The gospel is so simple that I think we sometimes dismiss it. "It can't be that easy, can it?"

It can.

Questions to Ponder: What lessons from the last few chapters have stuck with you the most? Which have stood out as things you can work on? What words of Christ have helped strengthen your testimony as you've pondered them the last week.

Daily Challenge: Spend some time pondering the words of Christ today from the last few chapters of 3rd Nephi. Reread them if you need to. Find a favorite verse, one that you can think about for the next few weeks or months.

Behold, It Shall Be Given Unto You

3 Nephi 18:18-23 - 18 Behold, verily, verily, I say unto you, ye must watch and pray always lest ye enter into temptation; for Satan desireth to have you, that he may sift you as wheat.

19 Therefore ye must always pray unto the Father in my name;

20 And whatsoever ye shall ask the Father in my name, which is right, believing that ye shall receive, behold it shall be given unto you.

21 Pray in your families unto the Father, always in my name, that your wives and your children may be blessed.

22 And behold, ye shall meet together oft; and ye shall not forbid any man from coming unto you when ye shall meet together, but suffer them that they may come unto you and forbid them not;

23 But ye shall pray for them, and shall not cast them out; and if it so be that they come unto you oft ye shall pray for them unto the Father, in my name.

I always wondered what "praying always" looks like in practice. It obviously can't be on your knees or verbally praying every waking hour of the day. Not only is that not feasible, we also don't have an example of that sort of method in the scriptures.

So what then? Is daily enough? 3 times a day? 5 times?

Is it something that can be measured that way, or not?

The part that I always omitted was that it says "*watch* and pray always". Read this way, I think it's more of a mindset, or a perspective. I take it to mean that in everything we do, checking to make sure it's a good thing. That it is in alignment with gospel teachings. That it is Christlike. That it reflects well on the Savior and his Church that we have covenanted to represent.

This is the only way I can realistically think to accomplish the command to "pray always." The example He gives is perfect here. If you're meeting at church and someone comes in that doesn't look, smell, dress, or act like you do, what's the right choice? If we take that and extrapolate it out to all aspects of our lives, we see that Christ just outlined how to live a Christ-like life. Sweet!

What's more, there are promised blessings for doing so. "And whatsoever ye shall ask the Father in my name, which is right, believing that ye shall receive, behold it shall be given unto you." WHATSOEVER THING.

I don't think we get how huge a promise that is. If we're "living right", watching our actions and our choices, if we're praying and living the gospel as obediently as possible, there are no limits to what the Lord will bless us with, as long as it "is right", of course. That is astounding! Honestly, it's beyond my comprehension, or at least my actions aren't currently lining up with my excitement over these beliefs. Something for me to work on.

Questions to Ponder: Why is it so hard to live this principle, to watch and pray always? Why is it hard at times to live the gospel fully, despite our fallen nature and all that? What can you do about it to get better and to be able to partake of these incredible promised blessings?

Daily Challenge: Take something ordinary today, an interaction at work or with your children, your driving habits, what kind of media you consume, and apply this principle. Watch and pray always.

To Be Let Into Temptation

> 3 Nephi 18:24-25 - 24 Therefore, hold up your light that it may shine unto the world. Behold I am the light which ye shall hold up—that which ye have seen me do. Behold ye see that I have prayed unto the Father, and ye all have witnessed.

> 25 And ye see that I have commanded that none of you should go away, but rather have commanded that ye should come unto me, that ye might feel and see; even so shall ye do unto the world; and whosoever breaketh this commandment suffereth himself to be led into temptation.

I really want to use this verse where he says "I am the light which ye shall hold up" as a way of persuading the world to stop taking selfies and caring so much about social media. But I'll digress before even going down that train of thought.

Except, that's the most applicable modern thing I can think of at this point. How many of us are so concerned about what the world thinks of us, how we look online, how we appear. Yet, the counsel from Christ is that we should be thinking about pointing to *Him*, not ourselves. We should be striving to come unto Him, not increasing our likes and subscriber numbers.

I have found it hard to live this principle. I've often felt like my vocational pursuits are at odds with this principle. I want to make movies, but the kind of movies I want to make aren't about Christ or gospel topics. Heck, I wrote a screenplay about what it would be like if Harry Potter grew up to become James Bond. With a sword.

Not a lot of crossover there.

How do we live this commandment to come unto Him, to have "our light" truly be Christ, and not something else?

The consequence of failing at this is that we suffer ourselves to be led into temptation. I think the first temptation is that we open ourselves up to pride, to feeling that we are über important and that the things we're doing are more important than Christ and the gospel. We can all extrapolate out where that leads... So how do we combat it? How do we overcome our fear or our hesitation to hold up the light that is Christ and let it shine to the world around us?

Questions to Ponder: How do you combat it? How do you overcome your fear or your hesitation to hold up the light that is Christ and let it shine to the world around you?

Daily Challenge in Three Tiers: a) Take a day off social media. b) take a WEEK off social media, see how it feels. c) delete social media apps from your phone. I just deleted the FB app again and I can't tell you how freeing it is. (Very. It's very freeing.)

For Unto Such Shall Ye Continue To Minister

3 Nephi 18:28-34 - 28 And now behold, this is the commandment which I give unto you, that ye shall not suffer any one knowingly to partake of my flesh and blood unworthily, when ye shall minister it;

29 For whoso eateth and drinketh my flesh and blood unworthily eateth and drinketh damnation to his soul; therefore if ye know that a man is unworthy to eat and drink of my flesh and blood ye shall forbid him.

30 Nevertheless, ye shall not cast him out from among you, but ye shall minister unto him and shall pray for him unto the Father, in my name; and if it so be that he repenteth and is baptized in my name, then shall ye receive him, and shall minister unto him of my flesh and blood.

31 But if he repent not he shall not be numbered among my people, that he may not destroy my people, for behold I know my sheep, and they are numbered.

32 Nevertheless, ye shall not cast him out of your synagogues, or your places of worship, for unto such shall ye continue to minister; for ye know not but what they will return and repent, and come unto me with full purpose of heart, and I shall heal them; and ye shall be the means of bringing salvation unto them

33 Therefore, keep these sayings which I have commanded you that ye come not under condemnation; for wo unto him whom the Father condemneth.

34 And I give you these commandments because of the disputations which have been among you. And blessed are ye if ye have no disputations among you.

First of all, how comforting to be known by the Lord, to be numbered by him. That simple truth can provide so much joy and hope. It can brighten up a rough, dark day in a matter of seconds if we really sit and think about what that means and how incredible it is.

Second, this is such a great set of verses about how we should treat others. I can think back to my early teens and recall experiences that I witnessed that were the cause of people leaving the church. While it may be true that we need to be aware of people that are taking the sacrament unworthily, our call is not to shun them, or make fun of them, or point fingers.

No. Christ teaches that "for unto such shall ye continue to minister." That is such an important part of this principle. Our job is not to judge or to turn people away, but to continue to minister to them. To help them feel welcome no matter what.

A friend of mine that I grew up with in Sacramento recently shared her story online, how she had left the church after coming out as attracted to other women. She ultimately fell in love and got married to a friend she met in college, and they started a family out in Oregon. She was kicked out of school at BYU and left the church because of the way she was treated here in Utah, but after years of being together, one day a pair of missionaries stopped by their house. Little by little, she began to open her heart to the gospel and the light of Christ. First by reading The Book of Mormon, then later by attending the local ward.

My favorite part of the story is how when she went to relief society in that ward in Oregon, she stood up and introduced herself, and included that her wife was at home and was not a member. No one in the room batted an eye. Rather, they befriended her, welcomed her, and loved her. They continued to minister. And just as Christ said in these verses, "they [knew] not but what they will return and repent, and come unto me with full purpose of heart, and I shall heal them; and ye shall be the means of bringing salvation unto them."

This sister ultimately ended up taking the discussions, coming back to full fellowship in the church, and, incredibly, her wife took the discussions as well, gained a testimony, and ended up joining the church. How? They had to go through a process of separation and ultimately divorce in order to be living the gospel fully, but they did it because they knew that the gospel was true and that the Lord needed them to help him with the work. Their amazing story is one of many examples of this principle in action, that we never know who the Lord is working on and how our actions might help or hurt their progress.

Imagine what would happen if we all continued to minister to those around us, member and non member, active and inactive, sinner and saint.

Questions to Ponder: How many people do you know that have left the church because they were offended by the actions of another member or church leader? How would their lives been different if those members had followed more closely this guidance to continue to minister? How can we do more to treat others the way Christ would have us treat them?

Daily Challenge: Think of someone in your life, in your ward, or neighborhood or your life that you can "continue to minister" to, and do something small today to help bring the light of Christ into their lives.

His Soul Shall Never Hunger Nor Thirst

> *3 Nephi 20:8 - ...He that eateth this bread eateth of my body to his soul; and he that drinketh of this wine drinketh of my blood to his soul; and his soul shall never hunger nor thirst, but shall be filled.*

A great reminder of the importance and meaning behind the Sacrament that we have the privilege of participating in each week. To hear the Savior describe it adds a bit of extra weight and sacredness to the ordinance. The promise is what I love the most, and I'm a bit ashamed that I don't think about it more often.

I don't think about my soul that much, let alone feeding it. But we know that our bodies and our spirits are separate entities; one eternal, and one destined to age and to ultimately return to the earth at the end of our lives. We spend tons of time thinking about feeding our physical bodies, but do we think about our souls the same way? Do we think about what kind of spiritual diet we ingest, or what we're exposing our spirits to?

If we spend some time thinking about it I think it will add to the importance of the Sacrament ordinance, but also how we act and what we choose to partake of during the week as well. It would be incredible for our physical bodies to never hunger nor thirst, but imagine how it feels to have our souls filled in a similar manner.

Questions to Ponder: What do you do to feed your soul? How do you remember Christ during the Sacrament each week? What importance does the Sacrament have for you? How do you remember the covenants throughout the week?

Daily Challenge: Feed your soul today. Find something extra that you can abstain from or consume to benefit your soul.

Ye Ought To Search These Things

> *3 Nephi 23:1 - And now, behold, I say unto you, that ye ought to search these things. Yea, a commandment I give unto you that ye search these things diligently; for great are the words of Isaiah.*

I'm sure I could go back every single year of my life and feel the same way about this verse - inadequate. I even took a class on Isaiah while studying at BYU, and I feel like I've only scratched the surface of a little scratch that was already on the surface.

Yet, rather than feeling discouraged, it gives me a ton of hope. Why? Because you can't understand the entirety of The Book of Mormon, or the words of Isaiah, or the gospel on your first try. Sure, you can gain a testimony of the truth of these things rather quickly, but a full understanding? A perfect knowledge? Nope.

Again, it's not a discouraging thought. It means that I can open these scriptures every single day and get a new insight, a deeper understanding, one step closer to a perfect knowledge. There's no end to that process. That's incredible!

I'm grateful today for this reminder. I feel differently now than I did 13 years ago when I returned from my mission, and I felt differently then than I did when I was 14 and first felt the Spirit testify of the truthfulness of the scriptures. I look forward to how I'll see the scriptures and the gospel and my testimony in another 10, and 20, and 50 years, because I know that the gospel is set up in a way that we get back what we put into it.

Questions to Ponder: How has searching the scriptures helped you in your life? What experiences do you remember where the gospel helped you? When/how did you start to receive your testimony? When was the last time the Spirit touched your heart?

Daily Challenge: Search these things today. Open your scriptures, find a favorite verse. See how spending a little extra time adds even more to your day.

Whoso ... Endureth To The End

> *3 Nephi 27:6 - And whoso taketh upon him my name, and endureth to the end, the same shall be saved at the last day.*

We've all taken upon us His name, at least those of you who are reading these emails and are baptized members of the Church. It's the endure to the end part that's the variable. I feel like that's going to be the challenge during the last days, whether those days are now or hundreds of years from now.

We don't know what the future holds. We don't know what policies or changes in the Church are going to rock people's testimonies and cause them to question their beliefs. We don't know what stories will come out, what kind of tactics Satan will try to use to lure us away. We just know it will happen.

Why mention the importance of enduring to the end? So that we could start preparing now. So that we could learn how to endure through small temptations, short periods of trial and tribulation, so that we could get used to being tested and proven. Because the Lord needs us. He needs people with unwavering testimonies, with incredible faith, with eternal perspectives. He needs us.

Questions to Ponder: How do you maintain your testimony through hard times? What has been hard on you in the past? How did you get through it? How can you prepare today for the hard times that you'll face in the future?

Daily Challenge: Ask the Lord in your prayers today to bless you as you work on your testimony and your faith. If you think you're ready, ask for a trial so that that faith can be tested and proven and ultimately strengthened. Ask Him to use you, to put His trust in you, to give you opportunities to learn and to grow.

If He Endureth To The End

> 3 Nephi 27:16-17 - 16 ...whoso repenteth and is baptized in my name shall be filled; and if he endureth to the end, behold, him will I hold guiltless before my Father at that day when I shall stand to judge the world. 17 And he that endureth not unto the end, the same is he that is also hewn down and cast into the fire, from whence they can no more return, because of the justice of the Father.

The phrase "endureth to the end" pops up a bunch in The Book of Mormon, and for good reason. It's what sets us apart. It's how we show God our grit, what we value, that we want to live with him again.

When I talk with creatives and artists about their craft or their businesses, I often talk about what sets the professional apart from the amateur. Is it talent? Having a viral hit?

No. What sets apart the professional is that they do the work. Day in, day out, no matter what. The writer writes 1000 words a day whether she feels like it or not. The artist sketches in a notebook every single day, whether he's inspired or not. They do the work, the stuff that isn't glamorous or fit for social media. It's the behind the scenes stuff when no one is watching that makes a professional a professional.

It's the same for being a Latter-day Saint. It's the daily, behind the scene stuff when no one is watching. It's how we react to a social media post, or a change in policy, or a friend leaving the church. It's the small things that build on themselves from daily practice, like studying the scriptures, meditating, going to the temple, ministering. It's what sets us apart, helps us to progress, and become better.

Questions to Ponder: What could you do better at? How do you feel you're doing at "enduring to the end"? What would make you happier?

Daily Challenge: Go to the Lord with humility and ask for help to do the things He needs you for, to endure to the end, to be able to rise above any negativity or influence.

That Ye May Stand Spotless Before Me

> *3 Nephi 27:19-20 - 19 And no unclean thing can enter into his kingdom; therefore nothing entereth into his rest save it be those who have washed their garments in my blood, because of their faith, and the repentance of all of their sins, and their faithfulness unto the end. 20 Now this is the commandment: Repent, all ye ends of the earth, and come unto me and be baptized in my name, that ye may be sanctified by the reception of the Holy Ghost, that ye may stand spotless before me at the last day.*

These verses not only remind us to repent, but why. We cannot enter the kingdom of heaven on our own merits or by our own efforts, no matter how hard we try. We can't do it without a Savior and an atonement. It's just not possible.

I've had a number of conversations over the last week with friends who have left the church, and who feel that they are finding their own way. Whether or not they can make it into the kingdom without being an active member of the Church is not for me to judge. I'm sure each of us will be put in the context of what we had to deal with on earth. One thing that I know for certain though is that we cannot force our way into heaven. We can't bypass the need for an atonement and for a Savior. We have to rely on the atonement for our salvation.

I realize that I haven't had to deal with anything hard when it comes to remaining active. I haven't had to deal with sexism or inequality, I haven't ever had reason to doubt my leaders. But even given those obstacles to overcome, look at the promises in this verse. If we remain faithful, if we repent and come unto Him, we'll be sanctified, we'll stand spotless before God at the last day.

We're all going to have to confront difficult things that will test our faith and our testimonies. These verses provide a helpful perspective that refocuses our attention on what matters most.

Questions to Ponder: How has the gospel provided you with perspective in your life? How has that perspective helped you overcome obstacles and tough times in the past? What, if anything, are you currently struggling with? How can an eternal, Christ-centered perspective help you get through it?

Daily Challenge: Ask for help, either through prayer or from a friend, if you're struggling. If you're not, pray for or reach out to a friend who may be doubting or losing their faith, and see how you can help bring the Spirit into their lives and help.

Even As I Am

> *3 Nephi 27:27 - ...what manner of men ought ye to be? Verily I say unto you, even as I am.*

Can you imagine Christ saying this while standing in front of you, recently resurrected, descended from heaven, after preaching His incredible gospel to you and everyone around you?

Is there a simpler encapsulation of the gospel than this? A charge to be like Him, to live our lives as He lived His?

As I'm writing this around Easter time, I was thinking about how the last week of His life was an example of love and service, of humility and obedience. Even though He lived 2000 years ago, the principles he taught, the way He lived His life, the example He set is still perfectly applicable to our lives that are filled with social media, politics, the 9 to 5, keeping up with the Joneses, and everything else that's used to define our time. We can live our lives the same way, with love and service, humility and obedience. With faith. With hope.

How lucky we are to have this record of His time spent in America, to have the Bible and the Doctrine and Covenants and the Pearl of Great Price, to have modern, living prophets who can remind us on a regular basis the life that Christ led and the blessings that come into our lives when we try to live this verse. When we try to be Christlike.

Questions to Ponder: When you think of this charge, what do you think of? What part(s) of your life? What changes are you inspired to make? In what ways can you be more Christlike?

Daily Challenge: Go out of your way today to be more Christlike. Be slower to anger. Quicker to kindness. Serve. Be humble. Repent. Be obedient.

Ask And Ye Shall Receive

> 3 Nephi 27:28-29 - 28 ...And verily I say unto you, whatsoever things ye shall ask the Father in my name shall be given unto you. 29 Therefore, ask, and ye shall receive; knock, and it shall be opened unto you; for he that asketh, receiveth; and unto him that knocketh, it shall be opened.

I needed to read this one tonight. My problem with almost everything I do is that I try to do too much at once. Rather than one creative side hustle I have four or five. Rather than reading one book all the way through I pick at half a dozen, just look at my Goodreads account.

The surface level commitment, skimming but never really diving in, makes it seem like I do a lot, but in reality not much gets done at all. It's extremely frustrating, and something I've been consciously working on over the last year or so.

I think the problem I have really comes down to fear. Fear of failing, fear of what my life will look like if I actually succeed, fear of choosing the wrong path and ending up somewhere I never wanted to be.

But these two short verses provide SO MUCH comfort. "Whatsoever things." No limits other than they have to be good things that we can ask for in the name of Christ.

These two short verses have the ability to remove the fear that I have. They help me realize that it's okay to want things, to have goals, to want to improve, to help others, to be a writer and a film producer, to raise good kids, to make enough money to provide for my family.

I'm lucky that's all I have to deal with. But I've also experienced the comfort that comes when I've prayed for help coping with the loss of my mom, or the ending of my first marriage. It took time, but that comfort came. I needed help, and He provided it.

These two verses show the power of Christ's life, His gospel, His atoning sacrifice, and the truthfulness of this book of scripture. No matter what we need, we can ask, and we can receive.

Questions to Ponder: What do you need? What should you ask for help with? Do you believe these verses? Have you experienced their truthfulness in the past? What do you want to ask for but have been too afraid to?

Daily Challenge: Ask. You might just receive...

Few There Be That Find It

> *3 Nephi 27:33 - ... Enter ye in at the strait gate; for strait is the gate, and narrow is the way that leads to life, and few there be that find it; but wide is the gate, and broad the way which leads to death, and many there be that travel therein, until the night cometh, wherein no man can work.*

For the first time ever I read this verse and got a little sad. "Few there be that find it." Every one of us here on earth were part of the group of God's children who accepted the plan and decided to come here to progress, gain a body and experience, be tried and proven, and to hopefully, through our agency and the atonement, return and live with Him again as perfected beings.

Sounds simple enough, right?

But the reality is that those of us reading this are incredibly privileged. We found the gospel, we have testimonies of the gospel, a knowledge of the plan and an awareness of the atonement.

There are many that don't have those things. There are many who won't enter the strait gate.

That sadness then turned to a sense of responsibility. How wrong it would be to just sit here and not do anything to share this incredible gospel with others, to help others overcome their doubts of the Church and the gospel. To not try and spread the light of Christ as far and wide as possible.

This verse is a wake up call, at least upon this reading. How does it make you feel?

Questions to Ponder: What about this verse sticks out to you? How does it make you feel? What should you do about it? How does it feel knowing that few will find that strait gate?

Daily Challenge: Do something to spread the gospel today. Share this book, post a favorite verse from the scriptures on social media, call a friend.

He Will Not Receive Them

> *3 Nephi 28:34 - And wo be unto him that will not hearken unto the words of Jesus, and also to them whom he hath chosen and sent among them; for whoso receiveth not the words of Jesus and the words of those whom he hath sent receiveth not him; and therefore he will not receive them at the last day.*

Hearken is a word I never really paid attention to until I started working on this book. As I wrote the chapter on humility, it really came alive for me, and now it carries so much extra meaning. It's not just to listen, but to listen intently, with humility. There's a posture associated with it that matters just as much as the listening.

This verse provides a great reminder that we are to hearken to Jesus, but also to those whom he hath sent. We're in the midst of a great division in the Church, at least from what I can see, where many are leaving due to statements made and positions taken by the leaders of the Church. I'm not in a position to say whether it's a test, or a way for the Lord to separate His disciples from those that are unbelieving, or if it's just a case of men making some mistakes. All I can speak to are the effects, and they're disappointing to say the least.

It's hard to talk with friends who have so vocally and proudly left the Church, in part because of verses like this. I believe this verse is true, that there are consequences for not listening to the Lord and His servants. It's hard because I'm not okay with the decisions they're making - I know that they're wrong. But at the same time, I need to love these friends and family members, help them see the joy the gospel brings to my life, and not judge them or make them feel marginalized. It's a hard balance to strike.

Despite those feelings, there are eternal truths, and this scripture is just one example of the truths we need to live by in order to one day return to live with God and Christ again.

Questions to Ponder: How do you help those that have wandered away from the church? What is your responsibility in those interactions and relationships? How do you maintain your ability to hearken to the words of Christ and His chosen servants?

Daily Challenge: Think back to this verse and the things you've felt while reading this chapter the next time you're in a situation where you're interacting with a less active member, or someone who has chosen to leave the Church. Find ways to bring the light of Christ into the conversation and their lives.

He That Doeth This Shall Become Like Unto The Son Of Perdition

> *3 Nephi 29:9-7 - 5 Wo unto him that spurneth at the doings of the Lord; yea, wo unto him that shall deny the Christ and his works!*

> *6 Yea, wo unto him that shall deny the revelations of the Lord, and that shall say the Lord no longer worketh by revelation, or by prophecy, or by gifts, or by tongues, or by healings, or by the power of the Holy Ghost!*

> *7 Yea, and wo unto him that shall say at that day, to get gain, that there can be no miracle wrought by Jesus Christ; for he that doeth this shall become like unto the son of perdition, for whom there was no mercy, according to the word of Christ!*

I mean...yikes.

I hope this doesn't apply to anyone you know. It's a sad state of affairs to be lumped in with the son of perdition.

But think about the road that gets someone here. This isn't an overnight process. This doesn't happen out of the blue one day. It starts small, with questioning our local leaders, then the prophet and the apostles, then the gospel itself. How many of us know people who have done these things?

It's important to watch what we say and do. If we have doubts, we know that that's normal and to be expected, and we shouldn't feel ashamed or unworthy if those thoughts creep in, or even if they linger. What's important is how we handle those doubts. Do we lash out at the prophet? Or do we turn to study and prayer, asking others for guidance and help? Do we take a prideful approach or a humble one?

We're all going to deal with some amount of doubt, or questioning, or criticism. How we deal with it will determine our future happiness.

Questions to Ponder: What do you do when a doubt arises? How do you handle it? What's your process? What doubts are you dealing with now? Who do you know that's struggling that needs help?

Daily Challenge: Think about how you can strengthen your relationship with God, Christ, and the Holy Ghost, so that you can better hear and understand the promptings and the guidance that you seek.

Ye Need Not Suppose...

> *3 Nephi 29:9 - Therefore ye need not suppose that ye can turn the right hand of the Lord unto the left, that he may not execute judgment unto the fulfilling of the covenant which he hath made unto the house of Israel.*

Today, as I write this, was day one of the April 2018 General Conference, where we participated in a solemn assembly to sustain the new president of the Church, Russel M. Nelson. It was an incredibly moving experience for me - I don't think I've felt the Spirit that strongly in a while.

I'd like to share what I wrote in my journal about the experience:

> *Today we participated in a solemn assembly to sustain the new prophet of the church. President Eyering asked different groups to stand and cast a sustaining vote at different times. The spirit hit me as soon as the quorum of the twelve apostles stood. I immediately started tearing up. There's no doubt in my mind that they are called of God. Soon after they asked those that hold the Melchizedek priesthood to stand, wherever they are, and to cast a vote sustaining the prophet and the twelve. As soon as I stood, surrounded by my boys and my wife watching me, I broke into uncontrollable tears. I've never felt this way sustaining a leader before. Incredibly powerful, and an answer to prayers of mine over the last few weeks where I've felt...distanced?...from God and the Holy Ghost. I needed this today, and God provided an opportunity for me to feel this.*

I wanted to share that because leading up to the conference I had a number of friends talk about the reasons they felt like President Nelson wasn't qualified, or other dissenting comments about the leadership of the church. (I've since unfriended or muted those friends on social media, realizing the effect they had on me over the last little while.) I wouldn't say I doubted, but I definitely let the questions hang out for far too long, like an unwelcome guest who I didn't want to be rude and just kick out of my house.

We can't change the will of the Lord. We can't change truth. President Nelson was and is called by God to lead the Church, and no matter how we feel, it doesn't change that nor can it. Rather than spend our time and energy fighting against the truth, it's better to humble ourselves and gain a testimony of the things we're struggling with. It's hard to humble ourselves, but it's certainly better than being humbled later.

I'll add my testimony to those that were given today, that I know God leads this Church, and that he has called a modern day prophet and apostles to help Him here on earth. I know The Book Of Mormon is true and that Joseph Smith was a prophet of God as well, charged with restoring this Church and the gospel and the priesthood to the earth. I'm grateful for my testimony, and the opportunity I have to share it with so many of you.

Questions to Ponder: What were your main takeaways from General Conference, even if you're reading this months or years later?

Daily Challenge: Go back and watch the video of the solemn assembly that took place during the Saturday morning session. If you didn't write down your feelings then, take an opportunity now to write down your own thoughts and how it feels to be able to sustain a prophet of the Lord.

Repent Of Your Evil Doings

> *3 Nephi 30:2 - Turn, all ye Gentiles, from your wicked ways; and repent of your evil doings, of your lyings and deceiving, and of your whoredoms and of your secret abominations, and your idolatries, and of your murders, and your priestcraft, and your envying, and your strifes, and from all your wickedness and abominations, and come unto me, and be baptized in my name, that ye may receive a remission of your sins, and be filled with the Holy Ghost, that ye may be numbered with the people who are of the house of Israel.*

Who are the gentiles in this verse?

If we read the chapter heading, it says: "The latter-day Gentiles are commanded to repent, come unto Christ, and be numbered with the house of Israel."

Yep, that's us. And not just those of us living on the earth today, but those that are reading this book of scripture.

It's a humbling reminder that even though we're living righteously, that even though we're faithful and trying to become better followers of Christ, that there is always room for improvement. I don't think it means we should feel bad about ourselves, I think it means that we need to be vigilant. We need to remember to repent no matter what. Yesterday, as I write this, was General Conference, and my family and I sat and watched all three sessions. Where would I even find time to do something that I needed to repent for? Well, it wasn't hard, apparently. I still had things I needed to repent for when my knees hit the floor last night. (Don't worry, it wasn't murder or priestcraft...)

The blessing, again, is a wonderful one for going through the process of repentance: We "receive a remission of [our] sins, [are] filled with the Holy Ghost, [and] may be numbered with the people who are of the house of Israel."

Let us remember that part of living a righteous life, of being a disciple of Christ and keeping the commandments, is to repent often so that we can learn from our mistakes, be forgiven, and progress even more.

Questions to Ponder: Why would the scriptures be so hard on Latter-day Saints? Why not a gentle reminder to repent? What do you think the prophets saw when they saw our day?

Daily Challenge: Repent!

❖ ❖ ❖

MORMON

These Things Doth The Spirit Manifest Unto Me

> Mormon 3:20-22 - 20 And these things doth the Spirit manifest unto me; therefore I write unto you all. And for this cause I write unto you, that ye may know that ye must all stand before the judgment-seat of Christ, yea, every soul who belongs to the whole human family of Adam; and ye must stand to be judged of your works, whether they be good or evil;

> 21 And also that ye may believe the gospel of Jesus Christ, which ye shall have among you; and also that the Jews, the covenant people of the Lord, shall have other witness besides him whom they saw and heard, that Jesus, whom they slew, was the very Christ and the very God.

> 22 And I would that I could persuade all ye ends of the earth to repent and prepare to stand before the judgment-seat of Christ.

I'm still riding that post-conference high. This weekend was one of the most spiritual for me in a long time. It felt so wonderful to have so many confirmations from the Holy Ghost that the things I was hearing and feeling were true, that they are from God, and that if I follow those teachings it will help me live a better, happier life.

And, I can kind of relate to Mormon here in these verses. I (too) would that I could persuade all the ends of the earth to repent and prepare to stand before the judgment-seat of Christ. While I haven't put it in such scriptural language before, I definitely feel compelled to write each day. I imagine that it's easier for me than it was for Mormon, as I have had this incredible direct feedback from the readers of this book and the emails that comprise it. Mormon had to write and work on this record out of an insane amount of faith.

I'm glad he did.

I hope for those of you reading this that are struggling with your testimony or your faith, that these discoveries in The Book of Mormon have helped and are helping you believe the gospel of Jesus Christ, as that is really what this whole thing is about -- gaining a better/deeper understanding of the gospel through The Book of Mormon.

Questions to Ponder: What are your main takeaways from studying and pondering the scriptures every day that you've read this book? How has your life changed or - hopefully - improved?

Daily Challenge: Share the gospel with a friend, coworker, or even a stranger today. Pray for an opportunity and take advantage of it when it comes. Be ready with a pass along card or a copy of The Book of Mormon, or even just the website mormon.org. You'll never know what could happen unless you try.

The Judgments Of God

> *Mormon 4:5 - But, behold, the judgments of God will overtake the wicked; and it is by the wicked that the wicked are punished; for it is the wicked that stir up the hearts of the children of men unto bloodshed.*

Is it weird that I find this verse...comforting? It immediately removes all of that energy that I have spent thinking about evil people and politics and and renders it useless. It frees that energy up to be used for better things.

For example - I wrote for and produced a web show in the first half of 2017 called Zion Politics. The goal was to educate and to expand the political perspective of the viewers from a centrist, rational viewpoint. What it ended up being in reality, for me at least, was a ton of energy spent on being angry about the state of politics. That's not a political statement, it was reality. Every day I was spending time and energy stressing myself out about how to fix a broken system, how to combat lies masquerading as truths, and how to incentivize evil people to do good. It was wasted effort. I doubt I changed a single mind, but only reinforced opinions previously held.

I believe there are evil people in the world, and since the nature of prideful, wicked people is to get gain and to be seen of men, it makes sense that many of these people end up in politics. I'm not sure why I felt like it was somehow my responsibility to try and change things, but I tried nonetheless. Maybe I felt helpless and that I had to do something.

This verse teaches that it's not my job to stop people from doing evil things. That should be left for God to deal with, and the way He handles it will be much more effective than anything I can do.

When I finally let it go, turned off my news feeds and stopped paying attention, it finally freed up my creative aspirations and I had energy to pursue the goals and ideas that I had. Not only that, more ideas came each and every day, because there was finally room for them again.

I started working on the book. I wrote a screenplay. I found a job working on a TV show for BYUTV. So many opportunities that I wouldn't have seen otherwise because I was so focused on these negative parts of the world we live in. Things I now realize I have no control over. Surely there are people that can inspire change, I just don't think I'm one of them (when it comes to politics). That said, I strongly encourage you to get involved in the political process and fight for change, just learn from me and don't spend so much time focusing on the negative that comes along with it.

The principle can be applied anywhere in our lives. When you free yourself of the time and energy you spend on things that are out of control, you can then turn to things that will actually bring you happiness and help bring good into the world, whether it be through your art, your service, or your example.

Questions to Ponder: What things are you wasting energy on? What things that are out of your control take up too much of your mental and emotional energy? What would you do with that extra time and energy if you were to change what you spend that time on?

Daily Challenge: Answer these questions on paper or in a journal. Then make a concerted effort today and through the next week to give up one negative, wasteful thought and use that time and energy for something better.

Humble Yourselves Before Him

> *Mormon 5:24 - Therefore, repent ye, and humble yourselves before him, lest he shall come out in justice against you—lest a remnant of the seed of Jacob shall go forth among you as a lion, and tear you in pieces, and there is none to deliver.*

The prophets in The Book of Mormon really want us to repent and to live humble, obedient lives.

Why? Because it's a requisite principle of the gospel. We have to repent to qualify for the saving grace that comes from Christ's atonement.

And do we feel the same way about it that the prophets seem to? To the same extent? How do we talk about repentance and humility with our children, or our spouses, or our friends or neighbors in the ward? Do we see these principles with the same ferocity as Mormon in this verse?

Why not?

Questions to Ponder: Why do you think they were so intense in their reasons for repenting and being humble? What do you think they saw that would compel them to speak this way? What should you do about it?

Daily Challenge: Take an opportunity to repent. Turn it into a habit. Repentance requires humility, so you're killing two birds with one stone.

O Ye Fair Ones

Mormon 6:17-21 - 17 O ye fair ones, how could ye have departed from the ways of the Lord! O ye fair ones, how could ye have rejected that Jesus, who stood with open arms to receive you!

18 Behold, if ye had not done this, ye would not have fallen. But behold, ye are fallen, and I mourn your loss.

19 O ye fair sons and daughters, ye fathers and mothers, ye husbands and wives, ye fair ones, how is it that ye could have fallen!

20 But behold, ye are gone, and my sorrows cannot bring your return.

21 And the day soon cometh that your mortal must put on immortality, and these bodies which are now moldering in corruption must soon become incorruptible bodies; and then ye must stand before the judgment-seat of Christ, to be judged according to your works; and if it so be that ye are righteous, then are ye blessed with your fathers who have gone before you.

Imagine the scene here. Mormon is looking out at a battle scene unlike anything we've likely witnessed in our lifetime. If you have, I'm sorry you've had to experience that. Tens upon tens of thousands dead, slain in battle. Mormon has basically just witnessed the destruction of the entire Nephite nation.

It's easy to read these verses and feel like they're directed to us, but remember too that he was saying this about his people that had just gone to battle. Realize, though, that if it could happen to the Nephites, it can happen to us. No one is immune, so we have to be all the more vigilant.

You can really feel Mormon's emotions coming through these words. The nice thing is that if you are righteous, then you are blessed. It almost makes these verses easier to read. Almost.

I can't help but think that these words were written with the intent that we would read them one day. Today is that day for you.

Questions to Ponder: So what do you get from these words? How do they make you feel? What takeaways are there for you to act on today?

Daily Challenge: Prayerfully consider these words and then ask God to help you as you strive to be better.

That They May Know Of The Things Of Their Fathers

> *Mormon 7:1-2 - 1 And now, behold, I would speak somewhat unto the remnant of this people who are spared, if it so be that God may give unto them my words, that they may know of the things of their fathers; yea, I speak unto you, ye remnant of the house of Israel; and these are the words which I speak:*
>
> *2 Know ye that ye are of the house of Israel.*

Sums up the purpose of The Book Of Mormon nicely, doesn't it? The book exists and was preserved so that we could know the things our fathers knew. So we could know the gospel. So we could know of Christ and the Holy Ghost, of the plan of happiness, of so many other gospel truths.

It adds some extra weight to the book. It makes it feel that much more important. That perspective helps me cherish and respect it even more.

The first thing Mormon says is that he wants us to know that we're of the house of Israel. Even then he knew how important that lineage was, and what it meant.

We're lucky enough to be able to hold these records, these words, in our hands, to have access to them at all times. What does that mean about us?

Questions to Ponder: Why is lineage important? How important is it for you to know of and understand the Abrahamic Covenant? Why is it important to know of these words, these gospel truths contained in The Book of Mormon?

Daily Challenge: Offer a prayer of gratitude for The Book of Mormon and those that helped to bring it into the world.

Or Ye Cannot Be Saved

> Mormon 7:3 - Know ye that ye must come unto repentance, or ye cannot be saved.

Yet another prophet, another chapter, another book that reiterates the importance of repentance. It's that thought that got me writing the other book I'm writing, to figure out what a full picture would look like. If we took every single verse in The Book of Mormon that references repentance, and then compiled it together into an inclusive teaching about that principle, what would we learn? What would it teach us? How would our perspective change?

It's been a mind-blowing process of writing emails and working on the book, and if anything I feel like I'm not doing enough. I'm not giving the gospel enough time, enough focus, enough weight. I know that these blessings are true, yet my actions wouldn't always reinforce that statement, but rather undercut it.

That's the process at work though, isn't it? Being able to look at ourselves with that sort of clarity and then make choices to become better? Isn't that the gospel plan in a nutshell?

Verses like this one may seem repetitive, but I'm grateful for them and for the constant reminder of Christ, His grace and His atonement, and that I can be better.

Questions to Ponder: How do you feel now about repentance? Has it changed at all since you started reading this book? How?

Daily Challenge: Strive to be a little more humble, a little more obedient, a little more grateful for the atonement. Progress happens one day at a time.

Delight No More

> *Mormon 7:4 - 4 Know ye that ye must lay down your weapons of war, and delight no more in the shedding of blood, and take them not again, save it be that God shall command you.*

I think it's clear that while sometimes war is necessary, the Lord cares about our motives when war is concerned. "Delight no more..."

I wonder how the prophet and the Lord intended this verse to be taken today, with war all around us, and all of the other issues plaguing our time. Is this an eternal principle?

Questions to Ponder: What do you think this verse means for you today? About the choices you make as an individual and as a society? About the importance of war, or the way you should think about it?

Daily Challenge: Pray and ask the Lord about these questions or others you may have.

Lay Hold Upon The Gospel Of Christ

> *Mormon 7:5-8 - 5 Know ye that ye must come to the knowledge of your fathers, and repent of all your sins and iniquities, and believe in Jesus Christ, that he is the Son of God, and that he was slain by the Jews, and by the power of the Father he hath risen again, whereby he hath gained the victory over the grave; and also in him is the sting of death swallowed up.*

> *6 And he bringeth to pass the resurrection of the dead, whereby man must be raised to stand before his judgment-seat.*

> *7 And he hath brought to pass the redemption of the world, whereby he that is found guiltless before him at the judgment day hath it given unto him to dwell in the presence of God in his kingdom, to sing ceaseless praises with the choirs above, unto the Father, and unto the Son, and unto the Holy Ghost, which are one God, in a state of happiness which hath no end.*

> *8 Therefore repent, and be baptized in the name of Jesus, and lay hold upon the gospel of Christ, which shall be set before you, not only in this record but also in the record which shall come unto the Gentiles from the Jews, which record shall come from the Gentiles unto you.*

This last verse really sums up for me the "big idea" behind the other book I'm writing as well as this one: That our lives are blessed when we "lay hold on the gospel of Christ." There are blessings that come from heeding these words, blessings that every single one of us came to this earth for, blessings that will benefit us and our families.

My greatest fear at the end of 2016 when we finished up The Book Of Mormon curriculum in Gospel Doctrine was that we'd stop studying this incredible book of scripture, which really was just me projecting my own fear that I would stop reading and studying. I wanted to do something to not only keep me connected to the scriptures, but to help others who may struggle with studying every day, or who had a desire to read but maybe needed or wanted to look at the scriptures in a new way.

I know that this book has helped my life immensely when I take time to study and ponder the words and teachings it contains. I just hope it's doing the same for you.

Questions to Ponder: What are the main teachings you've learned from The Book of Mormon? How has it strengthened your testimony? Your desire to live the gospel? To repent? How have those things blessed your life?

Daily Challenge: Take some time to think about how you can incorporate The Book of Mormon into your daily life, and ponder how thinking about and reading it has benefited you over the last little while.

Ye Will Know Concerning Your Fathers

> *Mormon 7:9-10 - 9 For behold, this is written for the intent that ye may believe that; and if ye believe that ye will believe this also; and if ye believe this ye will know concerning your fathers, and also the marvelous works which were wrought by the power of God among them.*

> *10 And ye will also know that ye are a remnant of the seed of Jacob; therefore ye are numbered among the people of the first covenant; and if it so be that ye believe in Christ, and are baptized, first with water, then with fire and with the Holy Ghost, following the example of our Savior, according to that which he hath commanded us, it shall be well with you in the day of judgment. Amen.*

The obvious teaching here are about The Book of Mormon supporting the teachings of Christ in the Bible, the Abrahamic covenant, or the first principles and ordinances of the gospel.

But, what stood out to me is the promise that if we believe The Book of Mormon that we will know concerning our fathers, and also the marvelous works which were wrought by the power of God among them.

I recently took a gig working on the tv show *Relative Race* for BYUTV. It's been an eye-opening experience diving into the story with my contestant couple. I spent this last weekend in their hometown and in their home filming their "backstory" who they are, how they grew up, and (most importantly) who they are looking for on the show. My contestant is looking for her parents, as she was adopted at a young age and has almost no recollection of them.

At one point I asked her if she thought she would be able to recognize them if she saw either of them. Her reply? I'll tell you in a second.

The weekend reinforced how great a blessing it is to have a knowledge concerning our fathers. How lucky are we if we grew up in a family with a strong parental influence, with both parents in the home, with regular family vacations to visit aunts and uncles, grandparents and cousins? Even if you grew up with a single parent, you could consider that a huge blessing compared to some of the stories highlighted on this show.

Her response to my question broke me. I asked her if she'd recognize her parents, and she responded, "I can't remember their faces."

Can you imagine? I'm sure some of you can. I'm sorry if that rings too close to home. I write this tonight to help us that know our family and our relatives and ancestors see that this blessing is real. That there are those whose circumstances are different than ours. That the gospel is for everyone even if sometimes the blessings don't seem directed towards us and our situation, and that sometimes we may even run the risk of taking these blessings for granted.

Questions to Ponder: What other blessings in your life might you take for granted? How many blessings can you count in your life? What would your life be like without the knowledge that you have from the gospel?

Daily Challenge: Be kind today to everyone you meet. You never know what they're going through, but odds are that they are going through something.

Greater Things Than These

> Mormon 8:12 - And whoso receiveth this record, and shall not condemn it because of the imperfections which are in it, the same shall know of greater things than these. Behold, I am Moroni; and were it possible, I would make all things known unto you.

This verse sums up so much for me as I've been on this journey the last year and a half of trying to find and uncover these truths in The Book of Mormon. I've seen this principle validated time and time again, that if we receive the record - take it and spend time with it, study it, pray about it, rely on it - then more and more knowledge comes into our minds and hearts through the Holy Ghost.

Then, once you've received that knowledge, you start having a stronger and stronger desire to share the things you're learning, to "make all things known." (I wasn't planning on writing an email a night, let alone ultimately 300+ of them.) I wasn't planning on writing a book, but when I laid out in front of me all of the verses that I had highlighted during my research phase, I had a strong desire to seek out those greater things, and then also to share them. The email list and the book just seemed like the best way to accomplish it.

It comes down to the fact that The Book of Mormon makes our life better. No matter what we're going through, what we're struggling with, what questions we have or what the Lord is testing us with, we will always be better off if we're studying the gospel regularly and strengthening our relationship with God, Christ, and the Holy Ghost.

Questions to Ponder: What do you want to know? What greater things do you think could be waiting for you? How has studying and pondering the gospel through The Book of Mormon helped you over the last months that you've been reading this book?

Daily Challenge: Share your testimony with a friend or family member today.

God Knoweth All Things

> Mormon 8:17 - And if there be faults they be the faults of a man. But behold, we know no fault; nevertheless God knoweth all things; therefore, he that condemneth, let him be aware lest he shall be in danger of hell fire.

Another serious warning. I'm not recommending that anyone leave the Church, but if that's one's decision, at least be smart about it and skip the condemning the gospel part.

Why? Oh, you know, hell fire. Dangerous hell fire.

I was speaking with a coworker today who is no longer an active, practicing member of the Church. She's learned to stop condemning the Church when we chat because I've told her about verses like this, and also that I have no desire to have her speak ill of the leaders or the gospel.

The thing is, God knoweth all things. One way you could read this is that no matter what you think, it doesn't change what's true, and it doesn't affect the knowledge or the actions of God. He is the same from beginning to end, eternally consistent. Truth isn't affected by your desires and your opinions. Truth is eternal.

Depending on where one sits and what they or I may be going through, this is either a comforting thought or one that we feel is oppressive. How does it feel when you read it now? Could this verse have been included as a way to measure where we are with our testimonies and our devotion to the gospel?

It's a tough verse, but like it says in 2 Nephi, the guilty take the truth to be hard. I just hope that we remain humble enough to feel the guilt and change course, rather than become more hardened in our criticism and our doubts.

Questions to Ponder: Who do you know that has left the Church? Why did they leave? How did they change? Was it gradual or sudden? Do they criticize the Church? How can you live in a way that not only shields you from those influences, but also helps be a loving example to those who are hurting and need some extra light in their lives?

Daily Challenge: Pray for humility. Pray for opportunities to serve. Pray for love and for someone who needs it.

Neither Shall He Judge

> *Mormon 8:20 - 20 Behold what the scripture says—man shall not smite, neither shall he judge; for judgment is mine, saith the Lord, and vengeance is mine also, and I will repay.*

I wonder how many friends of ours would still be active members of the Church if we, collectively and individually, would heed the counsel in this verse. Judgement is God's job, His responsibility, not ours.

My personal feeling is that if we were truly trying to live like Christ, we would not judge others, put them down, make them feel like an outsider or disenfranchised, but rather we would go to them with charity and empathy and love in an attempt to welcome them and make them feel needed and wanted.

I have a friend in particular that comes to mind. He was an incredibly strong member of the Church, a friend whose testimony and spirit I looked up to in high school. We were in a performing arts group together, and when he would sing hymns at a fireside the spirit would fill the room and amplify his voice directly into the hearts of everyone who could hear.

A few years later while I was on my mission I heard that he had gone inactive. It wasn't until I returned home and then flew out to meet him that I heard his story. He was always a bit effeminate, but apparently that was something a few other "friends" and their families took issue with. He came out, but part of that decision meant that many people judged him and turned their backs on him. It pained me to hear him talk about it because at the time those wounds were still fresh.

I asked who, if anyone, he was still friends with. Besides his family, he said I was the only one who he had spoken to from our friends in over a year. I couldn't understand how something like that would change how people felt about him.

To this day we're still good friends, but he's still not able to see a way back to the Church because of how the members he knew treated him in that time. This story isn't to justify what we know as a sin, but to show that even in a situation like this, we can still love people, treat them as we would want to be treated, and help them feel like they aren't alone. Judgement doesn't help anything in these situations. If we truly understand that, we'd do as this verse suggests and leave the judgment to God.

Questions to Ponder: If you're not commanded to judge, what are you commanded to do? Is there a line that someone could cross that allows you to finally judge them? Is there a sin that would justify your judgement or other unkind actions? How can you love those that you feel are making wrong choices or hurting themselves and their families?

Daily Challenge: Love. Try to be more Christlike today and focus on love in every single interaction you have, and see how your day goes.

You Would Be More Miserable

> *Mormon 9:4 - Behold, I say unto you that ye would be more miserable to dwell with a holy and just God, under a consciousness of your filthiness before him, than ye would to dwell with the damned souls in hell.*

Perspective.

It's easy for us to justify our choices at times, thinking that we can just repent later, or it's not that big of a deal. The reality is that we'll have a very clear picture of all of our sins and our transgressions, all of our bad decisions, our prideful motives, our lies and deceptions and everything else.

I've mentioned a few times a friend who has gone inactive, and in her grand exit stated her plan to forge her own path to salvation and eternal life with God. I want to be loving and supportive, understanding that I'll never be able to understand the inequality, the judgement, the inappropriate comments, and everything else she's had to deal with inside the church. However, I can't not read this verse. The truth is the truth. Reality is reality.

We can't forge our own way. We can't shirk our covenants and then expect to be given a pass because our life was hard. (Again, I get that I'm speaking from an extreme place of privilege, being a middle aged white male living in America...). But what's hard for her may not be hard for me and vice versa. We all have things that are going to trip us up and make it hard to live the gospel to its fullest.

The question, and the test, is whether we will choose to be humble, to repent, to learn and progress with an open mind and a willing heart. Because when a prophet makes a statement warning us of how miserable it would be, I think I'd rather take his word for it than try and see if I can prove him wrong.

Questions to Ponder: Where is pride showing up in your life? What do you think you can do on your own, without needing or relying on God's help? How would life be different if God was helping us in all aspects of your life?

Daily Challenge: Ask for help during your prayer(s) today with regard to something you haven't asked for help with yet. Decide what you're going to do to get what you want and then ask for the Lord's help in making it happen.

Turn Ye Unto The Lord

> Mormon 9:6 - O then ye unbelieving, turn ye unto the Lord; cry mightily unto the Father in the name of Jesus, perhaps ye may be found spotless, pure, fair, and white, having been cleansed by the blood of the Lamb, at that great and last day.

Interesting that the prescription for the unbelieving is to pray. It's likely one of the first things they stopped doing, if my friends are any indication. It seemed like once they decided to leave, to stop believing, they cut all ties with the Lord and God and became not just "inactive Mormons", but full on atheists. I'm not sure why that is.

Similar to the call to "doubt our doubts," this prophet tells us to pray when we least feel like praying. If we're feeling like we are distanced from God, we merely need to reach out. There was a favorite song of mine that my friend from a few chapters ago used to sing in those firesides with the line "He's Never Farther Away Than A Prayer." The sentiments are similar to today's verse. All we need to do to rekindle that relationship and to know that He is there, that He's aware of us, that He knows us and loves us, is to pray.

Questions to Ponder: Have you gone through a period in your life where you stopped praying? What do you think caused that? How did you start praying again? Why do you pray now?

Daily Challenge: Pray! Spend some time each day with your Heavenly Father in humble prayer and give yourself time to hear and feel the answers and his presence through the Holy Ghost.

# If So, He Does Not Understand Them

> *Mormon 9:8 - Behold, I say unto you, he that denieth these things knoweth not the gospel of Christ; yea, he has not read the scriptures; if so, he does not understand them.*

I love when the prophets speak plainly like this. There's no room for confusion. If you've read the scriptures and can still deny that there is a Christ, if you can deny the truthfulness of the book, of its principles and teachings, then you do not understand them. Period.

I'm sorry I keep harping on my no-longer-active friends, but it seems like this is who these verses were written for, at least when I read them. The same coworker I mentioned previously likes to throw little jabs out at me about The Book of Mormon. "If you only knew the things I know..." she says.

I think she means, "If you only read the things I've read..." because you and I both know that the things out there on the internet are nothing more than philosophies of men trying to lead us astray.

The truth is very simple. The book is true. Its teachings are true. It contains the fulness of the Gospel, and "men (and women) would get nearer to God by abiding by its precepts, than by any other book." Anything that would lead us away from God obviously doesn't come from Him.

So, what should we do with this verse? I think we use it to help us keep the proper perspective. We know that these things are true, and we're not going around denying them. But, it helps us know that it is important to understand them.

I'm reminded of the words from our new prophet and seer, President Nelson, in the April 2018 conference that "in coming days, it will not be possible to survive spiritually without the guiding, directing, comforting, and constant influence of the Holy Ghost." This is also taught in The Book of Mormon, and we need to make sure we maintain a relationship with each of the members of the Godhead.

Read the scriptures. Understand them. Know God.

Questions to Ponder: What are the things that keep you from reading & studying, from praying and repenting? What can you do to maintain those habits?

Daily Challenge: Find and read a scripture that has had an impact on you in the past. Find that feeling again, and feel the Holy Ghost as you do so. Try and find that as often as possible.

A God Who Doth Vary

> *Mormon 9:10 - And now, if ye have imagined up unto yourselves a god who doth vary, and in whom there is shadow of changing, then ye have imagined up unto yourselves a god who is not a God of miracles.*

The principle behind this verse is a comforting one - that God, our Heavenly Father, is unchanging. He doesn't vary. He's consistent, eternally the same.

What does that mean, though? It means that we know that if we live the gospel that has been given to us as a way to be happy, to progress, and ultimately live with Him again, that it will work. If we believe that God is an unchanging God, it becomes that much easier to trust Him and to have faith in Him.

This quality is something that my wife and I have tried to implement in our home and how we raise our three boys. We knew that we would have to have consistency, both as parents as well as individually. Meaning, if there is a consequence for an action, it needs to be received by both parents 100% of the time.

What I've seen though is that we are really proud of the young men our small boys are becoming. They understand the rules. They know that doing good things brings good outcomes, and that making not-so-great choices brings undesired consequences. They're understanding how the world works and making choices based on that knowledge.

The same goes for us. The gospel lays out the rules, as well as the blessings and the consequences. We're given the ability to make choices in every aspect of our lives. The most important part besides that agency is the fact that we can rely on those outcomes. We know they won't change. We know the rules won't be altered.

It is an essential quality to have a God that doesn't change or vary.

Questions to Ponder: Do you believe this verse? How do you picture your Heavenly Father? Does the plan of salvation seem fair? How does the principle in this verse help with your faith in God?

Daily Challenge: Dig deeper. Go on a scripture chase, starting in the Bible Dictionary or the Topical Guide, and find some other attributes of God.

The Reason Why He Ceaseth To Do Miracles

> Mormon 9:20-21 - 20 And the reason why he ceaseth to do miracles among the children of men is because that they dwindle in unbelief, and depart from the right way, and know not the God in whom they should trust.

> 21 Behold, I say unto you that whoso believeth in Christ, doubting nothing, whatsoever he shall ask the Father in the name of Christ it shall be granted him; and this promise is unto all, even unto the ends of the earth.

Again, a consistent, unchanging God. If it seems like God has changed - he "ceaseth to do miracles," for example - that it is because of our faith, not because God stopped allowing miracles to exist.

It comes down to our humility, our desire to believe, and acting on that desire in the form of faith. We have to believe in Christ, in the power of prayer, and that those prayers can and will be answered. If we're not getting the desired effect, then we need to assess our side of things rather than questioning the power of God to answer those prayers.

I've often wondered how my faith compares to those we read about in the scriptures. I haven't had to go through much. I was raised in the Church, had a relatively short stint of inactivity which was more laziness and pride rather than disbelief, and feel very blessed where I'm at now. I'm sure at some point my faith is going to be truly tested and that it will be a very difficult time, but I can't really point to anything at the moment.

That said, I'm not sure that I could heal someone the way people were healed in the scriptures. Or move mountains. Or any number of things. I have faith that works for my life right now, but if I were thrown into different circumstances, I wonder how I'd do.

What I do know is that God is an unchanging God, and that prayers are answered. I wonder how that faith would hold up if it were really tested.

Questions to Ponder: Do you believe that your prayers can and will be answered? That God is an unchanging God? How do you nurture that faith? Why is doing so important?

Daily Challenge: Pray for the things you feel you need. Have humility and faith and ask God what He needs from you in order to have those things realized in your life as you work toward them together.

Doubting Nothing

> *Mormon 9:23-25 - 23 And he that believeth and is baptized shall be saved, but he that believeth not shall be damned;*

> *24 And these signs shall follow them that believe—in my name shall they cast out devils; they shall speak with new tongues; they shall take up serpents; and if they drink any deadly thing it shall not hurt them; they shall lay hands on the sick and they shall recover;*

> *25 And whosoever shall believe in my name, doubting nothing, unto him will I confirm all my words, even unto the ends of the earth.*

This echoes the last chapters' thoughts about belief. Where do you feel your faith is? How strong is it? How much doubt is there?

The blessings of our belief and our faith are numerous and incredible. The things we've been promised that we can do... I mean... it seems unbelievable. Yet, that says more about my belief than of reality. We know that miracles exist, that they happen every day. We know that the only limit to these miracles is our belief and that they are constrained to "good" things - meaning we're not going to have the miracle of making tons of money in order to buy more stuff and be seen of men as a great success.

Questions to Ponder: So what holds you back? What prevents you from having this level of belief in God and His promises? What blessings and miracles do you seek in your life that aren't happening because of your belief? And how do you strengthen that belief?

Daily Challenge: Whip out your journal or even a loose sheet of paper, and write down the things you believe. Then read it, and listen and wait for the Spirit to testify of the truthfulness of those beliefs.

Be Wise In The Days Of Your Probation

> Mormon 9:27-29 - 27 O then despise not, and wonder not, but hearken unto the words of the Lord, and ask the Father in the name of Jesus for what things soever ye shall stand in need. Doubt not, but be believing, and begin as in times of old, and come unto the Lord with all your heart, and work out your own salvation with fear and trembling before him.

> 28 Be wise in the days of your probation; strip yourselves of all uncleanness; ask not, that ye may consume it on your lusts, but ask with a firmness unshaken, that ye will yield to no temptation, but that ye will serve the true and living God.

> 29 See that ye are not baptized unworthily; see that ye partake not of the sacrament of Christ unworthily; but see that ye do all things in worthiness, and do it in the name of Jesus Christ, the Son of the living God; and if ye do this, and endure to the end, ye will in nowise be cast out.

The overarching principle here is to be wise. I wonder what would happen if we just took a month and focused on being wise in every single aspect of our lives, every part of our day.

What would that look like?

Would we speed down the freeway? Would we have an organized workspace? Would we watch uplifting content rather than the kind that closes us off to the spirit? Would we treat others with more kindness?

How would it look in your life, to be wise all the time...?

By living by that one principle, I think everything else would just take care of itself. We certainly wouldn't be baptized or partake of the sacrament unworthily. That would be the least of our worries.

Sounds like it would be worth trying.

Questions to Ponder: How can you apply wisdom to your daily life? What changes would you make? How would your day be different? Is it something you can try for the next week? Month?

Daily Challenge: Take some time thinking about and writing down what "be wise" would look like for you, and apply it for a set amount of time that you decide.

ETHER

Serve God, Or They Shall Be Swept Off

> Ether 2:9-12 - 9 And now, we can behold the decrees of God concerning this land, that it is a land of promise; and whatsoever nation shall possess it shall serve God, or they shall be swept off when the fulness of his wrath shall come upon them. And the fulness of his wrath cometh upon them when they are ripened in iniquity.

> 10 For behold, this is a land which is choice above all other lands; wherefore he that doth possess it shall serve God or shall be swept off; for it is the everlasting decree of God. And it is not until the fulness of iniquity among the children of the land, that they are swept off.

> 11 And this cometh unto you, O ye Gentiles, that ye may know the decrees of God—that ye may repent, and not continue in your iniquities until the fulness come, that ye may not bring down the fulness of the wrath of God upon you as the inhabitants of the land have hitherto done.

> 12 Behold, this is a choice land, and whatsoever nation shall possess it shall be free from bondage, and from captivity, and from all other nations under heaven, if they will but serve the God of the land, who is Jesus Christ, who hath been manifested by the things which we have written.

I always appreciate when these scriptures are so clear. There are promises for keeping the commandments, and consequences for iniquity. Keep the commandments, reap the blessings. Sin and ignore God, be swept off. It is the everlasting decree of God.

But what do we do when we as a people are living in a state of iniquity? Should we fear? Should we worry? Should we wander outside and start calling everyone we pass to repentance?

These verses underscore the need for each of us to have humility in our approach to how we live our lives. I don't think we're asked to go and call repentance to everyone, but I do believe that we need to be vigilant both personally and in our sphere of influence.

As a father or mother. As a member of a ward. As a Bishop or a Relief Society president.

I'm not sure what ripened in iniquity means, or what the threshold for ripeness is, but I'm fairly confident that the way to combat that is humility.

Questions to Ponder: What do these scriptures say to YOU? What impressions come to mind as to what actions and even changes should happen in your life? What is your responsibility when the world around you grows more wicked?

Daily Challenge: Study humility in the scriptures. See what they teach you at this point in your life.

My Spirit Will Not Always Strive With Man

> *Ether 2:15 - ...for ye shall remember that my Spirit will not always strive with man; wherefore, if ye will sin until ye are fully ripe ye shall be cut off from the presence of the Lord.*

It is important to note that the thing that causes the Spirit to withdraw is... us. Our own sin and iniquity. The promise when we are baptized, that we covenant each week in remembrance when we take the sacrament, is that the Spirit will always be with us. That's the promise, as long as we keep the commandments.

There are promised blessings that accompany each commandment, and consequences associated with breaking them. If we feel that we can get through life without keeping the commandments, that's our choice to make, but the consequences don't go away. They're as connected to those choices as anything else; we cannot escape them.

I wonder if we do enough to teach this to our children. I'm not sure I fully understood this concept until confronted with it's harsh reality. When I was briefly inactive, there was nothing I could do that made me anywhere near as happy as when I was living the gospel, studying the scriptures, regularly conversing with my Heavenly Father, and fully keeping my covenants.

It's important that we understand this concept so that we know that there are consequences to our actions.

Questions to Ponder: What other attributes of the gospel should you learn and prioritize in your life? What attributes of the Spirit should you know and believe in? How can this knowledge help you?

Daily Challenge: Spend some extra time studying today. Find a favorite verse or chapter in the scriptures, or go on a chase starting with a topic in the Topical Guide or the Bible Dictionary.

The Winds Have Gone Forth Out Of My Mouth

> *Ether 2:24 - ...Nevertheless, I will bring you up again out of the depths of the sea; for the winds have gone forth out of my mouth, and also the rains and the floods have I sent forth.*

It's been a while since we had a reminder of the power of God. It's nice to get them every so often. For me at least, it isn't something I think about often. I get up, write, get ready for work, work, head home, hang out with the kids, get them to bed, and write some more. I'm not sure why that would preclude any thoughts about God, but it often does.

Even now I haven't really optimized my life in any way to think about God more than when I was writing the daily emails at night and thinking about them in the morning.

While I may think about it more than the average person, it still feels like a long time since the last time I reflected on God's power, and what that means in my life. Like, if my kid got hurt, would I have the faith in that moment to give him a blessing and believe that he could be healed? I can sit here and write to you that I do believe that is possible, but how would that work in the moment?

All I can say with surety is that when I went through a divorce from my previous marriage, I didn't handle that faith crisis well. I felt like a failure, like I had broken my covenant with God and my ex, and that it was my fault that the relationship ended. Shame and then some mild depression set in, and I "fled," for lack of a better word. I stopped going to church. I stopped studying the gospel. I stopped praying.

While I believed that it would get better, and that I could be happier if I just did the things I knew would bring happiness, my actions didn't align with those beliefs.

I think that's where many of us in the Church are at, or at least that many of us have experienced a similar time.

Questions to Ponder: What do you do when your faith is tried? What do you really believe about the power of God to work miracles in your life, to comfort you, to guide you, to teach you, to save you? And do your actions align with those beliefs?

Daily Challenge: Act with faith today. Study the scriptures. Pray. Serve. Pay tithing. Do the thing that you're afraid of. Converse with God about what you're struggling with and ask for help.

We May Receive According To Our Desires

> *Ether 3:2 - ...because of the fall our natures have become evil continually; nevertheless, O Lord, thou hast given us a commandment that we must call upon thee, that from thee we may receive according to our desires.*

What do you think this means, that our natures have become evil continually? And does that destine us for failure?

Yes, actually. We're fallen creatures. We cannot live with God again without an atonement. That's the whole reason for an atonement, because of our fallen, evil natures. Upon first reading I was almost...offended?...by this verse. How unfair! But then I reread the verse. That second half is equally if not more important, that we have a way to overcome that evil, fallen nature. That we have a Savior. That there was an atonement made. That part of the plan of salvation is that we can receive according to our desires.

I didn't catch any limitations in that verse. I honestly have come to believe that as long as your desires are "good" or "righteous" desires, that you can receive anything. You can work to live the gospel and keep the commandments, work hard toward the things you desire, and as long as they're good you can achieve them.

That means financially, with your physical and emotional health, your knowledge and education, your ability to help others and reach people far and wide.

This is a beautiful verse, and an important reminder that we need to remember, especially if and when our lives get a little dark, and we're letting too much of the negative parts of the world in. Remember that we have a choice to seek out our Savior's help, both for our salvation and in our day to day lives.

Questions to Ponder: What does it mean to you that you (and I, and all of us) have a fallen, evil nature? What do you do about that fact? How does it affect the way you live your life? How important is the Savior and the atonement in your life, and how does that importance translate into daily action?

Daily Challenge: Study the Atonement. Read about our Savior's sacrifice in the scriptures, and think about how huge an influence that act has on our lives.

In Me Shall All Mankind Have Life

> *Ether 3:14 - Behold, I am he who was prepared from the foundation of the world to redeem my people. Behold, I am Jesus Christ. I am the Father and the Son. In me shall all mankind have life, and that eternally, even they who shall believe on my name; and they shall become my sons and my daughters.*

Around Easter time, a coworker asked if I, as a Mormon, believed in Christ. I answered with an emphatic, "YES!"

It's verses like this one that help cement that belief, and connect it to the hope that I have for me and my family to have happiness in this life and to live together through eternity. To say I believe in Christ is an understatement, because I not only believe *in* Christ, I *believe* Christ. I believe His gospel, His promises, His teachings.

The Book of Mormon has been such an incredible book to study over the last year and a half, and it makes me excited for what I still have to learn. I'm grateful for the testimony of Christ that it provides through the words of the prophets contained in its pages. I know that our lives will be blessed as we read and study its teachings.

Questions to Ponder: What do you love about The Book of Mormon? What attribute of Christ do you think of the most, or find most important? What do you think life would be like if you didn't have the knowledge you have of the gospel?

Daily Challenge: Seek out opportunities to share your testimony and your beliefs with others. Find ways to bring the light of Christ into other people's lives so they can start receiving more of the same blessings you experience in your life.

Man Have I Created

> Ether 3:15-16 - 15 ...Yea, even all men were created in the beginning after mine own image.

> 16 Behold, this body, which ye now behold, is the body of my spirit; and man have I created after the body of my spirit; and even as I appear unto thee to be in the spirit will I appear unto my people in the flesh.

These verses help give so much clarity to our lives here on earth. I can't imagine what life would be like if I didn't know of the plan of salvation, of an eternal Father in Heaven, of our infinite characteristics.

When I start feeling lazy, or incapable, or weak, I've started to actually focus on my spirit, and telling my body what to do, rather than letting my laziness dictate my actions. It works, which is probably unsurprising to you as you read this.

Think of all of the things our Heavenly Father is capable of. How much power He holds, and the fact that He has endowed us with similar power. What is possible if you have faith? If you remember the power you've been blessed with?

Questions to Ponder: What's something you've wanted to do? Something you can't find the motivation or the physical strength to do? Do you believe you're capable? Do you believe you've been created in God's image? What does that mean to you?

Daily Challenge: Surprise yourself. Do some physical exercise and push yourself further than normal. Wake up early, because you can. Eat healthy, because you can. Act in faith, and prove to yourself that you can do anything.

Having This Perfect Knowledge Of God

> Ether 3:19-20 - 19 And because of the knowledge of this man he could not be kept from beholding within the veil; and he saw the finger of Jesus, which, when he saw, he fell with fear; for he knew that it was the finger of the Lord; and he had faith no longer, for he knew, nothing doubting.

> 20 Wherefore, having this perfect knowledge of God, he could not be kept from within the veil; therefore he saw Jesus; and he did minister unto him.

Why do you think this story was included in The Book of Mormon? To make us feel good? (To make us feel bad?) To teach us?

I think it poses at least two very important questions: 1) Do you believe this actually happened? and 2) Do you believe it's possible for you?

I like to think I believe both. It's a hard thing to measure, belief. How do we know if we actually believe something? When we see the outcome of that belief? How are we supposed to know where we're at on that spectrum between belief and perfect knowledge?

Perfect knowledge is an important principle, and what better way to teach us that truth than to include a story like this one, where the brother of Jared saw Christ? I can't think of a better reward for that faith and belief, or a better example to get us motivated to try to perfect our own knowledge.

I don't think it's weird to want something like a perfect knowledge. But, for whatever reason, it's not something I really ever talk about. I don't think my wife and I have had a deep conversation about that desire. (Sorry April!)

But I do. I want that. I want to have a perfect knowledge. I think there are benefits that come from pursuing it, and for living life in a way that would allow that to happen. I think it's possible. I think it could happen to any one of us if we worked hard enough to be as obedient and faithful as possible. So, if it's possible, why not try?

Questions to Ponder: Do you think the story actually happened? Do you think it's possible for you?

Daily Challenge: Do something today to be extra obedient or faithful. Spend some time pondering the big picture, what you want out of life, and how you need to live in order to achieve it.

❖ ❖ ❖

If He Would Believe In Him

> Ether 3:26 - For he had said unto him in times before, that if he would believe in him that he could show unto him all things—it should be shown unto him; therefore the Lord could not withhold anything from him, for he knew that the Lord could show him all things.

The only thing asked of the brother of Jared in that moment was if he believed in Christ. We know the answer, but the takeaway for me is that this was a man who spent a lifetime strengthening that belief. This wasn't a random encounter where the Lord asked, "Hey, do you by chance believe in me" and then the brother of Jared was like, "uh, yeah. Sure. I guess."

It reinforces what I was thinking yesterday though - that it's possible, that we have a path laid out in front of us to gain this perfect knowledge (the process is laid out in The Book of Mormon), and we have an example of one potential outcome of that belief and pursuit of it. We can be shown all things, nothing withheld from us.

Pretty incredible. That perspective helps us as we go through our daily lives. Do we choose to break a commandment, or maintain our belief and our righteousness? Do we skip our scripture study and prayer for the day? Or are those extra minutes of sleep worth giving up in order to learn and grow closer to our Heavenly Father?

We, too, can have similar experiences as the brother of Jared, but it takes a long time of consistent effort to get there.

Questions to Ponder: What do you want? What do you want more than perfect knowledge? How do your daily actions support that desire?

Daily Challenge: Do something extra. Get up early. Study your scriptures a little longer. Go to the temple. Give up a vice. Show the Lord what you truly care about through your actions.

Exercise Faith In Me

> *Ether 4:7 - And in that day that they shall exercise faith in me, saith the Lord, even as the brother of Jared did, that they may become sanctified in me, then will I manifest unto them the things which the brother of Jared saw, even to the unfolding unto them all my revelations, saith Jesus Christ, the Son of God, the Father of the heavens and of the earth, and all things that in them are.*

I'm glad this story wasn't just a single chapter's worth. It's been so enlightening to go verse by verse this way, picking out the promises from this incredible experience the brother of Jared had.

This verse caps the story with some incredible promises: Sanctification, manifestation of everything the brother of Jared saw, and the unfolding of all of the Lord's revelations. Sign me up.

I keep saying "I want that" because I feel like if I say it enough times in as public a way possible, maybe my actions will start catching up and I'll start seeing more progress. I have felt some incredible leaps through the process of writing these chapters. Think about how just a few minutes a day can have such a meaningful effect. Spending this little bit of time every day getting some truth from The Book of Mormon and then thinking about it throughout the day actually makes a difference.

Imagine if we spent even more time. I have started to wonder what's next, what I'm going to do after this book is out into the world.

All I know is that the Lord has promised us so many incredible things in the scriptures, and hasn't asked much from us in order for us to receive them. Here, again, in this verse, He's made some amazing promises for those who exercise faith in Him.

So, will we?

Questions to Ponder: What amount of faith do you think is needed for these blessings to happen? Is it worth working towards? What changes would you need to make in order for that to happen?

Daily Challenge: Think about the habit you've started by reading this book every day. What other habits can this transition to, or could you add?

These Things Are True

> *Ether 4:9-12 - 9 And at my command the heavens are opened and are shut; and at my word the earth shall shake; and at my command the inhabitants thereof shall pass away, even so as by fire.*

> *10 And he that believeth not my words believeth not my disciples; and if it so be that I do not speak, judge ye; for ye shall know that it is I that speaketh, at the last day.*

> *11 But he that believeth these things which I have spoken, him will I visit with the manifestations of my Spirit, and he shall know and bear record. For because of my Spirit he shall know that these things are true; for it persuadeth men to do good.*

> *12 And whatsoever thing persuadeth men to do good is of me; for good cometh of none save it be of me. I am the same that leadeth men to all good; he that will not believe my words will not believe me—that I am; and he that will not believe me will not believe the Father who sent me. For behold, I am the Father, I am the light, and the life, and the truth of the world.*

My mind gets really satisfied when verses like this pop up on big milestones (This is the 300th chapter, if I'm not mistaken.) I've never spent this much time or this long a period on a project. These verses sum up a portion of why that is.

Every other time I've tried to consistently write a blog, I've failed. This is different because it's based on truth, not on my ability to come up with something true.

You can probably also see how you've changed, how you've progressed, how you're better for having the scriptures in your life every day. The time we spend on these things is not wasted. It's bringing us closer to our Heavenly Father because these things come from him. Every verse we read and every minute spent pondering brings us closer to Him because we are learning and internalizing more truth.

I've experienced the promise in verse 11, that those who believe these things will be visited by the Spirit, and the result of that is being persuaded to do good. That's the only reason I'd ever be able to keep up a daily writing habit for 300+ days, to write over 100,000 words, (and nearly another 100,000 words for the *other* book,) both in the course of a year.

The things we can accomplish with the help of the Spirit are truly miraculous. The process is laid out for us in these scriptures. If we believe, if we strive to do good, there's no limit to what is possible.

Questions to Ponder: What has the Spirit taught you throughout your life because of your desire to believe and working towards learning it? What blessings have come into your life from seeking out the good?

Daily Challenge: What "good" are you being persuaded to do? What does the Lord need from you right now, and can help you if you'll ask? Go and start today. Start now.

Come Unto Me

> *Ether 4:13-16 - 13 Come unto me, O ye Gentiles, and I will show unto you the greater things, the knowledge which is hid up because of unbelief.*
>
> *14 Come unto me, O ye house of Israel, and it shall be made manifest unto you how great things the Father hath laid up for you, from the foundation of the world; and it hath not come unto you, because of unbelief.*
>
> *15 Behold, when ye shall rend that veil of unbelief which doth cause you to remain in your awful state of wickedness, and hardness of heart, and blindness of mind, then shall the great and marvelous things which have been hid up from the foundation of the world from you—yea, when ye shall call upon the Father in my name, with a broken heart and a contrite spirit, then shall ye know that the Father hath remembered the covenant which he made unto your fathers, O house of Israel.*
>
> *16 And then shall my revelations which I have caused to be written by my servant John be unfolded in the eyes of all the people. Remember, when ye see these things, ye shall know that the time is at hand that they shall be made manifest in very deed.*

There are great things laid up for us from the foundation of the world. All we have to do to have them manifest in our lives is come unto Christ, and believe.

This goes back to the motivation we have for living any aspect of the gospel, to why we have decided to be members of this church, to live in this "peculiar" way, to make any choice at all. Why do we choose good? Why do we sometimes choose bad?

My belief is that the more we learn, the more our perspective grows and becomes more focused. We can then make choices as to what outcomes we want for our lives, and then we can act accordingly.

Just as someone who wants to be an artist needs to paint every day and someone who wants to be a dancer must learn and grow in her craft. If we want to know God, to have eternal life with our families, to become perfected, our daily actions have to align with those desires as well.

Questions to Ponder: What blessings could you be missing out on because of your "unbelief"? What desires are you working towards that could benefit from a more focused, daily effort?

Daily Challenge: Think of how you can show your belief and put together a daily action plan, so to speak, to accomplish those goals.

Blessed Is He That Is Found Faithful

> *Ether 4:18-19 - 18 Therefore, repent all ye ends of the earth, and come unto me, and believe in my gospel, and be baptized in my name; for he that believeth and is baptized shall be saved; but he that believeth not shall be damned; and signs shall follow them that believe in my name.*

> *19 And blessed is he that is found faithful unto my name at the last day, for he shall be lifted up to dwell in the kingdom prepared for him from the foundation of the world. And behold it is I that hath spoken it. Amen.*

So many blessings for those that believe. It seems super applicable to where we're at as a nation and as a church right now. There have been many incidents lately that have caused many to doubt and to question, and many have left their faith because of them.

I wonder how many were actively working on their faith at the time. Not in an accusatory way, but out of sheer curiosity. What makes the same situation the straw that broke the camel's back for some, and a non-issue for others? It's a matter of perspective and expectations not being met. My assumption, as unfair and potentially judgmental as it may seem, is that these situations are tougher for those that aren't actively working on their faith by studying the scriptures every day, or strengthening their beliefs rather than letting them go dormant

The blessings for working on that faith and for living according to those beliefs that we hold are many and they are wonderful. Those who choose that path will be lifted up to dwell in the kingdom prepared for them. Can any of us really fathom what a kingdom is or feels like? The closest I can imagine is seeing the insanely huge palaces on recent trips to Europe, and yeah, it's more than any of us would ever need to be happy. Yet, there it is, promised in The Book of Mormon, so that we had something to work towards, a reason for that faith and that belief.

What's more, by constantly nurturing our faith, we are also better prepared for when those moments come where our faith is tested.

Questions to Ponder: What are the reasons that you care about and nurture your faith? What can you do to prevent faith crises in the future? How can you help those that are struggling with their faith or belief.

Daily Challenge: Pray for strength, and for the opportunities to help others that may be struggling or who have left their faith because of incidents in the past.

Surely This Thing Leadeth Into Captivity

> Ether 6:22-23 - 22 And it came to pass that the people desired of them that they should anoint one of their sons to be a king over them.
>
> 23 And now behold, this was grievous unto them. And the brother of Jared said unto them: Surely this thing leadeth into captivity.

Here's another story warning us about kings and what happens when a people desire to be led in that way. "Surely this thing leadeth into captivity." While this book is barely starting to reach an international audience, I do want to speak specifically to those in the US, so, apologies.

One thing that we've seen over the last few decades in our political atmosphere is the rise of the "imperial presidency." The short version is that since the 1930s and especially since the 1970s, the president has been acquiring more and more executive authority and power. It's not a party issue either, the problem persisted through Clinton, Bush, Obama, and now through Trump. The concern is what we're seeing now: checks and balances no longer working. The president using executive orders to get around congressional support. Launching attacks on foreign countries without congressional support.

So what happens when our institutions become eroded to the point where they no longer have any ability to prevent a president from taking advantage of the situation? Captivity. This isn't me stoking fear, but rather saying that we have seen this exact situation play out in The Book of Mormon a number of times, each with the same outcome.

While the news media may not be a place you want to spend too much time in these days (believe me, I know), we still need to make sure that we're doing what we can to vote in a way that will protect our institutions and the constitution of our nation. We can't allow evil men and women to continue to usurp power and consolidate it in a way that would allow an individual to rise to power akin to becoming a king or a tyrant.

God provided this land for the building up of His church and kingdom on the earth. It's up to us to preserve it and safeguard it for Him.

Questions to Ponder: What is it about having a king that leads to captivity? How do we prevent it from happening? What is our responsibility as citizens?

Daily Challenge: Make sure you're registered to vote, and commit to do so in upcoming and future elections.

They Began To Prosper

> *Ether 7:26 - And because the people did repent of their iniquities and idolatries the Lord did spare them, and they began to prosper again in the land...*

Repentance leads to prosperity. Iniquity and idolatry leads to hardship and failure.

Like anything in life, there is opposition in all things, and there is also a choice. We can choose between the two options in every instance.

You can use this principle to reverse engineer the life you want. Ask yourself: "How would I describe my life right now? Hard, or prosperous?" Depending on the answer, you know what to do. If you're feeling prosperous, keep on the path and find ways to improve where you can. If you're feeling like life isn't working out the way you'd hoped, find ways to humble yourself, seek the Lord's help, and make sure you are repenting often, as that has been promised to lead to prosperity and the Lord's hand in your life.

I've seen it in my own life. It's a true principle. The hard part is being humble enough to observe your life that way, and then make the decision to repent rather than rebel or become angry. It's a choice, sometimes a hard one, but one we can make if we try.

Questions to Ponder: How would you describe your life right now? Heading the way you'd hoped? What can/should you do about it?

Daily Challenge: Pray, either with gratitude or for help. Repent either way, it's a proven way to help us progress and find what we're looking for in this life.

The Lord Worketh Not In Secret Combinations

> *Ether 8:19 - For the Lord worketh not in secret combinations, neither doth he will that man should shed blood, but in all things hath forbidden it, from the beginning of man.*

The last few times I read through The Book of Mormon, I did it in chronological order. Then while teaching it in 2016 we went in order through the book, as I did when I reread it again in early 2017. I hadn't realized until today how big of a leap in content the book of Ether is, meaning that the topics are so different than what the book is surrounded by with Mormon and Moroni. It's an interesting choice Mormon made to include it where he did in the book.

Yet, looking at it now, I'm glad for the reminders it's providing. Repentance. Fear of having a king. Awareness of secret combinations... these are incredibly important topics that The Book of Mormon teaches us about that are easy to forget once we get a ways deeper into the book. Mormon didn't want us to forget these important lessons, so he included another group of people that dealt with the same problems as the Nephites and the Lamanites.

If they're so important, they must be for us as well, to have these records and to be able to learn from them.

Questions to Ponder: Why are secret combinations so pernicious? Why do you think we are reminded and taught about them so often in the scriptures? What forms do secret combinations take today?

Daily Challenge: Read Ether chapter 8 in full to read about the secret combinations and the warnings given to us modern readers.

They Shall Be Destroyed

Ether 8:22-26 - 22 And whatsoever nation shall uphold such secret combinations, to get power and gain, until they shall spread over the nation, behold, they shall be destroyed; for the Lord will not suffer that the blood of his saints, which shall be shed by them, shall always cry unto him from the ground for vengeance upon them and yet he avenge them not.

23 Wherefore, O ye Gentiles, it is wisdom in God that these things should be shown unto you, that thereby ye may repent of your sins, and suffer not that these murderous combinations shall get above you, which are built up to get power and gain—and the work, yea, even the work of destruction come upon you, yea, even the sword of the justice of the Eternal God shall fall upon you, to your overthrow and destruction if ye shall suffer these things to be.

24 Wherefore, the Lord commandeth you, when ye shall see these things come among you that ye shall awake to a sense of your awful situation, because of this secret combination which shall be among you; or wo be unto it, because of the blood of them who have been slain; for they cry from the dust for vengeance upon it, and also upon those who built it up.

25 For it cometh to pass that whoso buildeth it up seeketh to overthrow the freedom of all lands, nations, and countries; and it bringeth to pass the destruction of all people, for it is built up by the devil, who is the father of all lies; even that same liar who beguiled our first parents, yea, even that same liar who hath caused man to commit murder from the beginning; who hath hardened the hearts of men that they have murdered the prophets, and stoned them, and cast them out from the beginning.

26 Wherefore, I, Moroni, am commanded to write these things that evil may be done away, and that the time may come that Satan may have no power upon the hearts of the children of men, but that they may be persuaded to do good continually, that they may come unto the fountain of all righteousness and be saved.

During the 2016 election, I heard arguments from "both sides" about how the candidate from the other party was evil and corrupt.

That they each represented a modern-day version of the secret combinations we read about in the scriptures.

Whether you believe it or not about either of those politicians, the fact that the parallel can be drawn by many people is concerning to me. Why? Because of what it says here about nations that uphold such secret combinations. You know, stuff like destruction...

No thanks.

So what are we to do? Repent of our sins. Work to make sure the secret combinations don't gain too much power. To humble ourselves and to be aware of the reality of the situation. It's very clear what they look like and how they operate, but it's also clear what we need to do to fight it.

The only way to prevent the destruction that comes from these prideful, secret combinations is humility and repentance. The consequence for apathy or ignoring them is literal destruction of entire nations of people. THIS is how Satan wins, by taking down a group when he can't get to a single individual, using the "status quo" to lull people into justification and thinking that these actions are normal and that everything is fine.

These verses were written for us, so that we could choose to do good continually rather than allow secret combinations to destroy our nations.

Questions to Ponder: What is our responsibility as saints when secret combinations arise? Do you think they ever fully go away? Why is humility a remedy for the problem of secret combinations?

Daily Challenge: Pray for humility, for awareness. Repent. We have to establish that habit if it is going to have the desired, combined effect.

The People Began To Repent

Ether 11:8 - And the people began to repent of their iniquity; and inasmuch as they did the Lord did have mercy on them.

Here is another reminder of what happens when we repent. The blessings always come. The promises in The Book of Mormon are just that, promises from a Savior who is eternal and unchanging. So much so that if the desired outcome isn't happening, it's likely a sign that we need to look inward, to see what we can do differently. Do we need more humility? To lower or change our expectations? To accept the results, knowing the Lord has other plans for us?

Probably a mixture of all of the above. Some would call those answers a cop out, but I would argue that we benefit more from humility and introspection than from anger and frustration for results that never come.

Questions to Ponder: Again, why is humility so important in the gospel? How does it change you for the better? How can you work on your humility and grow better at it? How are humility and repentance related?

Daily Challenge: Repent! It's the ultimate act of humility you can perform.

Faith, Hope, and Belief

Ether 12:6-22 - 6 And now, I, Moroni, would speak somewhat concerning these things; I would show unto the world that faith is things which are hoped for and not seen; wherefore, dispute not because ye see not, for ye receive no witness until after the trial of your faith.

7 For it was by faith that Christ showed himself unto our fathers, after he had risen from the dead; and he showed not himself unto them until after they had faith in him; wherefore, it must needs be that some had faith in him, for he showed himself not unto the world.

8 But because of the faith of men he has shown himself unto the world, and glorified the name of the Father, and prepared a way that thereby others might be partakers of the heavenly gift, that they might hope for those things which they have not seen.

9 Wherefore, ye may also have hope, and be partakers of the gift, if ye will but have faith.

10 Behold it was by faith that they of old were called after the holy order of God.

11 Wherefore, by faith was the law of Moses given. But in the gift of his Son hath God prepared a more excellent way; and it is by faith that it hath been fulfilled.

12 For if there be no faith among the children of men God can do no miracle among them; wherefore, he showed not himself until after their faith.

13 Behold, it was the faith of Alma and Amulek that caused the prison to tumble to the earth.

14 Behold, it was the faith of Nephi and Lehi that wrought the change upon the Lamanites, that they were baptized with fire and with the Holy Ghost.

15 Behold, it was the faith of Ammon and his brethren which wrought so great a miracle among the Lamanites.

16 Yea, and even all they who wrought miracles wrought them by faith, even those who were before Christ and also those who were after.

17 And it was by faith that the three disciples obtained a promise that they should not taste of death; and they obtained not the promise until after their faith.

18 And neither at any time hath any wrought miracles until after their faith; wherefore they first believed in the Son of God.

19 And there were many whose faith was so exceedingly strong, even before Christ came, who could not be kept from within the veil, but truly saw with their eyes the things which they had beheld with an eye of faith, and they were glad.

20 And behold, we have seen in this record that one of these was the brother of Jared; for so great was his faith in God, that when God put forth his finger he could not hide it from the sight of the brother of Jared, because of his word which he had spoken unto him, which word he had obtained by faith.

21 And after the brother of Jared had beheld the finger of the Lord, because of the promise which the brother of Jared had obtained by faith, the Lord could not withhold anything from his sight; wherefore he showed him all things, for he could no longer be kept without the veil.

22 And it is by faith that my fathers have obtained the promise that these things should come unto their brethren through the Gentiles; therefore the Lord hath commanded me, yea, even Jesus Christ.

I love this section so much. I feel like you could study these verses your whole life and still find new insights each time you read through it, similar to the temple endowment. I want to spend a lot of time and a lot of words on these verses, so I figured I'd put the whole section up today so we have some context, and then over the next week or two we can go verse by verse.

There are some key takeaways in this chapter that can help us with our faith and our belief, and I'm excited to dive in with you.

Questions to Ponder: What stands out to you on this time through these verses? What made you pause and reread, or think extra hard? What insights or takeaways occurred? What questions do you have about these topics?

Daily Challenge: Pray and ponder on these verses as we prepare to go through them together over the next two weeks!

After The Trial Of Your Faith

> *Ether 12:6 - And now, I, Moroni, would speak somewhat concerning these things; I would show unto the world that faith is things which are hoped for and not seen; wherefore, dispute not because ye see not, for ye receive no witness until after the trial of your faith.*

There's a maxim that I've tried to live by for the last year or so, but especially the last six months. It's that "everything you want is on the far side of hard work." I heard it again just yesterday in a podcast, so it seems like a fairly universal truth if it's not just me living by it.

As with most truths in business or life found in self help books, the principle can also be found in the scriptures. You "receive no witness until after the trial of your faith" is just another way of putting it.

The question I have been pondering is "where does hope originate?" Is it a mental thing? A physical thing? A thought or a feeling? Oddly enough, it isn't mentioned in the four gospels in the New Testament. It doesn't show up until the book of Acts. There's also a blurred line between faith and hope. Hebrews 11:1 says, "faith is the substance of things hoped for." Does that mean that hope is only in our minds?

I'm sorry I don't have answers for any of this stuff. I'm just someone, like you, who is searching for more light and knowledge by studying the scriptures.

The key takeaway for me from this verse though is how it helps us set our expectations. It helps us define faith - that it stems from things that are hoped for and not (yet) seen, that this life requires work and faith and action and that we aren't just going to be given everything if we don't put in some effort on our own to make things happen, to figure things out, to learn, to act without knowing the outcome.

Questions to Ponder: Where does hope come from? Why is hope an important part of the gospel? What is the relationship between hope and faith? What should you do based on what this verse teaches?

Daily Challenge: Study and ponder these topics, see what answers you can find.

It Was By Faith

> *Ether 12:7 - For it was by faith that Christ showed himself unto our fathers, after he had risen from the dead; and he showed not himself unto them until after they had faith in him; wherefore, it must needs be that some had faith in him, for he showed himself not unto the world.*

There is a power that comes from faith, or the act of faith. Miracles come after faith, not the other way around. We've seen many times in the scriptures how men like Laman and Lemuel saw angels and felt the power of God in miraculous ways, yet still never gained any faith from those experiences. On the other hand, because of the faith of the brother of Jared, he was able to see the Lord.

It was faith that allowed the disciples to see Christ after his resurrection. The question that comes to my mind is one of possibility: "What miracles are waiting for me after I show my faith?"

Questions to Ponder: What is possible with faith? Are there any limitations? What must our faith be rooted in? Why don't miracles produce faith in people? How are we to gain and strengthen our faith?

Daily Challenge: Study faith, pray for faith, and act in faith.

Because Of The Faith Of Men

> *Ether 12:8 - But because of the faith of men he has shown himself unto the world, and glorified the name of the Father, and prepared a way that thereby others might be partakers of the heavenly gift, that they might hope for those things which they have not seen.*

This expands the definition and power of faith. It shows that our faith can grow to the point where we not only bring miracles into our own lives, but into the lives of others. Our families. Our wards. Our neighborhoods. Our states and our nations.

It is another reason to strive to nurture, cultivate, and grow our faith. My analytical brain wishes there were some "faith metric" that we could use to measure where we are on a scale from "lacking in faith" to "Seeing God" level. Am in in the bottom 10%? The middle 50%? The top 1%?

I'm fairly sure I'm not in that last category, but still, it would be nice to know. That aside, there is always room for improvement and growth, no matter where we are on that spectrum. Even at the highest levels of faith, even with a perfect knowledge, we can still expand our faith to the point where it starts reaching and benefiting the lives of others.

Questions to Ponder: Where are you at with your faith? Do you feel like you're lacking? Like there's room for improvement? What should you do about it?

Daily Challenge: Go back and read Alma 32 to refresh yourself on the process of obtaining more faith and knowledge, and make a conscious effort to try and implement something today.

Ye May Also Have Hope

> *Ether 12:9 - Wherefore, ye may also have hope, and be partakers of the gift, if ye will but have faith.*

This is part of the reason I wanted to go verse by verse through this chapter in Ether. We have already talked about how faith grew out of hope, yet now it's saying that hope also comes out of faith. A sort of virtuous circle, or a loop that feeds on itself as we contribute more to it. More hope leads to more faith, which leads to more hope, which leads to more faith.

More hope?

The more faith we show, the more we are rewarded for that faith. All of a sudden, new things to hope for appear, things that we wouldn't have thought to hope for before. The gifts come after our faith has been realized. Along with those gifts, the reward for our faith, comes more hope. Interesting thought.

Hope > Faith > Reward > More Hope > More Faith > Greater Reward > and so on...

Questions to Ponder: What new insights are coming to you as you study these verses? How does hope lead to faith which leads to more hope? Does it make you want to have more hope and faith?

Daily Challenge: Check out the talk "The Infinite Power of Hope" by President Uchtdorf in the October 2008 General Conference.

It Was By Faith

> *Ether 12: 10-11 - 10 Behold it was by faith that they of old were called after the holy order of God.*

> *11 Wherefore, by faith was the law of Moses given. But in the gift of his Son hath God prepared a more excellent way; and it is by faith that it hath been fulfilled.*

I don't know that I've given much thought up to this point about how faith has played a part in basically every story we have in the scriptures. Someone had faith, and that's where the story starts. Nephi and Lehi had faith - that kicks off The Book of Mormon. We wouldn't even have The Book of Mormon if it weren't for the faith of all of those in it, as well as Mormon, Moroni, and Joseph Smith, to name just a few.

So what about our own lives? What's the takeaway here?

When we look back on our lives, we can probably see good times and bad, some highlights and low points. Is there a common thread to the good times and the great experiences? Could that common thread be faith?

The happiest times in my life can be directly linked to faith. How I got my testimony was going out into the woods (unoriginal as it may be) and praying to God in faith. Serving a mission was an act of faith and to this day is one of the most rewarding experiences of my life. Having friends join the church were acts of faith on both of our parts. Marrying in the temple is a massive act of faith. Serving in the Church, again, stems out of faith.

From a 30,000 foot view, though, there are longer periods of happiness and even some of discouragement and frustration. I can directly point to the amount of faith as a causing factor. Sometimes I could even point you to the exact day or moment where I made a choice to act in faith, or to act out of pride, or fear, or laziness. Those daily decisions can lead to incredible times of happiness, or really tough times of darkness.

Faith is the constant throughout all of it, which is why it's such an important recurring topic in The Book of Mormon. Other than the verses about Christ, Faith was the topic I highlighted most in my research. I don't think that's a coincidence.

Questions to Ponder: Why is faith so important? How often are you conscious of your faith and how it's a part of your life? What are you doing to nurture and strengthen your faith on a daily basis?

Daily Challenge: Study faith. Try to find something you can do to provide a daily reminder to work on and grow your faith in the Lord.

Wherefore They First Believed

> *Ether 12:12-18 - 12 For if there be no faith among the children of men God can do no miracle among them; wherefore, he showed not himself until after their faith.*

> *13 Behold, it was the faith of Alma and Amulek that caused the prison to tumble to the earth.*

> *14 Behold, it was the faith of Nephi and Lehi that wrought the change upon the Lamanites, that they were baptized with fire and with the Holy Ghost.*

> *15 Behold, it was the faith of Ammon and his brethren which wrought so great a miracle among the Lamanites.*

> *16 Yea, and even all they who wrought miracles wrought them by faith, even those who were before Christ and also those who were after.*

> *17 And it was by faith that the three disciples obtained a promise that they should not taste of death; and they obtained not the promise until after their faith.*

> *18 And neither at any time hath any wrought miracles until after their faith; wherefore they first believed in the Son of God.*

Continuing on with the same principles from the last few days, we see that faith has been a part of everything we read about in the scriptures, whether because of incredible amounts of faith or the complete lack of it.

Again, I wonder what is possible in my own life if I only had more faith. Reading through these verses this way - under a microscope, so to speak - makes me want to try harder, to study more, to act in faith more, to hope more, to desire more out of my life. I'm by no means disappointed by my life right now, but look at all of these incredible possibilities. Look how many people we could influence or affect with our faith if we work on it this way.

Questions to Ponder: What do these verses say to you? Do you find them inspiring? Daunting? Unrealistic? Do they make you want to grow your faith? How can you become like these examples in your own life, and what would the outcome be?

Daily Challenge: Act in faith today. Study the scriptures. Pray. Repent. Serve. Find a way to show your faith and see what happens as a result.

An Eye Of Faith

> *Ether 12:19-21 - 19 And there were many whose faith was so exceedingly strong, even before Christ came, who could not be kept from within the veil, but truly saw with their eyes the things which they had beheld with an eye of faith, and they were glad.*

> *20 And behold, we have seen in this record that one of these was the brother of Jared; for so great was his faith in God, that when God put forth his finger he could not hide it from the sight of the brother of Jared, because of his word which he had spoken unto him, which word he had obtained by faith.*

> *21 And after the brother of Jared had beheld the finger of the Lord, because of the promise which the brother of Jared had obtained by faith, the Lord could not withhold anything from his sight; wherefore he showed him all things, for he could no longer be kept without the veil.*

One of the audio books I've been listening to on my commute to and from Salt Lake every day is a book called The Master Key System, by Charles Haanel. It is a collection of 24 or so lectures he gave in the early 1900s, and is seen by many as the original self-help book. (I'd make an argument for The Book of Mormon, the translation of which predates *The Master Key System* by nearly 100 years, but was written hundreds if not thousands of years prior.)

One recurring thing he talks about is the concept of visualization and ideation, that in order for anything to be realized in our lives we have to be able to fully picture it in our minds first.

Sound familiar?

Those with faith, verse 19 says, truly saw with their eyes the things which they had beheld with an eye of faith. They saw it in their minds first. Their faith was so strong that they could not be kept from within the veil.

So how do we gain that level of faith? The only obvious answer I can think of is through practice. It isn't something that would ever occur overnight, unless the Lord really needed that person on his side, as we saw with the sons of Mosiah, Alma, and others who had quick turnarounds. But for us, it's most likely going to be a long, dedicated process of practicing our faith daily for our entire lives.

Still, the promise of no longer being kept without the veil is pretty motivating.

Questions to Ponder: What motivates you to practice your faith? How do you feel it's working out? How do you use that concept of seeing with an eye of faith in your life to achieve the outcomes you want?

Daily Challenge: Spend some time pondering or meditating. Try to start practicing the ability to see with the eye of faith.

Obtained The Promise

> *Ether 12:22 - And it is by faith that my fathers have obtained the promise that these things should come unto their brethren through the Gentiles; therefore the Lord hath commanded me, yea, even Jesus Christ.*

This is a reminder that faith comes first. It precedes the promises, the blessings, the rewards. We have to act first, then receive. The fulfillment of promises is the reward of faith, which inspires us to hope for more, to exercise more faith, and receive greater and greater rewards from our Savior and Heavenly Father.

Questions to Ponder: What has the Lord commanded you to do? Where does He need your faith focused? Where does He need your help? How can you rise to that occasion and add your faith to His work?

Daily Challenge: Ponder this awesome chapter. Write down your thoughts about faith, hope, and belief, and then find ways you can turn those impressions into actionable items you can add to your life.

That They May Be Humble

> *Ether 12:26-29 - 26 And when I had said this, the Lord spake unto me, saying: Fools mock, but they shall mourn; and my grace is sufficient for the meek, that they shall take no advantage of your weakness;*

> *27 And if men come unto me I will show unto them their weakness. I give unto men weakness that they may be humble; and my grace is sufficient for all men that humble themselves before me; for if they humble themselves before me, and have faith in me, then will I make weak things become strong unto them.*

> *28 Behold, I will show unto the Gentiles their weakness, and I will show unto them that faith, hope and charity bringeth unto me—the fountain of all righteousness.*

> *29 And I, Moroni, having heard these words, was comforted, and said: O Lord, thy righteous will be done, for I know that thou workest unto the children of men according to their faith;*

It kinda feels like we're sitting side by side with Moroni as he's getting this information, learning these new truths. Like we're in a gospel classroom together with Christ as the teacher.

Verse 27 was a breakthrough verse for me last year. It teaches that humility is a prerequisite for every other aspect of the gospel. We have to be humble in order to learn and gain knowledge, to repent, to have faith, to act in faith, to believe and to have hope, to live the gospel. It's a foundational gospel principle that unlocks the fountain of all righteousness.

Yesterday I attended a brown bag at the Maxwell Institute library with about a dozen others. It was such a cool conversation about a talk everyone had read by Neal Maxwell from a few decades ago. One in the group brought up the analogy of the chess board that Elder Rasband used in a recent conference, and many in the group felt it was a troubling analogy. They didn't like the idea of being a pawn on a chess board, with no agency and no ability to determine our fate.

As I listened to the conversation progress, I started to feel the opposite, that it was a perfect metaphor. God is an infinite being, all knowing from eternity to eternity. He doesn't dictate our every move, unless we let Him. In an ideal world, we would make the single, humble choice to become like a chess piece, letting Him in His infinite wisdom guide our moves to a victorious end. How prideful to think that with our limited perspective - sitting on a chess board - that we would be able to make better decisions than a "chess master" who's "played the game" so many more times than we have.

Yet, we have agency. We can make our own moves. The great thing about God is that He, being all knowing, can adapt and go with us, so that even if we make a wrong move that sets us back, He can still guide us once we become humble again.

Perhaps not the perfect metaphor, but I think it works. If we want the desired outcome in this life - to become perfect as He is perfect, to have immortality and eternal life - then we must humble ourselves and be willing to let Him guide and direct us. That doesn't take away our responsibility to do the work and to act in faith, but it is a prerequisite so that the actions we take are directed properly.

Questions to Ponder: Why is humility such an important principle? Why isn't it talked about more in the scriptures? How do we become more meek and humble? What are the blessings for doing so?

Daily Challenge: Ask God in prayer for more humility, and for opportunities to learn and grow and progress.

After They Have Faith

> *Ether 12:30-31 - 30 For the brother of Jared said unto the mountain Zerin, Remove—and it was removed. And if he had not had faith it would not have moved; wherefore thou workest after men have faith.*

> *31 For thus didst thou manifest thyself unto thy disciples; for after they had faith, and did speak in thy name, thou didst show thyself unto them in great power.*

This is a quick reminder from our verses earlier this week that our faith has to come first. "We receive no witness until after the trial of our faith," and again here, "thou workest after men have faith." It's a true principle that's being reinforced over and over with a number of examples in this chapter.

Questions to Ponder: What is possible in our lives if we act in faith? How do we strengthen our faith so that we can receive more of these blessings and even miracles in our lives? How can we start small, today?

Daily Challenge: Find something today where you can act in faith. Say a prayer or repent. Serve someone. Go out of your way and minister. Ask the Lord for inspiration and then act on it quickly.

A More Excellent Hope

> *Ether 12:32-35 - 32 And I also remember that thou hast said that thou hast prepared a house for man, yea, even among the mansions of thy Father, in which man might have a more excellent hope; wherefore man must hope, or he cannot receive an inheritance in the place which thou hast prepared.*

> *33 And again, I remember that thou hast said that thou hast loved the world, even unto the laying down of thy life for the world, that thou mightest take it again to prepare a place for the children of men.*

> *34 And now I know that this love which thou hast had for the children of men is charity; wherefore, except men shall have charity they cannot inherit that place which thou hast prepared in the mansions of thy Father.*

> *35 Wherefore, I know by this thing which thou hast said, that if the Gentiles have not charity, because of our weakness, that thou wilt prove them, and take away their talent, yea, even that which they have received, and give unto them who shall have more abundantly.*

Lest we start to think that it's just faith or just humility, we also need to have hope and charity to inherit the place mentioned here. I think there is a present concern in the Church, at least from conversations I've had or overheard, that we're asked to do too much. It seemed like a prevalent topic in the last one or two General Conferences as well.

We all have a different capacity for these different qualities. My wife is infinitely more charitable than I am. I feel like I do a pretty good job with being disciplined and I'm trying hard lately to live with faith and to be led by the spirit in my life.

While at times it can seem like the gospel is an insurmountable list of to do's and expectations, that's not what the gospel feels like when it's presented in the scriptures. I'm not sure if it's a cultural issue, or Satan trying to influence and take down some of us, but it's not a gospel principle that there is some quota, some high bar that we have to clear.

While there are commandments and ordinances that we have to participate in for our salvation, the bulk of the gospel is how we live our daily lives. Each of us will be judged on the capacity that we have, and for trying. If we forsake that responsibility, there are consequences, but - in my experience at least - the Lord blesses us with each and every small step in the right direction we take. We shouldn't feel overwhelmed by it all, but rather see it as an incredible blessing. There are so many ways that we can help others and show the Lord that the gospel matters to us. All we have to do is take little steps as often as we can and try to make progress every day. That's all that's asked of us.

Questions to Ponder: What do you hope for? What should you hope for? How does hope help you reach the outcomes you desire in your life? What blessings have come into your life when you've had hope and faith?

Daily Challenge: Write down your hopes and the things you desire. Work toward them every day.

Seek This Jesus

> *Ether 12:41 - And now, I would commend you to seek this Jesus of whom the prophets and apostles have written, that the grace of God the Father, and also the Lord Jesus Christ, and the Holy Ghost, which bearers record of them, may be and abide in you forever. Amen.*

This is such a beautiful request - to seek this Jesus, to find Christ and follow Him. That single verse might be the best advice we could possibly receive, as it would lead us to everything that is good in this world. We would study the gospel and the words of the prophets, because they teach of Christ. We would attend church to partake of the sacrament and to learn and to serve. We would treat others with kindness to try and be like Him. That single choice to seek this Jesus would bring such incredible joy and blessings into our lives.

Let's commit to do this, now, together. Let's be a force for good. Let's seek out this Jesus of whom the prophets and apostles have written.

Questions to Ponder: How does seeking this Jesus bring the Holy Ghost into your life? How do you seek him? What does that look like on a daily basis?

Daily Challenge: Do it! Seek Him out! Read about His life, pray, serve, do whatever you feel would bring you closer to Him today.

MORONI

With Real Intent

> Moroni 6:8 - But as oft as they repented and sought forgiveness, with real intent, they were forgiven.

Two things here. First, there's a promise that forgiveness comes with repentance. It's a powerful promise that can help us if we try to seek that perspective when we've slipped up or sinned. It will help us feel loved and known by our Heavenly Father in those times where we may feel unworthy of those emotions.

Second, the addendum "with real intent." I know there have been nights in my life when I've "repented" in word only, lacking that essential element of real intent. The real intent, I believe, refers to the desire to change and to not sin again. If we are going through the motions over and over again, but we never actually change, then our intent is insincere. The repentance doesn't work and we don't receive the powerful forgiveness that we are hopefully seeking.

We must repent with real intent if we are to progress and remove the sin from our lives.

Questions to Ponder: What does real intent look like for you? Have there been times when you've repented without real intent? Did it work? Did it have the desired effect you were seeking?

Daily Challenge: Repent!

By Their Works Ye Shall Know Them

> Moroni 7:5-19 - 5 For I remember the word of God which saith by their works ye shall know them; for if their works be good, then they are good also.

> 6 For behold, God hath said a man being evil cannot do that which is good; for if he offereth a gift, or prayeth unto God, except he shall do it with real intent it profiteth him nothing.

> 7 For behold, it is not counted unto him for righteousness.

> 8 For behold, if a man being evil giveth a gift, he doeth it grudgingly; wherefore it is counted unto him the same as if he had retained the gift; wherefore he is counted evil before God.

> 9 And likewise also is it counted evil unto a man, if he shall pray and not with real intent of heart; yea, and it profiteth him nothing, for God receiveth none such.

> 10 Wherefore, a man being evil cannot do that which is good; neither will he give a good gift.

> 11 For behold, a bitter fountain cannot bring forth good water; neither can a good fountain bring forth bitter water; wherefore, a man being a servant of the devil cannot follow Christ; and if he follow Christ he cannot be a servant of the devil.

> 12 Wherefore, all things which are good cometh of God; and that which is evil cometh of the devil; for the devil is an enemy unto God, and fighteth against him continually, and inviteth and enticeth to sin, and to do that which is evil continually.

> 13 But behold, that which is of God inviteth and enticeth to do good continually; wherefore, every thing which inviteth and enticeth to do good, and to love God, and to serve him, is inspired of God.

> 14 Wherefore, take heed, my beloved brethren, that ye do not judge that which is evil to be of God, or that which is good and of God to be of the devil.

> *15 For behold, my brethren, it is given unto you to judge, that ye may know good from evil; and the way to judge is as plain, that ye may know with a perfect knowledge, as the daylight is from the dark night.*

> *16 For behold, the Spirit of Christ is given to every man, that he may know good from evil; wherefore, I show unto you the way to judge; for every thing which inviteth to do good, and to persuade to believe in Christ, is sent forth by the power and gift of Christ; wherefore ye may know with a perfect knowledge it is of God.*

> *17 But whatsoever thing persuadeth men to do evil, and believe not in Christ, and deny him, and serve not God, then ye may know with a perfect knowledge it is of the devil; for after this manner doth the devil work, for he persuadeth no man to do good, no, not one; neither do his angels; neither do they who subject themselves unto him.*

> *18 And now, my brethren, seeing that ye know the light by which ye may judge, which light is the light of Christ, see that ye do not judge wrongfully; for with that same judgment which ye judge ye shall also be judged.*

> *19 Wherefore, I beseech of you, brethren, that ye should search diligently in the light of Christ that ye may know good from evil; and if ye will lay hold upon every good thing, and condemn it not, ye certainly will be a child of Christ.*

This is one of my favorite "sermons" in The Book Of Mormon, and one I've reflected on a ton over the last few years. Initially it was an outward thing - I was using it to judge others like those running for political office or business owners that I chose to work with. A marketing director can say all she wants that she values my work, but when it takes her 90+ days to pay an invoice, the actions speak louder than the words.

Then - and I'm not quite sure when it happened - I started using it more internally to judge my own actions against the things I claimed to value and to believe. Could I say that I valued the scriptures if I didn't read them often? Or say that I care about my relationship with God and the Holy Ghost if I didn't pray every day? The list went on and on and entered every aspect of my life. Could I say that I value saving money if my savings account reflected a different set of values?

This may be one of the most important sections I know of in The Book of Mormon, as it gives such important guidance on how to live our own lives as well as how to judge others. I urge you to study and read it carefully and frequently.

Questions to Ponder: Where in your life have you judged others unfairly? Where can you better align your actions with your values and your beliefs? How important are your actions and your works?

Daily Challenge: Reread this section and study the footnotes, the other verses it leads to, and prayerfully consider what it teaches.

All Things Which Are Good Cometh Of Christ

> Moroni 7:22-24 - 22 For behold, God knowing all things, being from everlasting to everlasting, behold, he sent angels to minister unto the children of men, to make manifest concerning the coming of Christ; and in Christ there should come every good thing.

> 23 And God also declared unto prophets, by his own mouth, that Christ should come.

> 24 And behold, there were divers ways that he did manifest things unto the children of men, which were good; and all things which are good cometh of Christ; otherwise men were fallen, and there could no good thing come unto them.

Quite the lede for this section. "God, knowing all things...sent angels to...make manifest concerning the coming of Christ."

Why would this information be so important to deserve such fanfare and effort from our Heavenly Father? The answer is obvious, but the real question is: do our lives and our actions support how much we claim to value that knowledge of our Savior, Jesus Christ?

It's only been in the last year that I've been working on these two books that the concept has started to really enter my daily life. I had an experience while working on a film project for the LDS Motion Picture Studios back in 2013 that really solidified my belief in our Savior, but - embarrassingly - it has taken nearly 5 years for that belief to turn into action. I've brought up my belief in God in more conversations with more people. I vocally attribute the "good things" in my life to a higher power rather than my own efforts.

Over the last few weeks I was able to shoot a season of the TV show Relative Race for BYUTV, where I work as a senior producer. It was months of preparation all leading up to two weeks of 16 hour days, 7 different states, and meeting more than a dozen relatives that my "team" has been looking for her whole life.

Despite our different religions, it was incredible to share this common belief in God and His mercy, that He chose me and my crew, and this time and under these circumstances, to bring this family back together. Each time someone would thank me I felt almost guilty. I was completely undeserving of any credit beyond putting in the time and prayers for all of this to come together. But it has become incredibly clear that this was God's plan all along, and that we were all just lucky to play a small part in it. There was no way that I or anyone else could have made this happen through their own effort. It has been a beautifully humbling experience and one that I will cherish forever.

It was one of the "divers ways" that God chose to manifest to ME, one of His children, that "all things which are good cometh of Christ."

Questions to Ponder: When in your life has God brought good things? What were those good things? Could they have happened any other way than through a loving Father in Heaven blessing you? How can your daily actions and prayers bring more good things into your life?

Daily Challenge: Offer a prayer of gratitude to God for all of the good things in your life, especially if you feel like this time in your life is a tough period.

Thus By Faith

> *Moroni 7:25 - ...and thus by faith, they did lay hold upon every good thing;*

Coming off of yesterday's verses, this verse teaches us a simple principle that can lead us to more of those good things that come from Christ. They come through faith.

Now that we're nearing the end of The Book of Mormon it might serve us to look back on all we've learned together over the last year. What have we learned about faith? About how it is grown and cultivated? About what it is and what it isn't?

As we strive to grow our faith, this perspective is one that can help motivate and guide us in the right direction. If every good thing comes from faith, it's worth understanding it well enough that we can also lay hold upon every good thing.

The principles in The Book Of Mormon are eternal and unchanging. They are as true for us today as they were for Nephi and Alma and Moroni. We too can have richly blessed lives, incredible relationships with our Heavenly Father, and eternal happiness and joy with our families and loved ones if we will live a life of faith.

Questions to Ponder: Where in your life can you show more faith in God? Where is your testimony lacking and could be strengthened? What actions can you take on a daily basis that will put that faith to work and allow you to lay hold upon the good things you are seeking and that your Heavenly Father has for you?

Daily Challenge: Ponder for a few minutes on faith in your own life. How would you improve your faith? What changes can you start making today?

Ask The Father In My Name

> *Moroni 7:26 - ...Whatsoever thing ye shall ask the Father in my name, which is good, in faith believing that ye shall receive, behold, it shall be done unto you.*

What's one of the simplest ways we can show our faith? Through prayer.

Prayer, at least for me, hasn't been a 100% success rate. It's not like every time I kneel and ask my Heavenly Father for something I receive it that same day. No, prayer doesn't work that way, as that would not require any faith at all. Just as we don't see results immediately from improving our diet or starting to save money for our children's futures, prayer is an act of faith. We believe that we shall receive, but it doesn't always happen. Sometimes it's the wrong time, sometime's it's that we lack the faith necessary to realize the thing we're seeking. Other times it's that God has something better in store that we still can't see.

Prayer is an act of faith, and the times when I do it regularly, when I take the time to listen, not just to talk, and when I am humbly seeking answers, they tend to come. I receive thoughts and impressions, or even direct answers. I have received comfort and counsel through the power of the Holy Ghost. I have felt even a few times that I was kneeling right at the foot of my Heavenly Father, and in the times where I've needed Him the most, He has given me feelings of love and protection that I never knew I could feel.

Prayer is a real principle of the gospel that can bring so many blessings into our lives. I firmly believe that we have merely skimmed the surface of the depths of what is possible through faith and prayer. That could make some people discouraged, but it gives me hope. Hope that as I keep working, keep striving, keep living the gospel the best that I can, that more and more blessings will come.

Questions to Ponder: What blessings are you seeking in your life? What blessings could be in store for you that you aren't receiving because you're not praying? What answers are waiting for you on the other side of a faithful prayer?

Daily Challenge: Pray!

❖ ❖ ❖

If Ye Will Have Faith In Me

Moroni 7:33-34 - 33 And Christ hath said: If ye will have faith in me ye shall have power to do whatsoever thing is expedient in me.

34 And he hath said: Repent all ye ends of the earth, and come unto me, and be baptized in my name, and have faith in me, that ye may be saved.

I recently started reading through The Book of Mormon again with my oldest son who turns 8 on his next birthday. It is interesting to me - but not surprising - that we get this verse toward the end of this volume of scripture that echoes a similar verse in 1 Nephi chapter 7:

12 Yea, and how is it that ye have forgotten that the Lord is able to do all things according to his will, for the children of men, if it so be that they exercise faith in him? Wherefore, let us be faithful to him.

Christ has power to do anything according to His will, which I read as "anything good and right," as long as we have faith in Him. What a powerful and amazing promise! There is no limit to the things that are possible when you combine the power of God and faith in Christ.

Questions to Ponder: What are you seeking? What do you need? What do you want? And how can you increase your faith in order to receive it?

Daily Challenge: Pray to God and ask Him how you can grow and increase your faith.

Angels Appear And Minister Unto Men

> Moroni 7:37-38 - 37 ...for it is by faith that miracles are wrought; and it is by faith that angels appear and minister unto men; wherefore, if these things have ceased wo be unto the children of men, for it is because of unbelief, and all is vain.

> 38 For no man can be saved, according to the words of Christ, save they shall have faith in his name; wherefore, if these things have ceased, then has faith ceased also; and awful is the state of man, for they are as though there had been no redemption made.

I take this section really hard. It's probably the part of my brain that is not ok not being the best at something that also says "if you're not seeing angels, your faith isn't as good as it should be." Now, should is a harsh word for my mind to use, but I'm conflicted with how I "should" actually feel about this statement.

> If these things have ceased...it is because of unbelief.

Does that apply to me individually as well as the Church/world as a whole? I think it does, as the Church is made up a whole bunch of individuals. And I don't know about you, but I haven't been hanging out with any angels lately.

Today's gospel doctrine lesson was about how we're living through a challenging time and there are so many influences vying for our time and attention. I believe that's part of the problem. Most of us aren't spending hours a day studying the scriptures, conversing with others about the gospel, etc. We have jobs, families, and other pursuits. However, that might just be the thing that has caused *these things* to *have ceased*.

I wonder how different my life would need to be in order for these things to become a part of my life. To be ministered to by angels. To have a much stronger relationship with the Holy Ghost. To have more faith. Or, maybe I'm doing alright except that I'm so distracted at times that I'm just failing to see the incredible things all around me.

Either way, I can honestly say that I want it. Yet, I can also say that my life as it is now doesn't align as well as it could with that stated desire. Some changes will certainly need to take place at some point if I ever want to realize these incredible blessings.

Questions to Ponder: Do you believe in angels and being ministered to by them? Do you believe it's possible in your life or in the lives of others today? Is it something you desire? What changes would you need to make in your life to allow the Lord to bless you this way?

Daily Challenge: Really ask yourself what you want, and what you're willing to do to get it.

Save He Shall Be Meek, And Lowly Of Heart

> Moroni 7:41-44 - 41 And what is it that ye shall hope for? Behold I say unto you that ye shall have hope through the atonement of Christ and the power of his resurrection, to be raised unto life eternal, and this because of your faith in him according to the promise.

> 42 Wherefore, if a man have faith he must needs have hope; for without faith there cannot be any hope.

> 43 And again, behold I say unto you that he cannot have faith and hope, save he shall be meek, and lowly of heart.

> 44 If so, his faith and hope is vain, for none is acceptable before God, save the meek and lowly in heart;

This is a great reminder of verses we've covered recently about faith and hope, but adds something so important, something I've come to learn through this process of studying and writing about The Book of Mormon.

Humility is a prerequisite for faith.

As it says in verse 43, "*he cannot have faith and hope, save he shall be meek, and lowly of heart.*"

It's a principle that is rarely taught, at least in my experience growing up in the gospel. I cannot remember a single lesson about the importance of humility. Sure, there were lessons about pride and the pride cycle, but the emphasis is on *avoiding pride* rather than *having humility* and using it as a way to have faith and hope and to stave off the influences that lead to pride.

It may be one of the most important lessons I've learned through this process. It's become something that I'm now acutely aware of in all the different parts of my life. Pride is such a pernicious and ubiquitous threat - in our homes, our relationships with our family, at work, and out in the world as we interact with others, both in person and online. It shows up in so many forms, from seeking followers to our social feeds, to how we're seen and appreciated at home, to what we think we deserve at work. Those expectations come out of being in a prideful state of mind, rather than a humble one.

Without humility, we cannot have faith, nor can we have hope. These principles are essential for our salvation, which just reinforces how imperative it is that we have humility. Going beyond that, we would never pray or repent, we wouldn't partake of the sacrament and seek a remission of our sins, and we wouldn't have any reason to rely on the Lord if it weren't for humility and lowliness of heart.

Without it, *[our] faith and hope is vain*. That's how essential humility is.

Questions to Ponder: How can you become more humble? What is the process for it? Why is it important? How does your level of humility and meekness affect your faith and hope?

Daily Challenge: Humbly go to God in prayer and ask Him how you can become more humble, where pride is seeping into your life, and how to make those changes so that your faith and hope can be at full strength.

That Ye May Be Filled With This Love

> Moroni 7:44-48 - 44 ...and if a man be meek and lowly in heart, and confesses by the power of the Holy Ghost that Jesus is the Christ, he must needs have charity; for if he have not charity he is nothing; wherefore he must needs have charity.

> 45 And charity suffereth long, and is kind, and envieth not, and is not puffed up, seeketh not her own, is not easily provoked, thinketh no evil, and rejoiceth not in iniquity but rejoiceth in the truth, beareth all things, believeth all things, hopeth all things, endureth all things.

> 46 Wherefore, my beloved brethren, if ye have not charity, ye are nothing, for charity never faileth. Wherefore, cleave unto charity, which is the greatest of all, for all things must fail—

> 47 But charity is the pure love of Christ, and it endureth forever; and whoso is found possessed of it at the last day, it shall be well with him.

> 48 Wherefore, my beloved brethren, pray unto the Father with all the energy of heart, that ye may be filled with this love, which he hath bestowed upon all who are true followers of his Son, Jesus Christ; that ye may become the sons of God; that when he shall appear we shall be like him, for we shall see him as he is; that we may have this hope; that we may be purified even as he is pure. Amen.

When I left my mission I was asked by my ward mission leader to write up a sort of "goodbye" note to be included in his weekly insert in the ward program. The thing I remember to this day was how much I learned about how much God loves His children. I was able to experience and share in some of that pure love of Christ for two years while I was out serving. It's a feeling I'll never forget, and one that pops up now and then.

I just finished up two weeks on the road filming the TV show Relative Race for BYUTV. As I was out on the road, that same feeling came over me on nearly a daily basis as God was connecting this family after decades apart. As we wrapped the last day, I took a moment to share with one of the contestants how much I know God loves her, and how special she is to Him. It was another moment of feeling this pure love of Christ, where I was blessed with the opportunity to be filled with the spirit of charity, and to understand, even if in just a small way, what charity feels like.

When Moroni writes that charity is the greatest of all, it's in these moments that I really believe him. There's nothing that compares to that feeling. So, I'll encourage you to do the same as Moroni asks of you - to pray with all the energy of heart to be filled with charity. And to remember that charity also requires lowliness of heart, meekness, humility. Lastly, it's interesting to note that charity seeketh not her own, meaning we cannot have charity for ourselves, only for others.

Questions to Ponder: When have you felt the pure love of Christ in your life, either from God or for others? How would you describe it? How good did it feel? How can you feel charity for others? What makes it the greatest of all?

Daily Challenge: Pray for more charity. Work to live with more charity for others, starting today.

Diligence

Moroni 8:8-17 - 8 Listen to the words of Christ, your Redeemer, your Lord and your God. Behold, I came into the world not to call the righteous but sinners to repentance; the whole need no physician, but they that are sick; wherefore, little children are whole, for they are not capable of committing sin; wherefore the curse of Adam is taken from them in me, that it hath no power over them; and the law of circumcision is done away in me.

9 And after this manner did the Holy Ghost manifest the word of God unto me; wherefore, my beloved son, I know that it is solemn mockery before God, that ye should baptize little children.

10 Behold I say unto you that this thing shall ye teach—repentance and baptism unto those who are accountable and capable of committing sin; yea, teach parents that they must repent and be baptized, and humble themselves as their little children, and they shall all be saved with their little children.

11 And their little children need no repentance, neither baptism. Behold, baptism is unto repentance to the fulfilling the commandments unto the remission of sins.

12 But little children are alive in Christ, even from the foundation of the world; if not so, God is a partial God, and also a changeable God, and a respecter to persons; for how many little children have died without baptism!

13 Wherefore, if little children could not be saved without baptism, these must have gone to an endless hell.

14 Behold I say unto you, that he that supposeth that little children need baptism is in the gall of bitterness and in the bonds of iniquity; for he hath neither faith, hope, nor charity; wherefore, should he be cut off while in the thought, he must go down to hell.

15 For awful is the wickedness to suppose that God saveth one child because of baptism, and the other must perish because he hath no baptism.

16 Wo be unto them that shall pervert the ways of the Lord after this manner, for they shall perish except they repent. Behold, I speak with boldness, having authority from God; and I fear not what man can do; for perfect love casteth out all fear.

> *17 And I am filled with charity, which is everlasting love; wherefore, all children are alike unto me; wherefore, I love little children with a perfect love; and they are all alike and partakers of salvation.*

This is quite the tirade on this topic. Given the circumstances, he was really upset about this distortion of the gospel. It wasn't easy to write on plates - it took tons of time and effort. Often, topics like this get covered in a single verse or two, not 20.

I think it's important for us to not just read the words and realize that baptizing babies is not the gospel, but to realize that this is an example of how we can sometimes distort the gospel to fit our needs. How many of us justify certain types of tea or coffee, or are essentially addicted to soda or other caffeinated drinks? How many of us have distorted the law of tithing, or the law of chastity, or any other of the commandments and justified our actions by doing so?

I'd venture a guess that all of us have done this in some form or another. Reading over these verses with a more personal version can cut really hard. But it's necessary for us to realize that when we distort the gospel, it prevents us from being able to receive the full blessings of the gospel. It is a form of pride, which we know is the opposite of the humility we should be cultivating in our lives.

As we progress in our lives and our commitment to living the gospel, it becomes more stringent and specific. But that's how we continue to progress and grow, by becoming more disciplined, more obedient, more humble, and more like our Savior and His perfect example.

Questions to Ponder: Where do you have room for more discipline in living the gospel? Where - if anywhere - are you justifying certain actions that might be flirting with the line a little bit? What are the blessings that come from the increased discipline and obedience if you choose to live that way? Do you think there's a reason that discipline is essentially the same word as disciple?

Daily Challenge: Think about where you can be more disciplined in your life when it comes to the gospel, and make a goal to do one thing in a more obedient, disciplined manner. See how it feels after a week, and after a month.

The Remission Of Sins

> Moroni 8:25-27 - 25 And the first fruits of repentance is baptism; and baptism cometh by faith unto the fulfilling the commandments; and the fulfilling the commandments bringeth remission of sins;

> 26 And the remission of sins bringeth meekness, and lowliness of heart; and because of meekness and lowliness of heart cometh the visitation of the Holy Ghost, which Comforter filleth with hope and perfect love, which love endureth by diligence unto prayer, until the end shall come, when all the saints shall dwell with God.

> 27 Behold, my son, I will write unto you again if I go not out soon against the Lamanites. Behold, the pride of this nation, or the people of the Nephites, hath proven their destruction except they should repent.

Do we value the remission of our sins that comes from the Atonement of Christ? We don't speak of it often, but every week we are able to take the sacrament and renew those covenants we made at baptism. Why? So that we can remember Him, so that we can always have His spirit with us.

But why? These verses teach us that the Holy Ghost brings hope and perfect love, which leads to charity and prayer.

The opposite is pride - to be so hung up on doing things our own way, ignoring the atonement and the Holy Ghost, and trying to tough it out on our own. He warns us of that option, that it has and will lead to destruction.

Questions to Ponder: How can you focus on the Savior's atonement more often? How can you be more humble, repent and pray more, and have a stronger relationship with the Holy Ghost? What are your reasons for wanting to do so?

Daily Challenge: Pray, and seek out the Holy Ghost more often. Take time to listen during your prayers for the answers that come.

For They Are Many

> *Moroni 10:3-8 - 3 Behold, I would exhort you that when ye shall read these things, if it be wisdom in God that ye should read them, that ye would remember how merciful the Lord hath been unto the children of men, from the creation of Adam even down until the time that ye shall receive these things, and ponder it in your hearts.*

> *4 And when ye shall receive these things, I would exhort you that ye would ask God, the Eternal Father, in the name of Christ, if these things are not true; and if ye shall ask with a sincere heart, with real intent, having faith in Christ, he will manifest the truth of it unto you, by the power of the Holy Ghost.*

> *5 And by the power of the Holy Ghost ye may know the truth of all things.*

> *6 And whatsoever thing is good is just and true; wherefore, nothing that is good denieth the Christ, but acknowledgeth that he is.*

> *7 And ye may know that he is, by the power of the Holy Ghost; wherefore I would exhort you that ye deny not the power of God; for he worketh by power, according to the faith of the children of men, the same today and tomorrow, and forever.*

> *8 And again, I exhort you, my brethren, that ye deny not the gifts of God, for they are many; and they come from the same God. And there are different ways that these gifts are administered; but it is the same God who worketh all in all; and they are given by the manifestations of the Spirit of God unto men, to profit them.*

Often overlooked is this last verse, which comes after some of my favorite verses in the entire Book of Mormon. We're promised that the Holy Ghost will manifest the truth of The Book of Mormon to us, but more than that that he has the power to help us know all things. The truth *of all things*.

We need to pause and take a moment to really let that statement sink in. "*By the power of the Holy Ghost ye may know the truth of all things.*" No limits. No conditions. No caveats or small text at the bottom of the page. This is a true statement. An eternal statement. A promise written for us so that we could hold it in our hands, read it out loud, pray about and receive confirmation that it is true.

And after that promise, the statement that we should *deny not the gifts of God, for they are many*. As if the Holy Ghost telling us the truth of all things is not enough, there are *more* gifts. They come the same way - through the Holy Ghost.

It is so important that we spend time thinking about these gifts, and the extent of the power of the Holy Ghost.

Questions to Ponder: How is your relationship with the Holy Ghost? Do you know his voice? Do you know how he speaks to you personally? What gifts have you seen come into your life through the power of the Holy Ghost? How can you strengthen that line of communication and receive more of those gifts on a more frequent basis?

Daily Challenge: Take some time during a prayer to just listen. About a year ago I started regularly meditating after my morning prayers, but in the last few months started incorporating that time into my prayers, and I've been surprised at how just adding in that time to listen has given me so much more insight, guidance, and inspiration from my Heavenly Father through the Holy Ghost.

Every Good Gift Cometh Of Christ

> *Moroni 10:18-19 - 18 And I would exhort you, my beloved brethren, that ye remember that every good gift cometh of Christ.*

> *19 And I would exhort you, my beloved brethren, that ye remember that he is the same yesterday, today, and forever, and that all these gifts of which I have spoken, which are spiritual, never will be done away, even as long as the world shall stand, only according to the unbelief of the children of men.*

I love this reminder that every good gift cometh of Christ. When we are struggling through times in our lives when we feel alone, we can look to these good gifts and realize that we have a loving Savior and a loving Father in Heaven who know us and love us.

It can be anything, large or small. A smile from a stranger on the way in to work. A neighbor who mowed your lawn while you were out filming a TV show for two weeks. A friend who stopped by just to talk. A bonus that came at an unexpected time from a grateful employer.

All of these things fall into this category of good gifts, and we learn here that they come from Christ. All good things come from Christ. It's one of the most consistent reminders we have that our Savior lived and that there is a plan of happiness in place for our salvation.

Questions to Ponder: When was the last good gift you received? When was the last time that you felt a prompting to do something nice for someone else, and be a good gift for them? How did it feel? How does the new ministering program in the Church align with this doctrine?

Daily Challenge: Find a good thing you can do today to be a gift in someone's life.

If Ye Have Not Faith

> Moroni 10:20-23 - 20 Wherefore, there must be faith; and if there must be faith there must also be hope; and if there must be hope there must also be charity.

> 21 And except ye have charity ye can in nowise be saved in the kingdom of God; neither can ye be saved in the kingdom of God if ye have not faith; neither can ye if ye have no hope.

> 22 And if ye have no hope ye must needs be in despair; and despair cometh because of iniquity.

> 23 And Christ truly said unto our fathers: If ye have faith ye can do all things which are expedient unto me.

We've been told dozens of times in The Book of Mormon how important faith is and what is possible with it. Here, however, we have a warning of sorts: "neither can ye be saved...if ye have not faith." There are consequences to not having faith, as well as blessings for having it.

There's a reason that faith is the first principle of the gospel. It is fundamental. It unlocks everything that comes after it, as every other principle and ordinance comes out of that faith.

It's also interesting to note that despair comes from a lack of hope, so if we're feeling discouraged or depressed, as hard as it may be, we can go back to the fundamental principles of faith and hope and try to look at our situation from a different perspective. A more eternal perspective.

The promise at the end is so encouraging, that we can do all things which are expedient unto Him. Again, this is an incredible truth that we have essentially unlimited potential with our faith, if we'll dedicate time to nurture and grow our faith, and if we'll live our lives according to the faith that we have.

Questions to Ponder: How do you get through times of despair? How can having a more eternal perspective help you out of those times? What is possible through faith? Why do you think that faith is such an important principle of the gospel?

Daily Challenge: Pray for opportunities to strengthen and grow your faith. Do something today that is an act of faith to show God that you value this great gift.

❖ ❖ ❖

Come Unto Christ

> Moroni 10:32-33 - 32 Yea, come unto Christ, and be perfected in him, and deny yourselves of all ungodliness; and if ye shall deny yourselves of all ungodliness, and love God with all your might, mind and strength, then is his grace sufficient for you, that by his grace ye may be perfect in Christ; and if by the grace of God ye are perfect in Christ, ye can in nowise deny the power of God.

> 33 And again, if ye by the grace of God are perfect in Christ, and deny not his power, then are ye sanctified in Christ by the grace of God, through the shedding of the blood of Christ, which is in the covenant of the Father unto the remission of your sins, that ye become holy, without spot.

These two verses bring back such incredible memories for me, both of my own journey to gaining a testimony of the gospel, as well as the times throughout my life that I was blessed with the opportunity to share the gospel with others. These verses contain so much truth and so much power that it can't be denied.

This is one of the greatest statement verses in The Book of Mormon. One of the most incredible promises that the book contains. Look at the statements that start with if:

If ye shall deny yourselves of all ungodliness, and love God with all your might, mind and strength...

If by the grace of God ye are perfect in Christ...

Yes, those are big ifs. They aren't meant to be simple statements, but the epitome of what the gospel offers us and what it asks of us. A perfect standard to work towards.

Then look at the blessings:

His grace is sufficient for you

By His grace ye may be perfect in Christ

Sanctified in Christ by the grace of God

Ye become holy, without spot

It hearkens back to the statement that we are saved by grace after all we can do. These verses give us a challenge and a promise. They provide a north star, a direction and a focus for our lives so that we know what choices are going to lead us to the desired outcomes. To become perfect. To become sanctified. To become holy as He is holy.

To become like God.

Throughout the last year, I've been immensely changed from writing this book. I think there has been an unknown or unrecognized desire to try to help as many people as I can that are working toward the same goal. It's motivated me to become a better person.

I'm so grateful for the promises in The Book of Mormon, and am excited for what's to come for all of us as we pursue this path.

Questions to Ponder: What is asked of you? What are the blessings that are promised if you choose to live your life that way? What are the promises in The Book of Mormon that have impacted you the most?

Daily Challenge: Decide or recommit today to live a life of faith, of righteousness, of hope and charity. One that will lead you closer to your Heavenly Father and your Savior, Jesus Christ.

Thank You

I'm not quite sure what to say at this point, so I apologize if this chapter is a bit unstructured.

First of all, thank you! I started the email series with the hopes of reaching a few friends and family, and the list grew to hundreds and hundreds of people all over the world. It's humbling and became such a huge responsibility.

This last year has just been life changing for me. I had no idea the changes that would come into my life because of this project, nor did I understand how fulfilling and inspiring it would be. I've grown closer to my Heavenly Father, my Savior, and the Holy Ghost, just as the book promises in its introduction. I have a stronger testimony now that this book will bring you closer to God than any other book.

I know that The Book of Mormon is truly a book of scripture, written and translated by prophets of God. It was meant for us, and the blessing that it is has never been more apparent in my life.

Thank you x 1000 for being a reader, for making it here to the end, for everything. I'm grateful for each and every one of you, because you have motivated me to keep writing, to keep sending emails every day, and to ultimately write this book. It's not something I could have ever done if it weren't for people like you. I hope that at some point we get to meet so that I can thank you in person. It's been incredible writing these emails for you every day and I hope that the experience on your end has been just as great.

If you want to keep in touch, as always feel free to send me an email at info@dailymormon.email (I read every one), or you can also find me online. I'm @darentsmith on pretty much every social network, and you can follow my other writing and what I'm working on at my website http://darentsmith.com.

I wish you all the best as you study the gospel.

Your companion on the path,

Daren Smith

www.ingramcontent.com/pod-product-compliance
Lightning Source LLC
Chambersburg PA
CBHW071144070526
44584CB00019B/2654